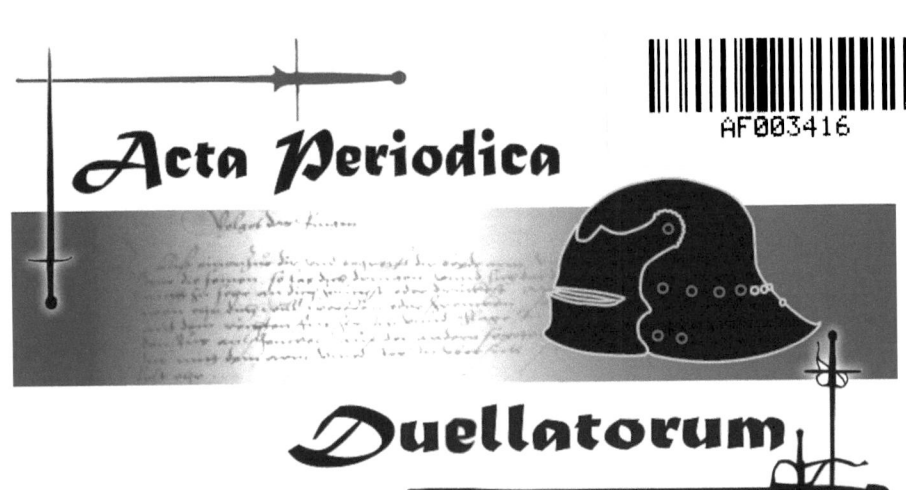

2016
Volume 4 - Issue 1
(Scholarly Volume)

2016 - Volume 4 - Issue 1 (Scholarly volume)

Acta Periodica Duellatorum

Editors

Daniel Jaquet, Max Planck Institute for History of Science

Mátyás Miskolczi, Acta Periodica Duellatorum Association

Scientific Committee

Prof. Sydney Anglo (emeritus); Prof. Jan Dirk Müller (Munich University); Prof. Paul Bowman (Cardiff University); Dr. Daniel Jaquet (Max Planck Institute for History of Science, Berlin); Dr. János Majár (University of Miskolc); Dr. Audrey Tuaillon-Démesy (University of Besançon); Dr. Bert Gevaert (Catholic University of Louvain); Dr. Eric Burkart (University of Trier); Dr. Ingo Petri (Deutsches Archäologisches Institut, Berlin); Dr. Marco Quarta (Stanford University); Dr. Matthias-Johannes Bauer (University of Duisburg-Essen); Dr. Reiner van Noort (IFE, Norway); Dr. Serge Vaucelle (University of Toulouse); Dr. Xavier Baecke (University of Ghent); Donald J. La Rocca (Metropolitan Museum, New-York); Robert C. Woosnam-Savage (Royal Armouries, Leeds); Claus Sorenson (Nyborg Museum, Denmark); Sixt Wetzler (Deutsches Klingenmuseum, Solingen); Jeff Lord (University of Massachussets); Dr. Julia Gräf (not currently affiliated); Dr. Ariella Elema (not currently affiliated).

Advisory Committee

Bartlomiej Walczak (PL); Christian Tobler (US); Devon Boorman (CA); Didier de Gernier (FR); Dierk Hagedorn (DE); Dieter Bachmann (CH); Gregory Mele (US); Guy Windsor (FI); Dr. James Robert (ZA); Jean Chandler (US); Jessica Finley (US); Dr. Jürg Gassmann (CH); Keith Farrell (UK); Kevin Maurer (US); Luis Preto (PT); Piermarco Terminiello (UK); Olivier Dupuis (FR); Rob Runacres (UK); Roberto Gotti (IT); Roger Norling (SE); Szablocs Waldmann (HU); Ton Puey (SP)

PARTNERSHIP Acta Periodica Duellatorum Association is grateful to its partners and individual donators: IFHEMA (International Federation for Historical European Martial Arts, www.ifhema.com); HROARR (Resources for Historical European Martial Arts, www.hroarr.com); MAM (Museum of Martial Arts, Botticino).

ABSTRACTED/INDEXED IN Baidu Scholar, Celdes, CNKI Scholar (China National Knowledge Infrastructure), CNPIEC, DOAJ (Directory of Open Access Journals), EBSCO, Google Scholar, Naviga (Softweco), Primo Central (ExLibris), ReadCube, Summon (Serials Solutions/ProQuest), TDOne (TDNet), WorldCat (OCLC).

The publisher, together with the authors and editors, has taken great pains to ensure that all information presented in this work reflects the standard of knowledge at the time of publication. Despite careful manuscript preparation and proof correction, errors can nevertheless occur. Authors, editors and publisher disclaim all responsibility for any errors or omissions or liability for the results obtained from use of the information, or parts thereof, contained in this work.

This work is licensed under the Creative Commons Attribution-NonCommercial-NoDerivatives 3.0 License. (CC BY-NC-ND 3.0)

All information regarding notes for contributors, subscriptions, Open access, back volumes and orders is available online at www.degruyter.com/view/j/apd and www.actaperiodica.org

© 2016 Acta Periodica Duellatorum Association, Switzerland

ISSN 2064-0404 – ISBN 978-0-0120-2573-4

TYPESETTING Arcanum Development LtD,
Baranyai u. 10, 1117 Budapest, Hungary

PUBLISHER De Gruyter Open,
Bogumiła Zuga 32A Str.,
01-811 Warsaw, Poland

PRINTING Books on Demand GmbH,
In de Tarpen 42,
2848 Norderstedt, Germany

LEGAL DEPOSIT May 2016

Table of Contents

EDITORIAL 1

ARTICLES 3

   Investigation on the collation of the first Fight book (Leeds, Royal Armouries, Ms I.33) (Fanny Binard) 3

   A Well Regulated Militia Political and Military Organisation in Pre-Napoleonic Switzerland (Dr. Jürg Gassmann) 23

   The French staff material from Johann Georg Pasch (Olivier Dupuis) 53

   The use of the saber in the army of Napoleon (Bert Gevaert) 103

   Income and working time of a Fencing Master in Bologna in the 15th and early 16th (Alessandro Battistini, Niki Corradetti) 153

   Pole-weapons in the Sagas of Icelanders: a comparison of literary and archaeological sources (Jan H. Orkisz) 177

RESEARCH NOTE 213

   Two late flying prints informing on the artist involved in the *Opera Nova* of Achille Marozzo and on the date of an original (lost) edition? (Roberto Gotti, Daniel Jaquet) 213

BOOK REVIEWS 221

   Jeffrey L. Forgeng, *The Art of Swordsmanship by Hans Lecküchner* (Daniel Jaquet) 221

   Jaser, Christian and Israel, Uwe (ed.), *Zweikämpfer. Fechtmeister – Kämpen – Samurai. [Duellists. Fencing masters - champions - Samurai]*. (Ingo Petri) 225

EDITORIAL

Acta Periodica Duellatorum has evolved since its first issue in 2013. In the past few years, we have built a strong network of both academics and martial artists supporting our aims. Through partnership and restructuring, we have improved quality, matching the high standards of scholarly publishing but still listening to the needs of the community of practitioners. Since late 2014, thanks to our publishing partner, De Gruyter, all of our issues are now open access and indexed with digital object identifiers (DOI), following the principles of the "Berlin Declaration on Open Access to Knowledge in the Sciences and Humanities" (22 Oct. 2003). We are also registered with the International Directory of Open Access Journals (DOAJ), allowing our articles to be referenced in all relevant indexes. Since late 2015, we have improved our international peer-review policy. Following the suggestion of the Committee on Publication Ethics (COPE, "Code of Conduct and Best Practice Guidelines for Journal Editors and Code of Conduct for Journal Publishers"), we established a double blind peer-review process, supported by an extended Scientific Committee and an Advisory Committee. From 2016 on, we will offer two issues per year, one issue entitled "Scholarly volume", intended for the broader academic audience, and a second one entitled "Hands On volume", intended for the practitioners of Historical European Martial Arts and the readers interested in pragmatic aspects of the rediscovery of these arts. We also expanded a partnership with the well-read HEMA blog "Hroarr: Resources for Historical European Martial Arts" (http://hroarr.com). The journal continues to pursue its primary goal of providing visibility to studies in this emerging field of research, bridging the gap between researchers and practitioners. Our attempts aim, particularly, to draw on expertise from both worlds (Academia and the community of HEMA practitioners), by aligning our guidelines and endeavours to best practices from both sides.

We are also proud to announce that our journal will sponsor two panels at the next International Medieval Congress in Leeds (IMC, July 4-7) entitled "Historical European Martial Arts Studies, I: Modern Practice and Its Connection to the Source Material, and II: The Art of Fighting in Context". A special issue will be dedicated to these proceedings. Lastly we introduce a new section in our standard issues: the "Research Notes", allowing researchers to present ongoing research projects and preliminary results in a digest format.

In tandem with open access publishing, we will now concentrate on our distribution with a new printing partner, BoD (Book on Demand) and to our new website with a reworked subscription system for individuals and institutions. In the long run, once our journal has reached the highest standards, we will aim to align with the Journal Impact Factor (JIF) requirements found in Thomson Reuters' annual "Journal Citation Reports", bringing HEMA studies to the forefront of the research landscape. For all of these achievements and dynamic developments, we are indebted to our readers and to the countless supporters and contributors who have helped shape the journal. Support us by subscribing to our journal and sharing our endeavours, and feel free to contact the Editorial Board with any suggestions, requests or projects. Thank you for reading.

Matyas Miskolczi and Daniel Jaquet, editors.

DOI 10.1515/apd-2016-0001

Investigation on the collation of the first Fight book (Leeds, Royal Armouries, Ms I.33)

Fanny Binard, Lugdunenses, binard.fanny@gmail.com

in collaboration with Daniel Jaquet, Max Planck Institute for History of Science, djaquet@mpiwg-berlin.mpg.de

Abstract: This paper investigates the collation of the first Fight Book, the Leeds, Royal Armouries, Ms I.33. It critically reviews previous hypotheses about the composition of the quires and the identification of the material lacuna, and proposes a new hypothesis. This investigation is based on observation of the original after restoration (2012) and the simulation of the previous hypotheses with a working document composed of laminated sheets into which reproductions were inserted. Bifolia were physically attached, forming quires by successive folds. This simulation phase allowed us to analyse textual and pictorial content according to the various postulates and to propose identification of the material lacuna. The pivot point allowing a new argumentation are the two counterfoils of the two flying leaves (fol. 19 and 26), which were not taken into account by previous researchers. Several synoptical diagrams of the representation of the quire are enclosed for the reader to follow the developments.

Keywords: Fight Book, Ms. I.33, Liber de arte dimicatoria, tower fechtbuch, Walpurgis fechtbuch, codicology, collation, manuscript studies.

The manuscript kept in the Royal Armouries of Leeds with the shelf mark I.33 is the first witness of the corpus of the Fight books[1]. As such, and for its many significant particularities, it has already received the attention of several researchers[2], as well as several editions and translations[3]. The manuscript is a unicum that has circulated among different owners; however, whole swathes of the history of its conservation remain obscure[4]. The researchers therefore questioned the current state of the object[5] (irregular quire construction and two half-sheets) compared to a hypothetical original state. Indeed, besides the current state of the composition of the quires (structural aspects), the content analysis suggests that it lacks material (textual aspects). Jeffrey L. Forgeng, James Hester, Franck Cinato and André Surprenant have all made assumptions about the composition of the manuscript, the current order of the quires, and possible material lacuna. It must be added that all studies conducted prior to the restoration in 2012 have been made on a manuscript that was tightly bound, implying difficulties for the codicological investigations.

Having reviewed the different hypotheses and confronted these to an analysis of the organisation of the content of both text and images, as well as with phases of practical interpretation, the necessity of further research on that matter became obvious. This article thus proposes on the one hand a critical description of the different hypotheses put forward by researchers; on the other hand, the exposition of our own hypothesis, relying both on observations made on the original and on our experiments with a working document allowing us to test the different possible configurations of re-organisation of the quires. Our work is accompanied by synoptic diagrams allowing to view the composition of the manuscript with the layout of the quires (Fig. 3-8), as well as a table

---

* We thank the Royal Armouries Library staff; Jeffrey L. Forgeng and Franck Cinato for their kindly provided critical comments, as well as the anonymous peer-reviewers who greatly contributed to the betterment of this paper; Olivier Gourdon for the assistance in the realisation of the Figs. 8 and 9; and Keith Farrell for his help in revising our English.

[1] Leeds, Royal Armouries, Ms I.33. The manuscript is also associated with alternative titles, including: Walpurgis Fechtbuch, Ms. I.33, Lutegerus Fight Book, Liber de Arte Dimicatoria.

[2] See the bibliography of Forgeng, *The Illuminated Fightbook*: vol. 2, p. 121-127. The following articles are not included in the cited bibliography: Cinato/Surprenant, 'L'escrime scolastique du Liber de Arte Dimicatoria' and ead. 'L'escrime à la bocle comme méthode d'autodéfense'.

[3] Forgeng, *The medieval art of swordsmanship*; id., *The Illuminated Fightbook* ; Cinato/Surprenant, *Le Livre de l'art du combat*. Many translations self published online, including in German, Czech, English, and Italian, the latest one being published (Morini/Rudilosso, *Manoscritto I.33*).

[4] Forgeng, *The Illuminated Fightbook*, p. 4-6, Cinato, *Le livre de l'art du combat*, p. xv-xxviii. Descriptions of half-sheets that have circulated independently feed the debates around the material lacunas, without succeeding in attesting, because of lack of sources. It should be noted here the manuscript's passage in private hands between years 1936 (exhibition at the Berlin Olympic Games, then kept in the library of Gotha) and its purchasing in 1950 by the Royal Armouries in a sale at Sothebies.

[5] For a material description of the manuscript, see Forgeng, *The Illuminated Fightbook*, p. 23-24.

presenting the different hypotheses discussed including pictures of the detail of the quire spine of the manuscript (Fig. 9).

I. METHOD

The working document used to test the hypothesis of re-organisation is composed of laminated sheets into which are inserted an A4 format reproduction of the manuscript, folio by folio. The sheets composing the original bifolia were physically connected (except for the half-sheets ff. 19 and 26, which were sewn on the quires) and placed in the order of the current state of the manuscript, forming different quires by successive folds. With this working tool, it is thus possible to experiment the different hypotheses regarding the place of the folios in the manuscript, the possible re-organisations of the composition or the order of the quires, and to determine the locations of potential material lacuna.

With the hypotheses simulated physically with this tool, it is possible to assess their relevance, based on the physical folding and sewing, as well on sequences of text and images, and on the beginnings of plays (*frustum*), marked with crosses[6]. In addition to objective criticism of the assumptions made, we were able also to formulate new hypotheses related to material lacuna, and even for some of those, to hypothesise the potential content missing.

II. DESCRIPTION OF THE CURRENT STATE OF THE MANUSCRIPT

The manuscript has five quires in its current state. The binding was restored in 2012 with conservation studies[7], prior to the production of the facsimile[8]. Various descriptions of the manuscript were offered, some with more and some with fewer details[9]. Table 1 presents the quires with diagrams of their state before and after restoration:

---

[6] Frustum are technical sequence of gesture, known as "plays", marked internally with crosses. See Cinato, *Le livre de l'art du combat*, p. 325: "Frustum: pièce, morceau, division du discours iconographique balisé par un signe de croix et jouant un rôle équivalent à celui d'un chapitre…"

[7] Unpublished report of the conservation studies conducted prior to the rebinding (Leather Conservation Centre, University of Northampton, 2012), consulted with permission of the Royal Armouries library.

[8] Forgeng, *The Illuminated Fightbook*, p. 23.

[9] Forgeng, *The Illuminated Fightbook*, pp. 23-29. Cinato, *Le livre de l'art du combat*, p. xv ; Leng, *Katalog der deutschsprachigen illustrierten Handschriften*, pp. 124-126 (n° 38.9.8).

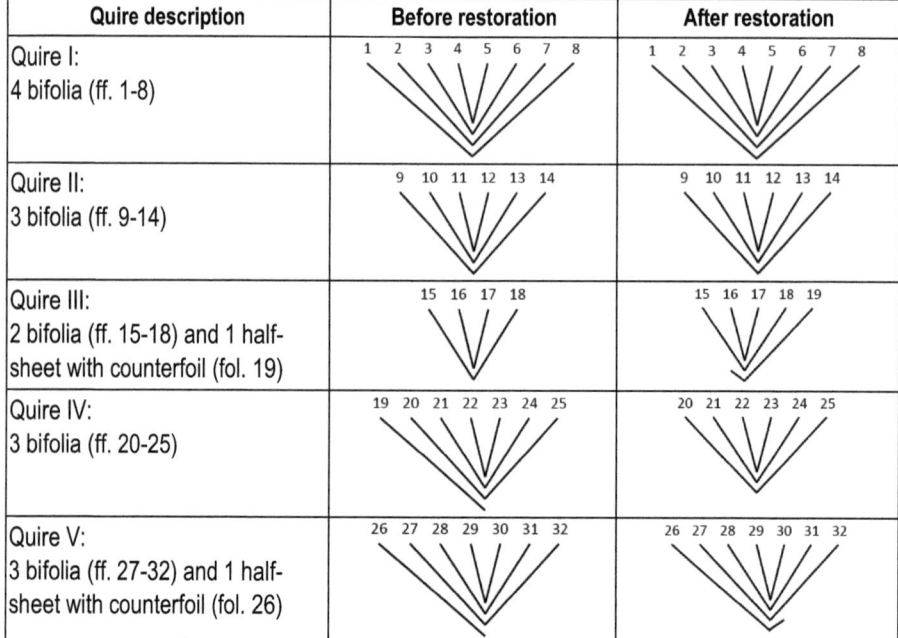

Figure 1: Table of the quires, with diagram of composition before and after restoration, realised after the conservation studies of 2012, with permission of the Royal Armouries Library

This collation is not consistent with Forgeng's description, which places half-sheets 19 and 26 respectively in quires IV and V, reflecting the state of the manuscript before restoration. He argues toward an original gathering of those, which he would locate in the quire IV (see below). The counterfoils of folia 19 and 26 are not reported in any previous description, but they might have been difficult to see in the state before restoration. Moreover, their folding may have been reversed compared to the current state (Fig. 2). We believe that they are crucial in the analysis of the collation of this manuscript and the identification of the material lacuna.

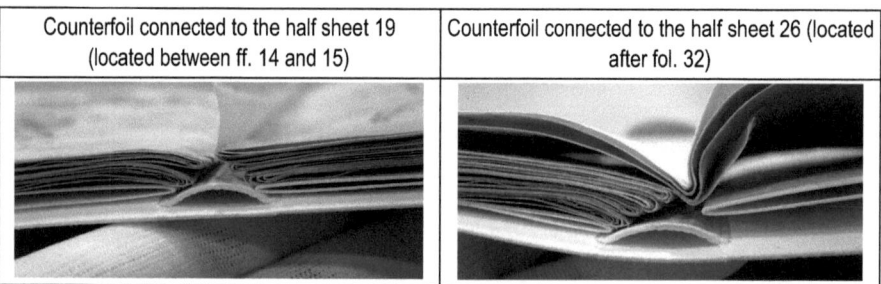

Figure 2: Details of the two counterfoils (ff. 19 and 26)
Pictures by F. Binard, with courtesy of the Royal Armouries Library.

III. DISCUSSION OF PREVIOUS HYPOTHESES

In their 2009 edition, Cinato and Surprenant suggest a reshuffle of the current state of the manuscript to create what they believe to be a more satisfactory thematic organisation, allowing an outline in seven parts following the sequences of the guards. They propose to keep the first two quires as they are, then to form a ternion with folia 26, 15 to 18 and 19, followed by the quire V, returned on itself by the fold, and finally the quire IV, but in the fifth position (Fig. 3)[10].

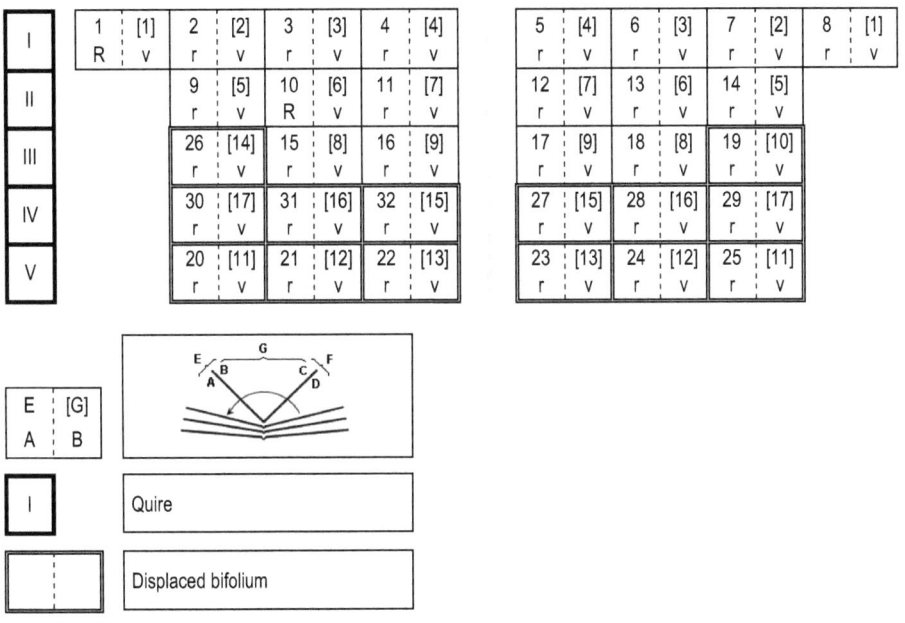

Figure 3: Synoptical diagram of the collation, according to the Cinato hypothesis (2009), with turnaround and relocation of the quire III to V.

The proposed reshuffle is disputable because of material contingencies, as indicated below. Even following this hypothesis, some discrepancies concerning textual and pictorial sequences can be observed when simulating the hypothesis.

At the end of the quire II, folio 14 ends with the beginning of a play, concerning the third guard opposed by the half-shield. The text ends with a note: "You will find here everything you had before, up to the next mark of the cross"[11]. The next folio of the new ternion (fol. 26) begins with the text: "The one who binds and the one who is bound are contrary and irate; The one who is bound flees to the side; I seek to pursue"[12], followed by the beginning of a play concerned with the opposition of the fourth guard to the special

---

[10] Cinato, *Le livre de l'art du combat*, p. XXXIII-XXXIV.

[11] Trsl Forgeng 2013, p. 74: *Que omnia prius habuisti invenies hic, usque ad proximum signum crucis.*

[12] Trsl Forgeng 2013, p. 97: *Ligans-ligati contrarij sunt et irati; Ligatus fugit ad partes laterum, peto sequi.*

guard of the Priest. However, we know that when the author states, on folio 14, that the actions are already covered above, we find them here until the next sign of cross[13], he refers indeed to binding (*religatio*), and to the shield-strike (*Schiltschlach*). These two actions are generally shown with three images[14], and not only one as proposed here, which depicts binding and pursuing. In addition, by moving folio 26, a play is pulled out of a set where the author starts by discussing the special guard of the Priest (*specificata custodia sacerdotis*) opposed with various guards. Finally, folio 26 ends with the beginning of a play. Yet, folio 15, attached just after, begins with another play.

Folios 12 to 14 relate to the fourth guard. The end of folio 14 is about the fifth guard, then folio 26 discusses the fourth and fifth guard. Folio 15 and the beginning of folio 16 focus on the fifth, then on the first, folio 17 on the sixth, and folia 18 and 19 on the seventh.

The end of the quire III (consisting of a reordered ternion) is followed by the quire V, upturned. Folio 19 is therefore followed by folio 30, with the beginning of a play that still concerns the fourth guard, but opposed with the special guard of the Priest. Folio 31 follows, with the same guard and the same opposition, then folio 32 with the second special guard of the Priest (*specificata custodia secunda sacerdotis*), still opposed by the special guard of the Priest. Next are folia 27 and 28, both describing the fifth guard opposed by this very same special guard. Finally, on folio 29, the author states: "two illustrations prior to this, the Student executed a thrust"[15]. Yet, checking previous images, no such thrust is to be found. Finally, the quire V (composed of the quire IV in the original order) continues with the seventh guard, followed by several specific guards.

This very important reshuffle implies several changes in the order of the guards' sequences and their internal development. Several inconsistencies are observable in textual and logical patterns. These assumptions were part of an ongoing research work and were made without having consulting the original; the author himself abandoned his hypothesis in his latest article (see below, Fig. 6).

In his contribution, Hester proposes another collation with up to 10 material lacuna identified, which he places according to the following diagram (Fig. 4)[16].

---

[13] Ibid.

[14] For example, fol. 13v to 14r, see ibid., pp. 72-74.

[15] Trsl Forgeng 2013, p. 103: *Prius quam superius in tertio exemplo ymaginum fixura quedam ducta est per scolarem.*

[16] Hester, 'A Few Leaves short of a Quire'.

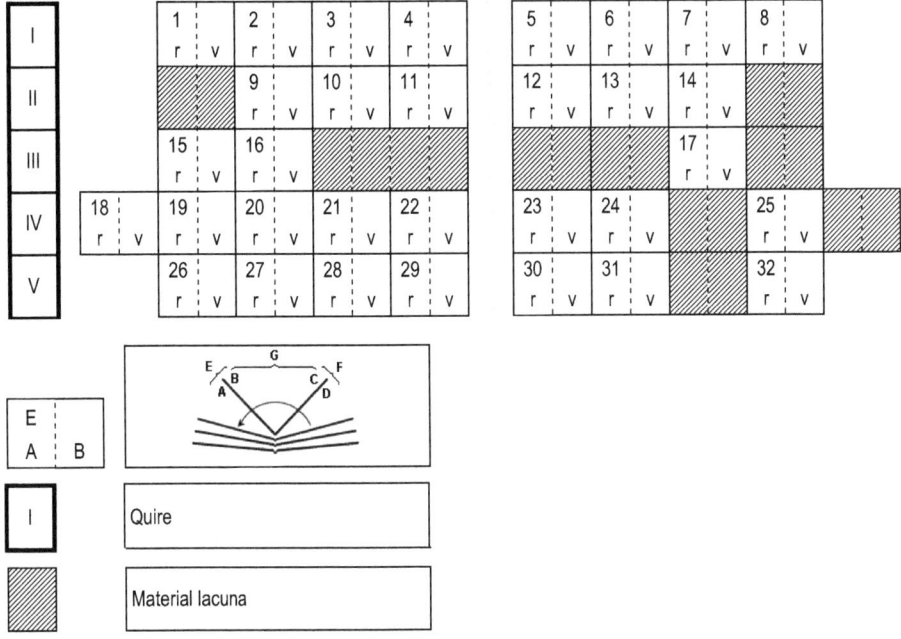

Figure 4: Synoptical diagram of the collation with location of the material lacuna, according to Hester hypothesis (2012)

The first quire is a complete quaternion. The second one is a quaternion consisting of the original ternion with the addition of a bifolium at the beginning of the quire (before fol. 9 and after fol. 14). The third quire is a quaternion, composed of only 3 original folia (fol. 15-17) with a missing folio attached to folio 15, which would be placed between folia 17 and 18. One more bifolium would be added to this quire, after folio 16 and before folio 17[17]. The fourth quire is a quinion composed by folia 18 to 25 with two missing folia, respectively between folia 24-25 and 25-26. The fifth is a quaternion composed by folia 26-32 in the present order, with a missing folio placed after the folio 31.

Before discussing the textual patterns after the hypothesis simulation, it is necessary to note physical contingencies that make this collation questionable. First of all, the author considers that a material lacuna sits between folia 17-18. This assumption is physically not possible, since folia 15 and 18 form a single bifolium (observable in the spine, the seam of the quire being between folia 16-17). Therefore, he also places folio 19 in the following quire (IV), while this half-sheet with a counterfoil is, according to our opinion, attached to the third quire. This assumption makes him consider the fourth quire as a quinion, the seam of the quire being situated between folia 22-23. He thus artificially adds two folia to the fourth quire. Finally, for the fifth quire, he considers that the missing folio lies between

---

[17] He justifies this reshuffling by assuming that the material lacuna would contain the fifth guard and the beginning of the sixth. Secondly, he proposes to substitute folio 17 to folio 18 in the quire order because the text of folio 18 is concerned with a bind (*ligatio*), which is represented in folio 17. Ibid., p. 23.

folia 31-32 after observing that the second bifolium would be incomplete. However, as the reader can see on the picture of Fig. 7, it is the first bifolium which is incomplete, the material lacuna will therefore follow folio 32, since the seam lies between folia 29-30.

The technique depicted in folia 24 and 25 appears to be rather complicated to the author, so that he implies that this might be a potential location for a material lacuna. As to the folio missing after folio 25, he therefore suggests that the illustration on folio 25r is a continuation of another technique that is missing[18]. By simulating this hypothesis, it is possible to observe the following points concerning the textual patterns (limited here to the analysis of quires IV and V).

Folio 24v ends with the special guard of the Priest opposed to the half-shield (*halbschilt*), which, for the guardian, consists of falling under the sword and buckler to come to the binding. The solution proposed after this technique is to make a shield-strike (*schiltschlach*) with a blow toward the head[19]. The text accompanying the image reads: "Here the Priest sets to the Student, as has often been seen before.[20]" The next technique (fol. 25) comes with the following text:

> Note that the Student here delivers the common blow that all ordinary combatants are accustomed to deliver in this situation, namely that when the one who binds and the one who is bound are wrangling, then the one who binds, who is above, goes toward the head and omits the Shield-Strike, leading to a blow; but the Priest enters as shown here.[21]

The author therefore explains simply that the student omits the shield-strike; he goes directly from the binding to the blow to the head, which is quite possible, without guarding himself from the Priest's sword. Thus, the Priest executes an entry, and thrusts the student in the face. The two images and the text therefore form a coherent set, and seem to form a very single play, contrary to the assumption of Hester.

Regarding the missing folio between folia 25-26, he implies that the images show too many differences in the positions of swords and in the depiction of fencers for the folia to follow one another[22]. In fact, in folio 25v, the Student is on the left side, and the Priest

---

[18] Ibid., p. 23: "The last sequence on fol. 24v has the Student's sword bound from below by the Priest. The sequence continued on fol. 25r shows the Student executing a failed upward cut toward the Priest's head; a move that would take quite a bit of maneuvering to arrive at from where we left the Student in the previous illustration. Thus it would be likely that the illustration on fol. 25r is the culmination of a different, now missing, technique."

[19] Trsl Forgeng 2013, p. 49: *Dum ducitur halpschilt, cade sub gladium quoque scutum. Si generalis erit, recipit capud : sit tibi stichslach. Si religat, calcat, contraria sint tibi schiltslac. Notandum quod ille qui iacet superius dirigit plagam post capud sine schiltslach, si est generalis. Si autem vis edoceri consilio sacerdotis, tunc religa et calca.*

[20] Trsl Forgeng 2013, p. 94: *Hic sacerdos ponit se ad scolarem, ut sepius prius visum est.*

[21] Trsl Forgeng 2013, p. 95: *Notandum quod scolaris ducit hic plagam generalem, quam consueverunt ducere omnes generales dimicatores ex supradictis proxime tactis, videlicet quando ligans et ligatus sunt in lite. Tunc ligans, qui est superior, vadit post caput et obmittit schiltslacmediante quo subsequitur plaga. Sacerdos vero intrat ut hic.*

[22] See Hester, 'A Few Leaves short of a Quire', p. 23: "The same is true for the sequence spanning fols. 25v and 26r. At the bottom of fol. 25v we have the Student binding the Priest's sword, whereas

on the right side. The Student is on the position of a right superior bind (*religatio*). On folio 26r, the Priest is on the left side, and the Student on the right side. This time, the Priest is doing the right superior bind. However, it is very simple to switch from one to the other, with a simple counterbinding. When analysing the text on folio 26r, it appears to be not specific to a peculiar sequence of technique[23], and may therefore not indicate whether or not the two images follow one another.

Forgeng offers a codicological description of the current state of the manuscript after restoration (2012). He then discusses the possible changes and material lacuna, which he places according to the following diagram (see Fig. 5)[24].

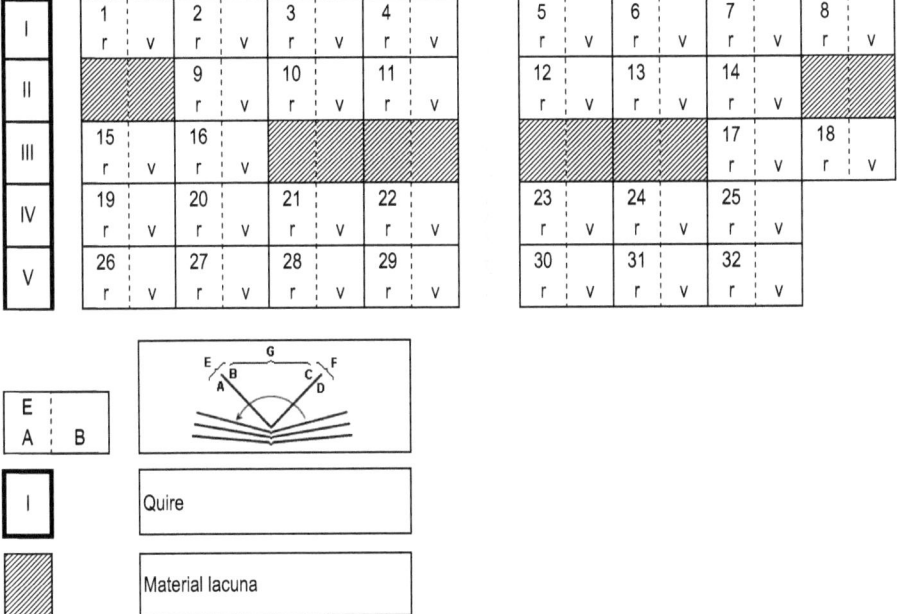

Figure 5: Synoptical diagram of the collation with location of the material lacuna, according to Forgeng hypothesis (2013)

The first quire is a complete quaternion. The second is a quaternion consisting of the original ternion with the addition of a bifolium at the beginning of the quire (before folio 9 and after folio 14). The third quire is a quaternion, composed of two originals bifolia

---

in the next illustration on fol. 26r it is the Priest who appears to be binding the Student. In both of these cases, the addition of currently missing content between these spaces would most likely make these sequences flow better and more sensibly."

[23] Trsl Forgeng 2013, p. 97: *Ligans ligati contrarij sunt & irati; Ligatus fugit ad partes laterum; petro sequi.*

[24] Forgeng, *The Illuminated Fightbook*, pp. 23-29. Here the collation is represented as described, corresponding to the original state. However, his hypothesis of the gathering of folia 19-26 are not represented on the diagram, since the author did not include it in his "V" diagrams (see Fig. 9), but discussed this re-organisation in the body of his text.

(fol.15-18) and two missing bifolia (between folia 16 and 17). The fourth quire is a quaternion formed by the original ternion (folia 20-25), wrapped by the two half-sheets with counterfoil (19 and 26) forming one original bifolium. The fifth quire is a ternion composed by folia 27-32 in the present order.

He suggests that folia 19 and 26 were originally a single bifolium, which belongs to the quire 4. This bifolium would have been separated in half during an unknown time in its conservation history and one folio would have served as a model in the faithful copy found in the compendium of Wolfenbüttel[25].

Applying this reshuffle (folio 26 being sewed to quire V), the quire V forms a ternion. This final structural irregularity seems plausible to the author. He assumes that no material lacuna could have been placed after folio 32, eventually in the middle of quire V, but not at the end. This assumption is based on the observed damage on folio 32v (indicating that the manuscript, or at least this quire, would have circulated for a long period of time as is) and on textual elements on this folio (the outcomes of this situation have already been covered)[26]. The end of folio 32 indeed marks the end of a play; not because he said earlier that everything that is seen here has already been processed in the first quire[27], but because the play ends on a shield-strike and a blow to the head, as in the first quire. Even following this argument, there is finally little evidence supporting that the treatise would end here, allowing us to hypothesise a potential lacuna after fol. 32v (see below).

Also, if the two half-sheets (19 and 26) formed originally one bifolium, it would be interesting to put this hypothesis to the test by checking if the counterfoils would match. Our preliminary observation let us doubt this hypothesis (see detailed pictures on fig. 1), but further research is to be done on this matter, with permission of the curator, since it would imply dismantling the quires.

Finally in his most recent article[28], Cinato proposes two new assumptions about the composition of the manuscript (Fig. 6). His first conforms broadly to that made by Forgeng, as discussed above (Fig. 5). However, he shared our doubts as to the location of folio 26, placing it in at the beginning of the quire V, thus aligning with our hypothesis and forming a quaternion and not a ternion as suggested by Forgeng. His second hypothesis is similar to his first, with the difference that he adds two material lacuna, bringing their number up to 10 (as Hester assumes)[29], thus turning the supposed

---

[25] Wolfenbüttel, Herzog August Bibliothek, Cod. Guelf. 125.16 Extrav., fol. 45r. Noted by Forgeng, The *Illuminated Fightbook*, pp. 5 and 28. Also noted by Cinato and Hester.

[26] Forgeng, *The Illuminated Fightbook*, p. 28. See conclusion for the discussion about the absence of damage on the counterfoil.

[27] Ibid., p. 109: *Et ex hiis generantur omnia que habentur de prima custodia, de quibus habetur in primo quaterno.*

[28] Cinato, 'Development, Diffusion and Reception of the Buckler plays'.

[29] He places a missing bifolium in the quire V between fol. 26-27 and after fol. 32, see ibid.

quaternion into a quinion. Due to lack of further evidence to support his first or second hypothesis, he left them open for discussion.

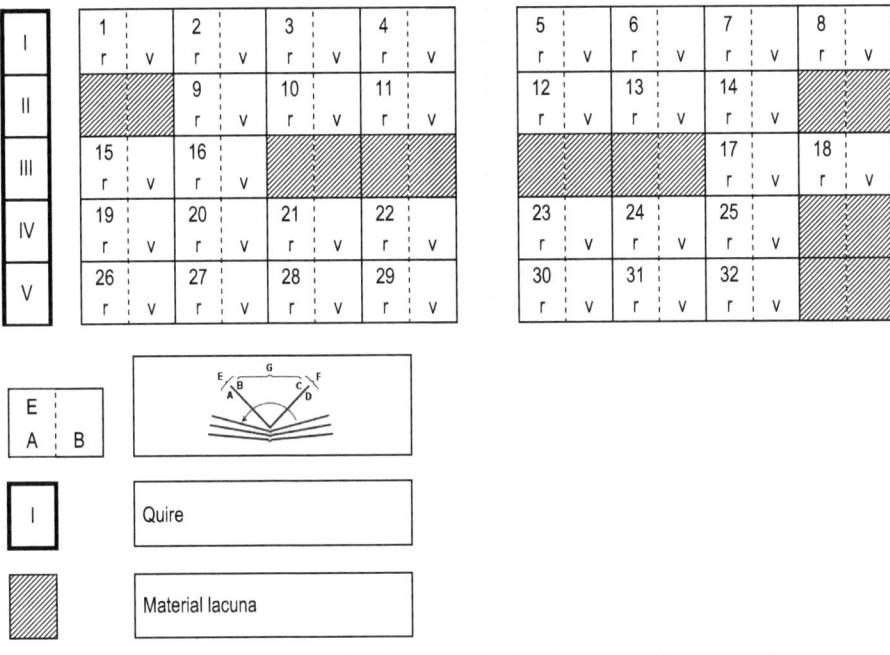

Figure 6: Synoptical diagram of the collation with location of the material lacuna, according to Cinato hypothesis (2016). Nota bene: the author did formalise a second hypothesis about quire V implying 2 more material lacuna, forming a quinion (this second hypothesis is not represented in the diagram).

IV. INTERPRETATIVE HYPOTHESIS OF THE QUIRES' LAYOUT

Our interpretation follows Forgeng, Cinato and Hester on the construction of the first two quires, but differs for the other quires. In the next section, we argue that previous researchers all locate fol. 19 and 26 incorrectly, which implies disputable hypotheses for the construction of quires 3-5 and the location of identified material lacuna.

We follow the postulate, according to which, the manuscript was originally composed by five quaternions, each quire being originally formed of 8 folia, as 4 bifolia folded in two, inserted into each other and sewn together. We therefore follow the actual order of the manuscript, realised after the restoration report of 2012. We then propose an identification of other potential material lacuna, crossing structural and textual evidences, by offering a quire-by-quire analysis below (see Fig. 7). We go even further by proposing the partial identification, subject to sufficient textual evidence, of the content of some of the material lacuna. We also hypothesise two material lacuna originally attached to folia with counterfoils (19 and 26), placed respectively in quires III and V (since they are currently sewn into the latter). The reader can follow the discussion by referring to Fig. 8 representing the content distribution throughout the quires. It presents the synoptical representation of the collation of the quire, and in the lower panel indication about the crosses and the content according to the guards' sequences (highlighting the hermeneutic structure).

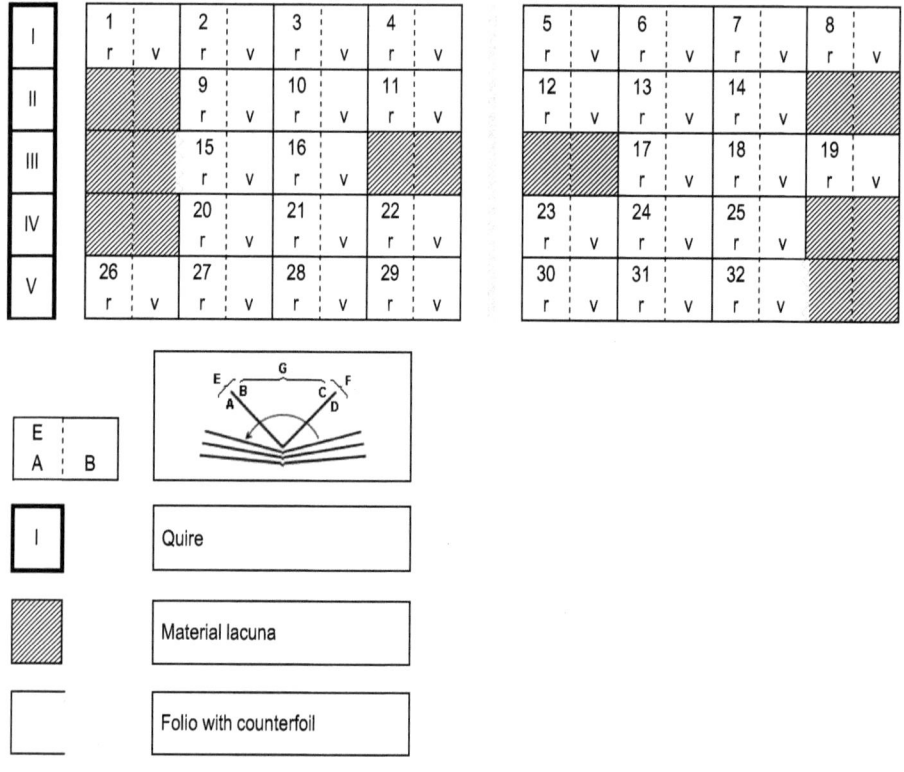

Figure 7: Synoptical diagram of the collation, with location of the material lacuna, according to Binard hypothesis (2016)

IV.1. First quire
This quire, consisting of 4 bifolia, is complete.

IV.2. Second quire
This quire consists of 3 bifolia. To form a quaternion, we propose to identify a material lacuna of a bifolium, placed between folia 8-9 and 14-15. This hypothesis can be supported by the text. Indeed, folio 8 ends on a play which reads: "Here we resume First Guard, and it is opposed with the first opposition, namely Half-Shield; and you will have

all the previous actions[30]"; followed by: "When Half-Shield is adopted, fall under the sword and shield.[31]" As a result of this action, the student must rebind, and then set up one of the five options at his disposal shown in the first quire:

- two for the Student: the shield-strike (*schilslach*), or to seize the Priest's arms with his left hand.

- three for the Priest: change of sword (*mutatio gladii*), stepping through (*durchtreten*), or with his right hand he can seize the Student's arms (*vel dextra manu comprehendere brachia scolaris*).

Both of the Student's options are explained and represented. As for the Priest, only the change of sword is explained. The capture of arms will be presented later in the treatise, on folio 12v. The analysis of the text and the deductions based on the pedagogical sequence suggests that explanations are lacking and reinforces the idea of a missing folio at this location. The material lacuna could thus include the explanation of the "stepping through" (*durchtritt*), or of the seizing of the arms with the right hand, even if it is repeated later. In addition, the following folio (9) begins by explaining the second guard, thus confirming that this guard was not seen before.

The hypothesis of the second part of the material gap (attached to the previously described folio) placed between folia 14-15 is also supported by the analysis of the textual content. The end of folio 14 reads:

> After we have dealt with the Third Guard, here we deal with the Fourth; the opposition to it will be Half-Shield. You will find here everything you had before, up to the next mark of cross.[32]

Comparing with the previous play to which the text return (third guard opposed with half-shield), the following action is therefore lacking: the fall under the sword and the shield, counterbind, and shield-strike. Assuming one image per action, we would have 3 missing images, covering three quarters of a potential missing bifolium (one folio contains two images).

IV.3. Third quire

The third quire is composed of 2 bifolia (15-18), 1 half-sheet with counterfoil (19), sewn into the third quire (the counterfoil is therefore placed between folia 14-15, see Fig. 1). The counterfoil is not cut cleanly: fibres are observable on the tear, suggesting a pull-out by hand. Unlike to what Forgeng and Cinato were able to postulate, this quire does not

---

[30] Trsl Forgeng 2013, p. 62: *Custodia prima resumitur hic et obsedetur cum prima possessione, videlicet halpschilt. Et habebis omnia priora.*

[31] Ibid.: *Dum ducitur halpschilt, cade sub gladium quoque scutum.*

[32] Trsl Forgeng 2013, p. 74: *Postquam determinatum est de tertia custodia, hic determinat de quarta, cuius obsessio erit halpschilt, que omnia prius habuisti invenies hic, usque ad proximum signum crucis.*

consist in the current state of only two bifolia. They place folio 19 in the next quire, thus shifting their assumptions about the location of the material lacuna.

The first lacuna in this quire lies before folio 15. The text here does not show enough indications to support this hypothesis. We can however assume that the lacuna could contain plays that still concern the fourth guard, because the text of folio 15r begins: "Here the Priest resumes the Fourth Guard.[33]"

To form a quaternion, it still lacks a bifolium. We locate this, as Forgeng, Cinato and Hester did, between folio 16 and 17, in the middle of the quire (where the seam lies). However, if all three researchers have identified the same location for the material lacuna, they have not suggested a material lacuna of a single bifolium, but of two.

The location of the material lacuna is justified by the content analysis:

> (fol.16v) Here the Student's sword is released by means of a Shield-Strike; and let the Priest beware lest the Student deliver a blow to the head or the common thrust that the Priest is accustomed to teach his students. And if the Student delivers a blow to the head, protect it with the sword and the shield held together in your left hand. And thus you will break the shield from your opponent's hand; see below in the next illustration.[34]

> (fol.17r) Here the Priest adopts the Sixth Guard, which is given to the chest. And note that you should only deliver the same thrust that is delivered from the Fifth Guard; see up to the next mark of the cross.[35]

It clearly lacks the shield-strike mentioned at the end of folio 16. The mention in folio 17 of a missing play, the thrust, confirms another lacuna. Since previous folia are introducing plays of the fourth guard, and folio 17 the sixth guard, we can suggest that the material lacuna is about the fifth guard.

IV.4. Fourth quire

The quire is composed of 3 bifolia. We hypothesise a missing bifolium, located between folia 19-20 and 25-26, the seam being located between folia 22-23. The analysis of the textual content supports the hypothesis.

---

[33] Trsl Forgeng 2013, p. 75: *Hic sacerdos resumit quartam custodiam*.

[34] Trsl Forgeng 2013, p. 78: *Hic relevatur gladius scolaris mediante schiltslac. Et caveat sacerdos ne scolaris ducat plagam capiti, sive fixuram generalem quam sacerdos consuevit docere discipulos suos. Preterea, scias quod si scolaris dat plagam capiti, protectionem duc gladio connexoque scuto quod habetur in sinistra manu. Et sic frangis scutum de manibus tui adversarii, ut patet infra proximo exemplo.*

[35] Trsl Forgeng 2013, p. 79: *Hic sacerdos ducit sextam custodiam que datur pectori. Et nota quod solum illa fixura est ducenda, que ducetur de quinta custodia usque ad proximum signum crucis.*

In folia 17, 18 and 19 of the third quire, the author talks about the bind. He first of all announces that there are four different binds: two on the right and two on the left. He discusses the superior right bind, then the inferior left bind on folio 19. Folio 20 addresses the superior left bind, and once again the superior right bind. One bind is missing, which could be contained in this missing folio, between folio 19 and 20: the inferior right bind.

The second part of the lacuna lies between folia 25-26. In the next folia, the author review the guards 3 to 5 opposed with the special guard of the priest. Folio 26 begins with the middle or end of a play. We know this because there is no cross to mark the beginning of the play here. We can then assume a lacuna at this point. Unfortunately, the text ("The one who binds and the one who is bound are contrary and irate; The one who is bound flees to the side; I seek to pursue"[36]) is too unspecific to relate it to a specific play. The next play addresses the third guard opposed with the special guard of the priest. Without too many risks, we can then suggest the hypothesis that the contents of the missing folio are about the first and the second guards opposed with the special guard of the priest.

IV.5. Fifth quire

This quire is composed of 3 bifolia (27-32), with 1 half-sheet with counterfoil (26), sewed in the fifth quire (the counterfoil is therefore placed after folio 32, see Fig. 1).

As well as folio 19, the counterfoil appearing on the other side of spine may have been torn by hand. It should be noted, as Forgeng pointed out that, the last folio of the manuscript is very damaged. The paper is obscured, possibly by the heat, and we can see some scorches. However, the counterfoil suffered no change of colour. In addition, fibres that come out from the counterfoil do not appear to have been affected by any heat. To theses physical observations, we should add textual comments. Folio 32 ends on a blow, it would therefore be consistent whether the end of the play with Walpurgis. No evidence can allow us to identify the potential content of this lacuna suggested by the presence of the counterfoil. The fact that this counterfoil does not have the same traces of wear as folio 32 lets us think, as suggested by Forgeng, that the quire has been reshuffled. However, we stand firm by our hypothesis. Indeed, it seems logical that folio 26 is in the right place since the author reviewed two oppositions (*obsessio*), then all the guards one after the other opposed with the special guard of the priest. Folio 25 concerns the "rare opposition" (*valde aliena obsessio*) opposed with the special guard of the priest, then there is a lacuna, that we suppose to be about the special guard of the priest opposed with first guard, then second guard. Indeed, folio 26 is about the special guard of the priest opposed to the third guard, then the fourth guard, and finally folio 27 is still about the special guard of the priest, opposed with the fifth guard.

---

[36] Trsl. Forgeng 2013, p. 97: *Ligans-ligati contrarii sunt et irati. Ligatus fugit ad partes laterum, peto sequi.*

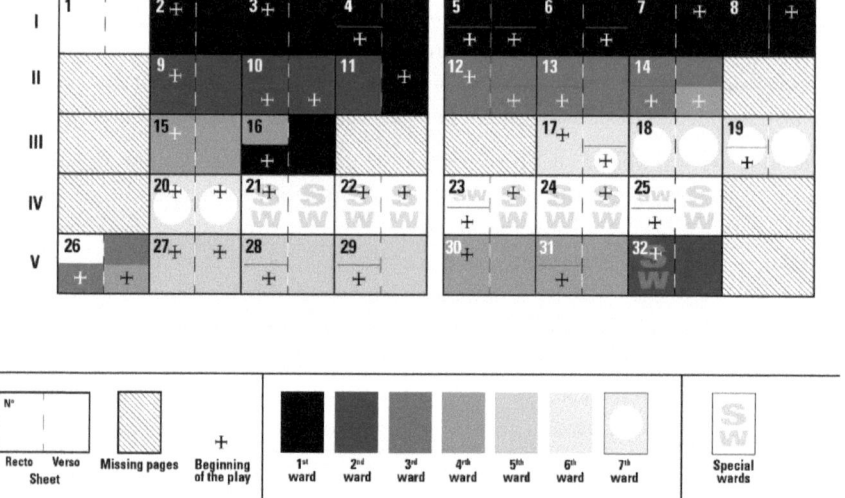

Figure 8: Content distribution throughout the quires, according to Binard hypothesis (2016)

V. CONCLUSION

After having reviewed the different hypotheses of previous researchers, simulated them with our working document, and confronted with material and textual evidences, we demonstrated some of the weaknesses of theses hypotheses, mainly about quires III to V. We believe that the current state of the manuscript represents the original order and the identification of material lacunas allows, in a certain way, to resolve the irregularities observed in the analysis of the text, reported and discussed by previous studies. Figure 9 offers a representation of the different hypothesis with the detail of the quires' spine, allowing the reader to make the same observations that have been presented in this article.

The discussion of the collation of the manuscript remains hypothetical of course, since it is based on the state of the manuscript, as it arrived in the collection of the Royal Armouries. The restoration of 2012 led to a relocation of the folio 19 from the quire IV to quire III, which we believe to be accurate. To our knowledge, there is no document allowing to retrace any previous collation or reshuffle, leaving any study about previous states of conservation open for discussion.

Therefore, the weakest point of our argumentation is the opinion we have about the last folio (32), divergent from Forgeng's or Hester's observations and assumptions[37].

---

[37] Forgeng, *The Illuminated Fightbook*, p. 28. He hypothesizes a ternion (see above, note 26). Hester notes a material lacuna between folia 31 and 32 (based on assumption that the material lacuna is attached to 26, but this is not possible considering the location of the sewing). He postulates this

Nevertheless, we believe that the association of the folio 19 with the fourth quire, as assumed by previous studies is actually altering the hypotheses about the composition of the manuscript. This point remains even so open for discussion and further research. It lies with the question of the location of the folia 19 and 26, and the direction of the folding of their counterfoil. Another collation of folia 19 and 26 at the beginning and end of the quire IV with a folding towards the inside of the quire might, for example, represent a previous state of conservation and explain the absence of damage on the counterfoils[38]. Moreover, other hypotheses might even lead to discussion about another material lacuna in the quire V, offering explanation about the conclusion of the work, which might be incomplete or have endured a change of auctorial project during production[39].

To conclude, this contribution offered a current state of research and a review of the previous studies concerning the collation of the manuscript with diagrams allowing the comparison between the different hypotheses. It proposes a hypothesis based on both the analysis of the material and the content, while leaving the issues about the location of the flying leaves and the composition of last quire open for discussion and further research.

---

would imply possible explanation about the lack of damage on 31 compared to 32, as well as to why the figure of Walpurgis appears instead of the Student without other comment, see Hester, 'A Few Leaves Short of a Quire', p. 24.

[38] This is a hypothesis formulated by Franck Cinato. We thank him for sharing his opinion on this matter.

[39] This would follow the second hypothesis of Cinato, 'Development, Diffusion and Reception of the Buckler plays', already hinted in his 2009 edition while observing that the authorial project might have undergone a reorientation during realisation.

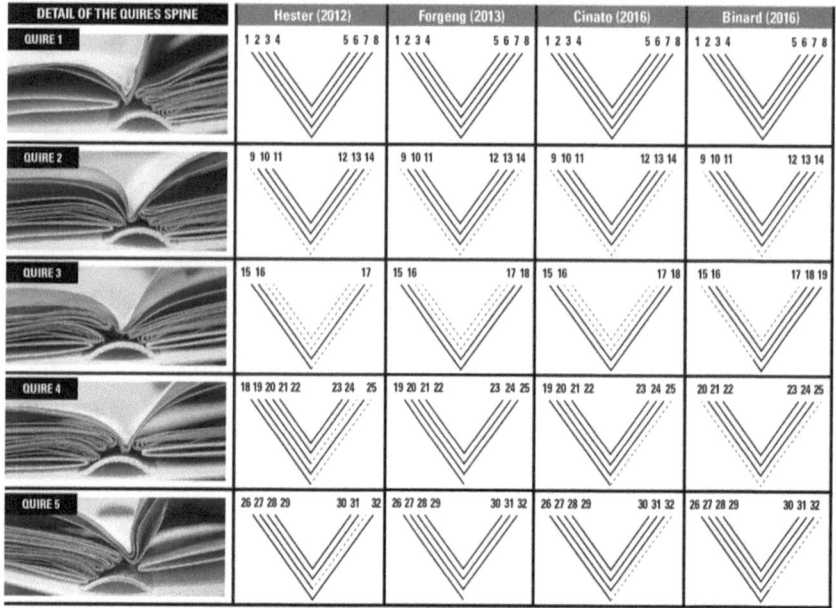

*Figure 9: Comparison of collation hypothesis with pictures of the edge of the quires
Pictures by F. Binard, with Courtesy of the Royal Armouries Library.
Diagram by F. Binard and O. Gourdon, reproduced or created according to the published
articles/monographs of the cited authors. Nota bene: the second hypothesis of Cinato is not
represented on the figure (see legend of fig. 6).*

VI. BIBLIOGRAPHY

VI.1 Primary sources

Anonymous, Liber de arte Dimicatoria, 1320-1330. Leeds, Royal Armouries, Ms I.33.

Anonymous, compendium (Hans Talhoffer Fight book), 17th c. Wolfenbüttel, Herzog August Bibliothek, Cod. Guelf. 125.16 Extrav.

VI.2 Secondary literature

Cinato, Franck, 'Development, Diffusion and Reception of the Buckler plays: A Fighting Art in the Making, a case study', in *Late Medieval and Early Modern Fight Books*, ed. by Daniel Jaquet, Timothy Dawson and Karin Verelst (Leiden: Brill, 2016).

Cinato, Franck, and André Surprenant, 'L'escrime à la bocle comme méthode d'autodéfense selon le Liber de Arte Dimicatoria', in *L'art chevaleresque du combat: Le maniement des armes à travers les livres de combat (XIVe - XVIe siècle)*, by Daniel Jaquet (Neuchâtel: Alphil, 2013), pp. 81–89.

Cinato, Franck, and André Surprenant, 'L'escrime scolastique du Liber de Arte Dimicatoria. Un cas de rationalisation par l'image', in *Quand l'image relit le texte: regards croisés sur les manuscrits médiévaux*, ed. by Sandrine Hériché-Pradeau and Maud Pérez-Simon (Paris: Presses Sorbonne Nouvelle, 2013), pp. 249–60.

Cinato, Franck, and André Surprenant, *Le Livre de l'art du combat (Liber de Arte Dimicatoria) : Édition critique du Royal Armouries MS. I.33*, Sources d'histoire médiévale, 39 (Paris: CNRS-éd, 2009).

Forgeng, Jeffrey L, *The Illuminated Fightbook: Royal Armouries Manuscript I.33*. 2 vols (Dorset: Royal Armouries and Extraordinary Editions, 2013).

Forgeng, Jeffrey L, *The medieval art of swordsmanship : a facsimile & translation of Europe's oldest personal combat treatise, Royal Armouries MS I.33* (Union City: Chivalry Bookshelf, 2003).

Hester, James, 'A Few Leaves Short of a Quire: Is the "Tower Fechtbuch" Incomplete?', *Arms & Armour*, 9 (2012), 20–24.

Leng, Rainer, Hella Frühmorgen-Voss, Norbert H. Ott, Ulrike Bodemann, Peter Schmidt, and Christine Stöllinger-Löser, *Katalog Der Deutschsprachigen Illustrierten Handschriften Des Mittelalters Band 4/2, Lfg. 1/2: 38: 38. Fecht- Und Ringbücher*, C.H. Beck (München: Bayerische Akademie der Wissenschaften, 2008).

Morini, Andrea and Riccardo Rudilosso, *Manoscritto I.33* (Rome: Il Cerchio Iniziative Editoriali, 2012).

A Well Regulated Militia
Political and Military Organisation
in Pre-Napoleonic Switzerland
(1550-1799)

By Dr. Jürg Gassmann
Artes Certaminis
jurg.gassmann@gassmannconsulting.com

Abstract – The period sees the transition of the ordinary fighter from feudal levy, yeoman or city burgher militia, to subject in an absolute polity, to today's concept of the free citizen in a democratic state. In the period, the Swiss Confederacy was the only major polity that was not monarchical, but republican, and at the same time eschewed a standing army in favour of continued reliance on militia throughout.

A commonwealth's military organisation is clearly one of fundamental importance to its own understanding of the nature of rule – its "constitution". The article traces the transition and relates it to the concept of government under the different theories of the period.

Keywords – Militia, democracy, absolutism, gute Policey, military organisation, Switzerland, 2nd Amendment, constitution, city-state, war, Natural Law

> *Da sprach der erste: »Kommandant! / Dort unten liegt mein Heimatland.*
> *Ich schütz es mit der Flinte mein. / Wie sollt ich da nicht lustig sein?«*
>
> *Der zweite sprach: »Herr Pestaluzz! / Seht ihr das Rathaus dort am Stutz?*
> *Dort wähl ich meine sieben Herrn. / Drum dien ich froh; drum leist ich gern.«*
>
> *Der dritte sprach: »Ich halt als Norm: / 's ist eine Freud, die Uniform.*
> *'s ist eine mutige Mannespflicht. / Da muß man jauchzen. Oder nicht?«*
> From Carl Spitteler: *Die jodelnden Schildwachen*[1]

I. OBJECTIVE, INTRODUCTION AND PROPOSITION

Even to contemporary writers, it was remarkable that within a sea of princely states which disarmed their own populace and instead paid standing armies, Switzerland was not only a republic, but also relied exclusively on locally-raised militia.[2] And yet, while the story of

---

[1] Carl Spitteler (1845-1924) won the Nobel Prize for Literature 1919 (<http://gutenberg.spiegel.de/buch/carl-spitteler-gedichte-1294/10>; accessed 23 October 2015).

[2] Sigg, *17. Jahrhundert*, p. 350.

Swiss mercenary service abroad has received intense scrutiny, the academic discussion, both at the time and currently, seems uninterested in going beyond that general statement – with some exceptions.

In this article, I propose to follow the methodology sketched out by Walter:[3] What was the relevant constitutional concept prevalent in Switzerland at the time? My approach is slightly different from Walter's: Walter's analysis was limited to the relationship between the Netherlands on one hand and Zurich and Berne on the other, but included topics other than the militia. I propose to focus on the issue of the militia, but widen the purview and pay more attention to the legal and constitutional dimension, to ask: What were the drivers for the concept of an armed populace organised in a militia, as the only armed force in the commonwealth?

II. SWITZERLAND IN THE RELEVANT ERA

II.1. Political Structure

Switzerland – after 1550 internally and externally roughly within the borders that exist today – was made up of three types of territories: First, a confederacy of Thirteen Cantons (*Orte*), full members, each of them sovereign within the Holy Roman Empire, bound together by a network of treaties and resolutions; the sole common institution was the *Tagsatzung*, a congress of ambassadors from the cantons. The Thirteen were selective, taking care to maintain a balance between city and rural, Catholic and Protestant cantons; after 1513 (Appenzell), no new full members were created until Napoleon re-arranged Switzerland.[4]

Secondly, the associate members, without vote in the *Tagsatzung* but allied with the Thirteen. Some of the associate members were sovereign republics in the HRE in their own right, others did not have the full panoply of privileges to rate as sovereign.[5]

---

[3] Walter, *Niederländische Einflüsse*, pp. 11-15.

[4] Simler, *Regiment der Eydgenoßschaft*, pp. 1-2; Wyß, *Politisches Handbuch*, pp. 117-221; Maissen, *Geschichte*, p. 111-113; comprehensive overview: Oechsli, *Orte und Zugewandte*. The *Dreizehn Orte* were: Zurich, Berne, Lucerne, Uri, Schwyz, Unterwalden, Glarus, Zug, Fribourg, Solothurn, Basel Stadt, Schaffhausen and Appenzell (after the Reformation split into Inner- and Ausserrhoden).

[5] Generally Maissen, *Geschichte*, pp. 113-115. Sovereign *Zugewandte* were the Grisons, the Valais, Geneva, Neuchatel, St Gallen city and some cities now integrated into the cantons (like Gersau or Biel). The Prince-Abbey of St Gallen and the Prince-Bishop of Basel (now the demicanton Basel-Landschaft), as ecclesiastical estates, could not have the full set of privileges. The Prince-Abbey was a significant estate, and in the *Defensionale* of Wil 1647 the fifth-largest contributor of forces, after Berne, Zurich, Lucerne and Fribourg – Menolfi, *Solddienst*, p. 205.

Finally, there were the subject territories; each was administered by one or more of the full members, and the chief function of the *Tagsatzung* was to share out among the full members the lucrative offices and the income derived from their exploitation.[6]

All cantons had republican forms of government; the city cantons[7] had essentially oligarchical structures, where leading patrician families or guilds populated privy councils that largely selected themselves and which were no less absolutist than the princely states.[8] Alongside the city cantons were the rural cantons, where a *Landsgemeinde* – a popular assembly of all citizens – elected magistrates and passed laws; though here, too, leading families emerged, the "oligarchisation" was more limited.[9] In these *Landsgemeinde* cantons, a clear link traditionally existed between citizenship (the right to vote), bearing arms, and military service, and in Appenzell Innerrhoden, male voters still today carry a side-arm to show their eligibility to vote in the *Landsgemeinde*.[10]

II.2. International Relations

Thanks to the comprehensive mercenary hiring treaties of 1516 and 1521, the undeniably closest external relationship was to France, with the Swiss sometimes seen as a protectorate of France. Especially after the revocation of the Edict of Nantes, France was clearly Catholic, and pre-1712 often intervened to preserve the Catholic preponderance

---

[6] Today the cantons of St. Gallen, Aargau, Thurgau, Vaud, Basel-Land, Ticino, and Jura; Maissen, *Geschichte*, pp. 111-113; Fehr, *Absolutismus*, pp. 197-200.

[7] Zurich, Berne, Lucerne, Fribourg, Solothurn, Schaffhausen, Basel; Neuchâtel, an associate member, was a hereditary principality – the only non-republican entity in the confederation, until 1707 part of the house of Orléans-Longueville, and then of Prussia.

[8] Peyer, *Verfassungsgeschichte*, pp. 110-116; Fehr, *Absolutismus*; Gmür, *Städte als Landesherren*, p. 191; Schläpfer, *Ausserrhoden*, pp. 57-65; Maissen, *Geschichte*, pp. 109-111 and pp. 129-130; Jeker, *Rechtsgeschichte Solothurn*, pp. 38-45. Josias Simler, *De republica*, ff. 121r-121v, recites the Aristotelian definition of forms of government: By the one (*rex*), the few (*optimates*), and the people (*totus populus*), and their lapsed forms *tyrannis* (a monarch ruling without the consent of the people), *oligarchia* and *populare imperiu[m] tumultus et anarchiae plenum* (a popular rule full of tumult and anarchy); he finds that Switzerland has a mixed form of government, some cantons governed by *optimates*, other by the *totus populus*. An instructive – though slanted to the point of propaganda – read is David Wyß' exposition of the Zurich constitution, written 1796 (*Politisches Handbuch*, pp. 51-54).

[9] Brändle, *Revitalisierung*. Uri, Schwyz, Unterwalden (both Ob and Nid dem Wald), Glarus and (both) Appenzell; Zug was technically a city canton, but organised like a *Landsgemeinde* canton.

[10] <www.ai.ch/de/politik/sitzung/>; Bischofberger, *Rechtsarchäologie Innerrhoden*, pp. 79-83; Schläpfer, *Ausserrhoden*, p. 42; Tlusty, *Martial Ethic*, p. 275; Brändle, *Revitalisierung*, pp. 605-606. In the city cantons, the authorities avoided a link since their rural subjects had no voting rights but still a service obligation; still, in Zurich, a man needed the proper equipment to join a guild (i.e. vote): Wyß, *Politisches Handbuch*, p. 225.

in the Confederacy.[11] Generally, the Catholic cantons maintained their own friendly relations with the Holy See and Catholic princes.

Especially for the Protestant cantons, the connection to the Netherlands was a particularly strong one, thanks to Calvinism. Initially, Geneva was a centre for Protestant studies by Dutch students, but as the Dutch founded their own universities, a veritable stream of Swiss students flocked to Leiden, Franeker, Groningen and Utrecht, not just to study theology, but also law and other subjects.[12] The Dutch also hired large numbers of Swiss mercenaries, especially in the Protestant cantons.[13]

The military reforms put in place by Maurice of Orange in the late 16th C, which enabled the Dutch to defeat Spanish Habsburg in the Eighty Years' War, were a model for all of Europe, and were copied in Switzerland as well.[14]

II.3. The Militia Principle

All of the cantons for their military relied on a militia, none had a standing army.[15] While in the 16th C recruitment was specific to a venture, by the early 18th C the militia were raised by a system of annual or at least regular musters, where military-age men were allocated to the units they would train with and their kit was regularly inspected.[16] The

---

[11] Peyer, *Verfassungsgeschichte*, pp. 81-84. Grosjean, *Kriegsgenügen*, pp. 162-163; Ulrich, *18. Jahrhundert*, p. 372: It is no accident that Villmergen II happened while the European powers' attention was focussed on the War of Spanish Succession peace negotiations.

[12] Walter, *Niederländische Einflüsse*, pp. 7-8, 87-97; at the time, the only Swiss university was Basel, founded 1460. Geneva, Zurich and Lausanne had religious (Protestant) colleges.

[13] Walter, *Niederländische Einflüsse*, pp. 82-87; Sigg, *17. Jahrhundert*, p. 359; despite Zurich's prohibition, Zurich was not able to stop – or chose to turn a blind eye to – Zurchers signing up for Dutch service.

[14] Walter, *Niederländische Einflüsse*, pp. 18-54; Jeker, *Rechtsgeschichte Solothurn*, p 78. Conversely, the Netherlands looked to Switzerland for inspiration on the constitutional organisation of the Seven Provinces; Walter, *Niederländische Einflüsse*, p. 7-8.

[15] Though purchasing mercenaries had been contemplated: during the Thirty Years' War, there were attempts to give the Confederacy the authority to hire a standing mercenary force and allocate the cost among the members, in accordance with the Dutch model, but the costs were daunting and the plan politically unpalatable – Peyer, *Verfassungsgeschichte*, pp. 94-96; Walter, *Niederländische Einflüsse*, pp. 55-81. Zurich had contingency plans to raise mercenaries if it had been drawn into the Thirty Years' War (Sigg, *17. Jahrhundert*, p. 352), and Berne actually did purchase some troops (Rodt, *Berner Kriegswesen*, II, p. 200-202; Grosjean, *Kriegsgenügen*, p. 155). Maissen, *Geschichte*, p. 120 points out that in 1732, Berne spent 4% of its budget on the military, France in 1700 75%, and a fair portion of that went to pay Swiss mercenaries.

[16] Simler, *Regiment der Eydgenoßschaft*, p. 406; Simler, *De republica*, p. 123v-124r: *Nam cum apud multos gentes plebi armorum usus interdicatur, contra in Helvetia etiam mercenarii & capite censi arma pro facultatum ratione sibi comparare & domi conservare coguntur* (For as with many peoples the common people are forbidden the use of arms, but in Switzerland even peddlers and labourers are obliged to buy and

change was forced by the transition from the *Gewalthaufen*, consisting of pike and halberd, where comparatively little training in weaponry or manœuvring was required, to the predominance of pike-and-shot and later flintlock units, where both the handling of the weapon and the evolutions of the battlefield formations required intensive training.[17] Authority mandates required regular compulsory meetings for drill and musket practice, and the authorities subsidised prizes for marksmanship competitions.[18]

Military service was compulsory for all able-bodied male inhabitants, usually from age 15 or 16 to 60, and a soldier had to purchase his uniform and weaponry – as defined by the authorities – himself.[19] The units were officered by the scions of the politically powerful families of the canton.[20]

---

keep at home arms in accordance with their means); in detail Wyß for Zurich 1796, *Politisches Handbuch*, pp. 224-227 and 231-236; Rodt, *Berner Kriegswesen*, II, pp. 282-300; Ziegler, *Milizen der Stadt St. Gallen*, for St Gallen city. Menolfi, *Solddienst*, pp. 213-216; Sonderegger, *Altappenzellisches Wehrwesen*, p. 30-32; Schläpfer, *Ausserrhoden*, pp. 128-129; Sigg, *17. Jahrhundert*, p. 358; Jeker, *Rechtsgeschichte Solothurn*, pp. 48-49 and 66-71; Nussbaumer, *Zuger Militär*, pp. 204-205 and 215-235.

[17] Walter, *Niederländische Einflüsse*, pp. 20-54; Maissen, *Geschichte*, p. 122; Sigg, *17. Jahrhundert*, pp. 352-353 and 358-359; Menolfi, *Solddienst*, p. 213; Sigg, *Promenade Militaire*, p. 26-34; Jeker, *Rechtsgeschichte Solothurn*, pp. 62-64; Grosjean, *Kriegsgenügen*, pp. 149-151; Ziegler, *Milizen der Stadt St. Gallen*, pp. 157-186. Drill was introduced and regulations written, initially on the Dutch pattern, later increasingly following French models – e.g. Hans Conrad Lavater, *Kriegsbüchlein* (Zurich, 1667 – particularly pp. 109-134); the *Reglement für die Herren Officiers Löbl. Grenadier-Compagnie zu Fuß* (St. Gallen, 1796) or the *Reglement vor die Land-Miliz lobl. Stands Zug* (1757).

[18] Schläpfer, *Ausserrhoden*, p. 130; Sonderegger, *Altappenzellisches Wehrwesen*, pp. 35-38; Menolfi, *Solddienst*, p. 214; Ulrich, *18. Jahrhundert*, p. 385; Nussbaumer, *Zuger Militär*, pp. 230-235; Jeker, *Rechtsgeschichte Solothurn*, pp. 75-76; Tlusty, *Martial Ethic*, pp. 191-196 and 204-206. Wyß, *Politisches Handbuch*, p. 246 – Zurich still has an annual *Knabenschiessen* (<http://www.knabenschiessen.ch>).

[19] Lavater, *Kriegsbüchlein*, pp. 65-68. Jeker, *Rechtsgeschichte Solothurn*, pp. 64-66 and 72-77; Ziegler, *Milizen der Stadt St. Gallen*, pp. 139-153; in Berne, the authorities initially tried to encourage uniforms through "*gute und freundliche Persuasion*" ("good and friendly persuasion"), but soon mandated them, while at the same time ensuring affordable cloth – Rodt, *Berner Kriegswesen*, II, pp. 242-247; Schläpfer, *Ausserrhoden*, pp. 128-129 (in Appenzell Ausserrhoden the required equipment was scaled by census); Nussbaumer, *Zuger Militär*, pp. 193-205; Schmidt, *Handfeuerwaffen*, pp. 121-128. A key concern was to ensure that all long arms had the same bore (Ahasverus Fritsch, *De iure lustrationis* p. 71), to rationalise the casting of shot; in Zug, this was not mandated until the 1750s (Nussbaumer, *Zuger Militär*, p. 79). In places, a man could not marry unless he produced the required kit and weapons: Rodt, *Berner Kriegswesen*, II, p. 233; Schläpfer, *Ausserrhoden*, pp. 128-129; Menolfi, *Solddienst*, p. 215; Nussbaumer, *Zuger Militär*, p. 204. In the 18th C, Zurich instituted that uniforms could be commissioned from franchised tailors, and arms and kit had to be purchased from the arsenal, both at regulated low prices: Wyß, *Politisches Handbuch*, pp. 238-239; Ulrich, *18. Jahrhundert*, p. 386.

[20] Nussbaumer, *Zuger Militär*, pp. 42-67; Sigg, *Promenade Militaire*, pp. 29-31; Sigg, *17. Jahrhundert*, pp. 359-361; Jeker, *Rechtsgeschichte Solothurn*, pp. 41-44 and 87-88; Ulrich, *18. Jahrhundert*, p. 387. For the practice in Zurich 1796, Wyß, *Politisches Handbuch*, pp. 228-231. There is a clear interdependency between political office, militia command and mercenary officer (which could result in considerable

Berne had the institution of the *äussere Stand* or "outer estate". The structure of the *äussere Stand* mirrored the structure of the *innere Stand* (the Grand and Privy Council), but without executive or legislative power; it served two functions: to familiarise the next generation of *Burger* with the processes and mechanics of wielding power, and to organise manœuvres for the militia, for which the *innere Stand* would allocate a budget.[21]

A Dutch-inspired novelty was the introduction by Zurich of military mustering and mobilisation districts (*Quartiere*). Not only did these new districts cut across the traditional feudal boundaries, discomfiting the subjects, but they also involved a military administration and command structure separate from the civilian general, fiscal and judicial administration, upsetting the formerly all-powerful bailiffs (*Vögte*).[22] Generally, in the 18th C both Berne and Zurich managed to thoroughly modernise both their militia and the administrative structure required to support it.

The forces consisted of infantry, artillery, cavalry, and specialised troops (pontooniers, sappers, supplies, etc.), to various degrees of sophistication and competence. A network of beacons assured prompt alarm.[23] Berne – far and away the largest and most powerful canton – could in the 18th C, fully mobilised, field an army of 78-80,000, all of them

---

wealth); on one hand, the ruling class could thus consolidate its political grip and keep its military know-how up-to-date, but it on the other hand preserved the civilian control of the military and prevented the emergence of a distinct "officer caste". In Berne, the institution of the *äussere Stand* (Fn 21) formalised the link between higher militia officer charges and political leadership; competent rural subjects had the opportunity to rise to officer rank – Rodt, *Berner Kriegswesen*, II, pp. 403-408.

[21] Mülinen, *Vom Aeusseren Stand*, pp. 5-8; Hidber, *Der äußere Stand*, pp. 5-8; Rodt, *Berner Kriegswesen*, II pp. 93-94; Adams, *A Defence*, p. 39.

[22] Ulrich, *18. Jahrhundert*, pp. 384-389. St Gallen city too reformed its military in the mid-18th c: Ziegler, *Milizen der Stadt St. Gallen*, pp. 108-109. Berne's reforms were no less intrusive and are elaborated in great detail by Rodt, *Berner Kriegswesen* (also Grosjean, *Kriegsgenügen*, pp. 159-161). Walter shows that Berne and Zurich were conscious that their reforms went beyond what the authorities could traditionally expect of their subjects, and carefully prepared their introduction in the early 17th C (*Niederländische Einflüsse*, pp. 35-37). Still, the separation of functions was a key step in the modernisation, by rationalisation and specialisation, of the cantonal administration.

[23] Sigg, *17. Jahrhundert*, pp. 351-352; Sigg, *Promenade Militaire*, p. 27; Wyß, *Politisches Handbuch*, pp. 237-238; Schläpfer, *Ausserrhoden*, pp. 127-128 (maintaining the beacons was the only military measure Appenzell Ausserrhoden took seriously, it comprehensively neglected mustering, equipment and training – Ibid., pp. 236-239); Sonderegger, *Altappenzellisches Wehrwesen*, pp. 21-29; in Zug, the beacons were so neglected that by 1733, no more trace of them could be found: Nussbaumer, *Zuger Militär*, p. 142; Jeker, *Rechtsgeschichte Solothurn*, p. 49.

uniformed and kitted out with standardised equipment supplied through a system of arsenals.[24] The rural and poorer estates might be able to field only infantry, with only a cockade or armband for identification instead of a uniform and without standardised kit.[25]

The infantry were by and large of reasonable to high standard. But there were huge differences in quality in both equipment and training among the cantons, which the authorities often lacked the political will or financial wherewithal to correct.[26] Both the cost of the personal equipment and the time required for drills fell on the individual, and with the generally tight economic situation in most of Switzerland from the mid-17th C onwards, individuals simply could not afford either.[27] Some estates – e.g. the City of St

---

[24] For a comprehensive overview over Berne's military: Rodt (the number of effectives – about 20% of the population! – *Berner Kriegswesen*, II, pp. 188-189). Berne understood the military cost of substandard kit and provided arms and uniforms to its draftees, though even there, the intent was that the individual should eventually purchase these: Grosjean, *Kriegsgenügen*, p. 162; Rodt, *Berner Kriegswesen*, II, pp. 231-232 (with prices). Zurich's service-age population 1679 was 21, 450, of which about 15,000 musketeers: Sigg, *17. Jahrhundert*, p. 356. The arsenals provided powder, lead, heavy weapons etc., and also a certain number of flintlocks or rifles to equip at least a rapid-reaction force – Wyß, *Politisches Handbuch*, pp. 239-241; Sigg, *Promenade Militaire*, pp. 32-33; Sigg, *17. Jahrhundert*, p. 357; Nussbaumer, *Zuger Militär*, p. 194. Peyer, *Verfassungsgeschichte*, pp. 129-130; Schläpfer, *Ausserrhoden*, p. 129; Sonderegger, *Altappenzellisches Wehrwesen*, pp. 33-34.

[25] Simler, *Regiment der Eydgenoßschaft*, p. 407. Peyer, *Verfassungsgeschichte*, pp. 128-130; Nussbaumer, *Zuger Militär*, pp. 209-214; Sigg, *Promenade Militaire*, pp. 29 and 35-36. For the weaponry and uniforms of the time: Schneider, *Vom Brustharnisch zum Waffenrock*.

[26] Mantel (*Zürcher Wehranstalten*, pp. 194-195) finds that in Zurich, efforts were made when trouble was on the horizon, but abandoned as soon as the crisis passed – in the 18th C, this changed with the *Quartier* system and concomitant measures: Ulrich, *18. Jahrhundert*, pp. 384-389. For Prince-Abbatial St. Gallen, Menolfi, *Solddienst*, pp. 213-216; Jeker, *Rechtsgeschichte Solothurn*, p. 40. Organisationally, too, there were deficits – centralisation would have benefited the military, but many cantons (e.g. Zug – Nussbaumer, *Zuger Militär*, pp. 33-42) left the matter to local authorities. Partly, the cantonal authorities couldn't be bothered, but the local communities also jealously guarded their role – in the case of Berne, after the disastrous campaign against Savoy 1589/90, the city asked the communities whether they'd be willing to contribute the cash to hire mercenaries, but the communities refused to allow the city that much power: Grosjean, *Kriegsgenügen*, pp. 154-155.

[27] Menolfi, *Solddienst*, pp. 215-218 – in Prince-Abbatial St. Gallen, draftees were instructed to show up with at least a hatchet. In Zug, a substantial number of draftees showed up with halberds right up the French Invasion in 1798: Nussbaumer, *Zuger Militär*, pp. 193-194. Complaints about defective, non-regulation or substandard equipment were perennial: Sigg, *Promenade Militaire*, pp. 32-33. In an annexe to his book on the law of muster and levy, Fritsch deals with the deficiencies in equipment and the cost of fixing them (*De iure lustrationis*, pp. 71-73). Pay was only due for active service; in Zug, the amount was dependent on the soldier's community's capability (Nussbaumer, *Zuger Militär*, p. 244-256), Berne had detailed regulation on pay (Rodt, *Berner Kriegswesen*, II, pp. 409-429). In any event, keeping militia in the field for a prolonged period was politically impossible, especially during harvest season, Sigg, *Promenade Militaire*, p. 37; therefore, preferably volunteers

Gallen – allowed a draftee to provide a replacement, resulting in the spectacle of aged men who had made a career of serving as replacements for others.[28]

Where artillery existed, it was also often of high standard, thanks to the pride the officers took in their art.[29] The weak point was generally the cavalry – many would-be troopers lacked the funds to equip themselves, and some could not even ride, having chosen the cavalry only to escape from the regular drills and practice demanded of the infantrymen and gunners.[30]

The authorities tended to rely on returning mercenaries, both officers and other ranks, to bring their training and experience with them and stiffen the inexperienced militia.[31] However, to keep the veteran other ranks friendly, they were often exempted from regular drill, somewhat defeating the purpose. Officers on the other hand tended to make a career of foreign service, reducing the number of returnees. Those that did return might inflict on their troops the latest uniform fashions, imposing further costs and causing resentment among their hapless recruits.[32]

---

were sought for campaigns: Schläpfer, *Ausserrhoden*, pp. 240-241; Schmidt, *Handfeuerwaffen*, pp. 60-61.

[28] Menolfi, *Solddienst*, p. 218; Jeker, *Rechtsgeschichte Solothurn*, pp. 64-65. In Zug, certain service-exempt persons had to provide stand-ins: Nussbaumer, *Zuger Militär*, pp. 164-165.

[29] Zurich: Sigg, *Promenade Militaire*, pp. 34-34; Sigg, *17. Jahrhundert*, pp. 355-356; Wyß, *Politisches Handbuch*, p. 245; Ulrich, *18. Jahrhundert*, pp. 386-387; St Gallen city: Ziegler, *Milizen der Stadt St. Gallen*, pp. 116-120; Berne: Rodt, *Berner Kriegswesen*, II., pp. 82-135; Berne paid stipends for artillery training abroad: Rodt, *Berner Kriegswesen*, II, pp. 322-331; Schmidt, *Handfeuerwaffen*, p. 87; Nussbaumer, *Zuger Militär*, pp. 205-209; Solothurn's artillery on the other hand was in a sorry state: Jeker, *Rechtsgeschichte Solothurn*, p. 86.

[30] Sigg, *Promenade Militaire*, pp. 27-28, Sigg, *17. Jahrhundert*, p. 358 – and this in Zurich! Jeker, *Rechtsgeschichte Solothurn*, pp. 85-86. Representational needs created a converse problem – in Ausserrhoden, e.g. the *Landsgemeinde*-town of Trogen regulary required guards of honour, and for this, the local worthies organised snappily uniformed mounted and grenadier units. The military value of these formations was dubious – Schläpfer, *Ausserrhoden*, pp. 239-240; St Gallen city also entertained a mounted grenadier unit: Ziegler, *Milizen der Stadt St. Gallen*, pp. 100-104. Jeker, *Rechtsgeschichte Solothurn*, p. 86-87: the treaties allowing France to raise troops also called for France to send cavalry and artillery in case Switzerland was attacked. Rodt, *Berner Kriegswesen*, II, pp. 62-82 – since it proved difficult to raise proper cavalry and even dragoons, Berne through the 17th C toyed with re-activating the feudal-law obligations regarding mounted troops, which proved less than satisfactory.

[31] Jeker, *Rechtsgeschichte Solothurn*, p. 79-80; Sigg, *17. Jahrhundert*, p. 359; Menolfi, *Solddienst*, p. 215; Grosjean, *Kriegsgenügen*, pp. 162-163; Wyß, *Politisches Handbuch*, p. 224; as Switzerland itself no longer offered opportunity to gain experience, Berne judiciously franchised out mercenary units – to Sardinia with the express purpose to train mountain warfare: Rodt, *Berner Kriegswesen*, II, pp. 300-303. Zurich too encouraged officers to gain experience abroad: Ulrich, *18. Jahrhundert*, pp. 384 and 390-391.

[32] Schmidt, *Handfeuerwaffen*, pp. 104-105; Grosjean, *Kriegsgenügen*, p. 165; Menolfi, *Solddienst*, p. 215; Maissen, *Geschichte*, p. 122; Appenzell Ausserrhoden did not have a significant mercenary business,

II.4. External Threat: The *Defensionalia*

After the defeat at Marignano 1515, the Confederacy itself was spared external attacks until Napoleon invaded in 1798.[33] The reasons for this were manifold and cannot be discussed here, but at the same time, the cohesion between the members of the Confederacy was weakening, due to the confessional divide, the disagreements over the mercenary business, diverging economic development and an increased focus of each canton on internal consolidation. Regional compacts on mutual defence (*defensionale*) were quite common, but the first comprehensive agreement, the *Defensionale* of Wil, was not achieved until 1647, by which time the Thirty Years' War was in its 29th and the peace negotiations in Münster and Osnabrück were in their second year.[34]

The *Defensionale* was renewed in Baden 1668, and this time, there was an embryonic effort at preparatory organisation, unified command and member obligations – which, however, did not go very far due to internal conflicts.[35] In 1702, under the impression of the War of Spanish Succession, a renewed effort to coordinate and integrate common defence was made, but the internal differences were too great.[36]

II.5. Internal Threat: The First and Second Villmergen Wars

If the Swiss avoided foreign wars, they still warred amongst each other – the two "hottest" contests were two Villmergen Wars. The First Villmergen War 1656 resulted from the Protestant cantons, principally Berne and Zurich, attempting to win predominance for the Protestant cause within the Confederacy. Bernese troops occupied the village of Villmergen without much resistance, proceeded to loot and carouse, and awaited the

---

so there was no infusion of up-to-date military knowledge from this side – Schläpfer, *Ausserrhoden*, pp. 241-243.

[33] Though there was danger enough – Oechsli, *Orte und Zugewandte*, pp. 118-143; for an overview of Switzerland's challenges during the Thirty Years' War: Jeker, *Rechtsgeschichte Solothurn*, pp. 12-27; Peyer, *Verfassungsgeschichte*, pp. 80-84; Kurz, *Schweizer Heer*, pp. 164-168 and 180; Ziegler, *Milizen der Stadt St. Gallen*, pp. 54-59.

[34] It merely set out the troop contingents the members had to contribute, but was silent on preparatory organisation, financing, and command: Peyer, *Verfassungsgeschichte*, p. 94-96; Oechsli, *Orte und Zugewandte*, pp. 127-131; Ziegler, *Milizen der Stadt St. Gallen*, p. 61. Wil was the administrative capital of the Prince-Abbey of St Gallen. Menolfi, *Solddienst*, p. 205; Nussbaumer, *Zuger Militär*, pp. 26-27. For a contemporary if rosy view of the *Defensionale* Wyß, *Politisches Handbuch*, pp. 222-224.

[35] Peyer, *Verfassungsgeschichte*, pp. 96-97; Oechsli, *Orte und Zugewandte*, pp. 133-139; Kurz, *Schweizer Heer*, p. 179; Ziegler, *Milizen der Stadt St. Gallen*, pp. 61-62. Baden was a Catholic-controlled fortress in the subject territory of the Aargau – within a few years, especially Catholic cantons exited the 1668 *Defensionale*; Nussbaumer, *Zuger Militär*, pp. 27-29. The 1668 *Defensionale* was activated in 1792 when the border near Basel was threatened; the called-upon cantons found excuses not to send any or not the required number of troops, (Schläpfer, *Ausserrhoden*, pp. 240-241; Nussbaumer, *Zuger Militär*, pp. 148-152); St Gallen city complied: Ziegler, *Milizen der Stadt St. Gallen*, pp. 64, 222-236.

[36] Nussbaumer, *Zuger Militär*, pp. 27-29; Oechsli, *Orte und Zugewandte*, pp. 138-143.

Zurich troops to join them. The Catholic forces, hastily assembled by Lucerne and Schwyz, saw this as an opportunity for a surprise attack during the night, and chased away the Bernese.[37]

The fact that the Catholic troops still relied on pike and halberd, and had routed the musket-equipped Bernese, at first led to a reversal of the movement toward firearms in the cantonal militias. But by the beginning of the 18th C, with the advent of the improved flintlock, especially Berne and Zurich replaced the ageing matchlocks and began to reorganise their military along modern lines.[38]

In 1712 then, trouble started in the Toggenburg, where the Catholic cantons were suspected of scheming to subvert the *status quo*. Zurich and Berne mobilised and successfully attacked the Abbey itself; the Catholic Five Cantons[39] then garrisoned the Catholic-controlled County of Baden in the Aargau, preventing Zurich and Berne from establishing a common border. Berne and Zurich prevailed here, too, and a peace was negotiated, which was rejected by the Papal nuncio. So the Catholic forces resumed hostilities in the Aargau, but were this time roundly beaten at Villmergen by Berne units that

---

[37] Luginbühl/Barth-Gasser/Baumann/Piller, *1712: Quellen*, pp. 49-50; Peyer, *Verfassungsgeschichte*, p. 98-99; Ziegler, *Milizen der Stadt St. Gallen*, pp. 198-201; Zurich's efforts were dogged by supply and organisation problems (Sigg, *17. Jahrhundert*, p. 357), and Berne by problems of training, leadership and discipline (Grosjean, *Kriegsgenügen*, pp. 153-157); Kurz, *Schweizer Heer*, pp. 177-179.

[38] Peyer, *Verfassungsgeschichte*, p. 94; Sigg, *17. Jahrhundert*, pp. 356-357; Schmidt, *Handfeuerwaffen*, pp. 84-85; Rodt, *Berner Kriegswesen*, II, p. 212-224; Grosjean, *Kriegsgenügen*, pp. 157-158; Ziegler, *Milizen der Stadt St. Gallen*, pp. 214-222. The nearly mystical faith in the halberd is illustrated by the Zug general Joseph Leonz Andermatt, confronting the French 1798! – cited after Nussbaumer, *Zuger Militär*, p. 193: *Unsere Infanterie kann der feindlichen an Fertigkeit im Feuern und an Geschwindigkeit im Manövrieren nicht beikommen. Die Halebardiere sind unsere grösste, und da wir keine Kavallerie haben, überaus notwendige Stärke. Die Leibeskräfte, mit denen die Natur die helvetische Nation vor allen anderen begabte, machen ein so bewaffnetes Korps jedem Feinde fürchterlich. Deswegen zielt unsere ganze Taktik darauf ab, mittels der Jäger, Artillerie und Infanterie die Zeit und den Ort zu gewinnen, wo die Halebardiere in's Spiel gebracht werden können, die sodann den Ausgang der wichtigsten Schlacht entscheiden und den vollkommensten Sieg erhalten können* (Our infantry is not able to compete with the enemy's in terms of accomplishment in firing or speed of manœuvre. Our halbardiers are our chief and, since we have no cavalry, eminently necessary prowess. Physical strength, which nature has lavished on the Helvetic nation before all others, renders a so armed corps terrible to every enemy. That is why our whole tactics aim to use riflemen, artillery and infantry to win the time and place where the halbardiers can be brought into play, who can then determine the result of the most important battle and achieve the most complete victory).

[39] Uri, Schwyz, Unterwalden, Lucerne, and the Valais (associate member). Fribourg, Solothurn and Appenzell Innerrhoden, as well as associate member the Prince-Bishop of Basel, all also Catholic, remained neutral; the Prince-Abbot of St. Gallen had been neutralised. The mostly Protestant Toggenburg has its own complicated history: Dierauer, *Das Toggenburg*.

outmatched the Catholics – who still relied on 17th C infantry equipment and tactics, without any cavalry and only minimal (but skilfully deployed) artillery.[40] Though the outcome was not a foregone conclusion, the military lessons of Villmergen II were clear. While rural cantons like the formerly powerful Schwyz lacked the resources to modernise their militia, Zurich and Berne put in place a new organisational infrastructure and improved equipment. Deficits remained, especially in training, where the political will to follow through was lacking. The parlous state of training led to the formation of private associations of officers who, out of patriotic motivation, sought to improve the training of field and staff officers. However, despite some spirited resistance and a few successes, the Swiss militias 1798-99 proved no match for (and were outnumbered by) Napoleon's armies.[41]

---

[40] Luginbühl/Barth-Gasser/Baumann/Piller, *1712: Quellen*, pp. 51-67; Peyer, *Verfassungsgeschichte*, pp. 99-100; Sigg, *Promenade Militaire*, pp. 34-39; Kurz, *Schweizer Heer*, pp. 191-201; Rodt, *Berner Kriegswesen*, II, pp. 444-562; Grosjean, *Kriegsgenügen*, pp. 161-164; Ulrich, *18. Jahrhundert*, pp. 372-374; Ziegler, *Milizen der Stadt St. Gallen*, pp. 62-63. Zurich's forces were competent but not yet up to scratch – at a joint camp of Berne and Zurich forces 1712, the Zurich commandant was embarrassed by the scruffy and shambolic appearance of his camp and troops when compared to the spit-and-polish Bernese: Sigg, *Promenade Militaire*, pp. 30-31.

The Catholic cantons attempted a re-run of Villmergen in the *Sonderbund* War of 1847, but were quickly and sparingly, but decisively beaten by the Protestant cantons. This paved the way for the first Federal Constitution in 1848 – Maissen, *Geschichte*, pp. 196-204. A final chapter was written in 2006, when thanks to the Good Offices of the Swiss Federal Government, Zurich and St Gallen agreed a settlement with regard to rare books and the magnificent celestial globe, which Zurich had looted from the famed St Gallen College Library in 1712 – Flury/Schmuki/Tremp, *Von der Limmat zurück an die Steinach*, pp. 9-17.

[41] Maissen, *Geschichte*, pp. 159-160; Rodt, *Berner Kriegswesen*, II, pp. 562-694; Nussbaumer, *Zuger Militär*, pp. 42-43, 140-144; Sigg, *Promenade Militaire*, p. 31; Kurz, *Schweizer Heer*, pp. 203-215; Ulrich, *18. Jahrhundert*, pp. 384-389; Ziegler, *Milizen der Stadt St. Gallen*, pp. 239-250. Cf. Wyß, *Politisches Handbuch*, pp. 223-224. Grosjean (*Kriegsgenügen*, pp. 166-171) has some criticism of Berne's preparations in the run-up to Napoleon, but it is hard to see what the Swiss could have done to defeat the French mass armies and operational doctrine.

In Prince-Abbatial St. Gallen, officers worried about the quality of the militia formed "free" or volunteer corps, which trained more frequently and seriously, but the authorities discouraged these as their members did not want to do regular militia service as well, and removing the crack soldiers from the militia would render this completely useless – Menolfi, *Solddienst*, 216. Zug actively promoted an *élite* "free corps" – Nussbaumer, *Zuger Militär*, pp. 172-173. Zurich had a special fund to pay for volunteer extracurricular manœuvres: Wyß, *Politisches Handbuch*, pp. 237 and 244-245; Ulrich, *18. Jahrhundert*, p. 385. In St Gallen city, there was rivalry between the regulars and the select grenadiers: Ziegler, *Milizen der Stadt St. Gallen*, pp. 92-99.

II.6. Internal Threat: Insurrection

In addition to fighting between the cantons, there were the occasional revolts and insurrections, where the rural subjects took up arms against their city lords. The most serious of these was the Peasants' War of 1653, which affected the cantons of Lucerne, Berne, Solothurn, Basel and the Aargau. The rural population insisted on the cities' respect for their feudal freedoms, rights and privileges, as well as economic relief. The revolt was put down quickly and brutally by the cities, with the help of the non-affected cantons.[42]

Though the peasants were armed and part of the militia, the officers were members of the city ruling elite, so the insurrectionists lacked expert leadership. Also, the city-based burghers and craftsmen had nothing in common with the peasantry, whom they considered their subjects. Even so – the various insurrections, "troubles" and revolts did not have the effect of disarming the rural populace. The principle of a self-armed militia remained in place.[43]

II.7. Mercenaries

Other than the subject territories, the issue that preoccupied day-to-day Swiss diplomacy and internal politics was the mercenary business; as practiced in Switzerland, a foreign prince needed to obtain, against a fee, the consent of a canton to raise troops, and once that consent was obtained, negotiate the final price with a mercenary entrepreneur franchised by the canton.[44]

That the mercenary business was huge is documented by the numbers – it is estimated that during the three centuries of the mercenary era, two million Swiss were in mercenary service for some time of their lives.[45] Whether the business benefited just the cantons and entrepreneurs, or the individuals as well, is contentious. The economic reality in

---

[42] Fehr, *Absolutismus*, pp. 187-188; Ziegler, *Milizen der Stadt St. Gallen*, pp. 60 and 197-198. Upto the 17th C, the *Tagsatzung* was also a forum for mediation between a canton's rulers and its subjects, estates, or subject territories, and so it initially functioned in the Peasants' War – the *Tagsatzung* recommended the satisfaction of the peasants' economic, but rejection of their political demands. However, the intervention did not bring a reconciliation. By the end of the Peasants' War, the cantonal authorities rejected *Tagsatzung* offers to mediate as interference with a canton's internal affairs: Peyer, *Verfassungsgeschichte*, pp. 101-103.

[43] Gmür, *Städte als Landesherren*, p. 191: the peasants did not revolt against the ruling structure, but against perceived infringements of their traditional (feudal) rights; in the Peasants' War, the financial demands were satisfied, the political ones not. For the (many) troubles see: Peyer, *Verfassungsgeschichte*, p. 134-141; Messmer, *Luzerner Patriziat*, pp. 70-72; Jeker, *Rechtsgeschichte Solothurn*, pp. 42-43; also Ziegler, *Milizen der Stadt St. Gallen*, pp. 57-59.

[44] Peyer, *Verfassungsgeschichte*, pp. 130-133; Jeker, *Rechtsgeschichte Solothurn*, pp. 42-44; Messmer, *Luzerner Patriziat*, pp. 73-93; Schläpfer, *Ausserrhoden*, pp. 136-142 and 241-243; Ulrich, *18. Jahrhundert*, pp. 389-391; Kurz, *Schweizer Heer*, pp. 138-139.

[45] Maissen, *Geschichte*, pp. 121-122; Kurz, *Schweizer Heer*, pp. 138-139 – among them 70,000 officers and 700 generals.

Switzerland at the time was that there was a surplus of manpower, and limited opportunities domestically.[46] Also, the nature of service changed; in the 16th C, mercenary troops were levied for a specific campaign, and spoils were an integral part of the pay. From the 17th C onward, the Swiss regiments abroad constituted part of the standing army of the employing prince. Actions were few and far between, and pay constituted the (meagre but regular) reward for service.

III. YEOMAN – SUBJECT – CITIZEN

III.1. Feudal Law

The lord's typical right in feudal law was the *Mannschaftsrecht* (*ius armorum; ius lustrationis et sequelae; Heerfolge; Reis und Folge*),[47] the right to call his vassals to arms. The expansionist Swiss cantons – especially Berne and Zurich, but it is probably generally true for all city cantons – saw the key advantage of territorial expansion in the acquisition of the *Mannschaftsrecht* over the acquired possessions.[48]

---

[46] Maissen, *Geschichte*, p. 108; Menolfi, *Solddienst*, pp. 206-211; Sigg, *17. Jahrhundert*, p. 361; Ulrich Bräker, the "poor man from the Toggenburg", wrote a popular account of his life in the second half of the 18th C, which included a stint as a mercenary in Prussia: *Lebensgeschichte und Natürliche Ebentheuer des Armen Mannes im Tockenburg* (1789); Menolfi, *Solddienst*, pp. 211-213.

[47] Josias Püttmann, *Elementa ivris fevdalis*, p. 47 (§71): *Primum inter iura regalia II.F.56. memorata locum occupant* armandia *a), quo vocabulo proprie ius armandi vasallos et subditos eosque sub proprio vexillo ducendi, hodie autem omne fere ius armorum significatur. In Capit. Caes. Art. XIX. § 6. Ius armaturae dicitur et cum iure sequelae (*der Heeresfolge *b), nec non iure fortalitiorum coniungitur* (The first place among the mentioned rights of rulership is the '*ius armandium*', which term signifies the right to arm vassals and subjects and to lead them under one's own standard, today though essentially any right related to arms. In … it is called the right to arm and is mentioned with the right of levy, and often with the right of fortification); Fritsch, *De iure lustrationis*.

Püttmann, *Elementa ivris fevdalis*, elaborates on the *feudal* military service obligation in §§425-436 (pp. 257- 264) - §429 (p. 259) suggests that the *feudal* obligation for non-knightly vassals was defensive, and that a vassal could legitimately refuse to comply with a call-up if the lord's war was manifestly unjust: *Quodsi enim a domino bellum manifesto iniustum geratur, vasallus seruitia haud iniuria denegat…*, but goes on to say that all that does not apply if the vassal is also a subject: *Fallit tamen hoc tunc, cum vasallus simul est subditus…* When during the Peasants' War 1653 (Section II.6) the *Tagsatzung* called on the cantons to send troops to help in subduing the peasants, the *Landammann* of Ausserrhoden sent two companies without consulting the *Landsgemeinde*; some Appenzeller objected and demanded a determination whether the objectives were just or unjust – Schläpfer, *Ausserrhoden*, pp. 59-60.

[48] Gmür, *Städte als Landesherren*, pp. 187-188; Schib, *Geschichte Schaffhausen*, p. 336; Studer Immenhauser, *Verwaltung*, pp. 202, 206; Bosshard, *Militärunternehmer Thurgau*, p. 18. The German Imperial cities limited their expansion so that the rural was at most equal to the city population (St Gallen city chose this route, which contributed to its second-rate status as a *zugewandter Ort* – Bührer, *Stadtrepublik St. Gallen*). To compare, at the end of the 18th C, Nuremberg, the largest German Imperial

In feudal law, that obligation was technically limited to the defence of the fief, it did not extend to an obligation to follow the lord on "foreign" adventures. In the subject territory of the Thurgau, for instance, the yeomen did not feel obliged to follow Zurich's levy to fight in the Burgundian Wars 1476, and it took authority mandates and *Tagsatzung* intervention to enforce the levy[49] – the transition from the autonomous yeoman, whose fighting obligations were linked to his feudal status, to the "subject", whose obligation to fight was rooted in authority mandates, was pursued vigourously by the authorities in both their subject territories and in the increasingly "subjectified" rural territories of the cities.[50] But the transition was not an easy one, and the population found ways to passively resist military service.[51]

The converse question was whether a prince had the right to disarm the populace – Ahasverus Fritsch (who specifically addresses the mustering (*lustratio*) and levy (*sequela*) in his *de iure lustrationis et sequelae* on the basis of Roman law) says that the prince has the right to disarm subjects (*subditi*).[52] Fritsch (like Justus Lipsius before him) recommends that a

---

city, had a territory of 1,400 km² and a total population of 35,000, with half in the city; in Berne, the city had 12,000 inhabitants, but the total Bernese population, on a territory of 9,000 km² or just over 20% of Swiss territory (including *Zugewandte* and subject territories), was 400,000 (Zurich 1,700 km², population 200,000, 11,000 in the city); in contrast, the total population of Venice, including the *Terra Ferma*, was over 2,000,000 – Gmür, *Städte als Landesherren*, pp. 182, 187 and 192.

[49] Bosshard, *Militärunternehmer Thurgau*, pp. 20-23; Grosjean, *Kriegsgenügen*, p. 133; similarly in the Toggenburg: Menolfi, *Solddienst*, pp. 216-217. In Zug, some communities refused to contribute their contingent to the cantonal force and instead kept their men for local defence: Nussbaumer, *Zuger Militär*, pp. 102-107. Interestingly, a New York militia contingent used the same argument in 1812: Kerby, *Militia System*, p. 114.

[50] The authorities based their claims on the purportedly old feudal law institution of the *Mannschaftsrecht*, but re-interpreted it to suit their absolutist conceptions – Bosshard, *Militärunternehmer Thurgau*, pp. 20-23; Schib, *Geschichte Schaffhausen*, pp. 336-337; Weissen, *Stuer*, pp. 142-143 and 168; Menolfi, *Solddienst*, p. 217. The service obligation was so matter-of-course that it was not laid down in any mandate – Nussbaumer, *Zuger Militär*, pp. 163-164; Jeker, *Rechtsgeschichte Solothurn*, p. 39. With Wyß (*Politisches Handbuch*, 1796), the obligation was defined purely as a citizen's obligation (*Staatsbürger*, differentiated as *Bürger* (i.e. a city burgher) and *Landmann* (i.e. a rural subject)) – p. 225. Püttmann differentiates between a vassal's obligations, which arise out of the feudal contract, and a subject's obligations: *Elementa ivris fevdalis*, §2 (p. 2).

[51] Nussbaumer analysed the situation in Zug and believes that the authorities simply did not have the organisational structure or the means to enforce the draft until the late 18th C (*Zuger Militär*, p. 165); see also Bosshard, *Militärunternehmer Thurgau*, pp. 20-23; Menolfi, *Solddienst*, pp. 216-218; Weissen, *Stuer*, pp. 169; Jeker, *Rechtsgeschichte Solothurn*, pp. 29 and 63-64.

[52] See DuCange, *subditi* – the word, as a legal technical term, refers to "subjects"; it could mean, more colloquially, persons that have been "subjected" or "conquered" due to e.g. losing a war, but the former, legal reading seems to me the better view. Fritsch writes (*De iure lustrationis*, p. 10): *Primò, qvod communi iure armorum usus privatis sit interdictus* (Firstly, that by common law [i.e. HRE Roman law] the use of weapons is prohibited to private persons); in Fritsch's opinion, the disarming of the populace is desirable since it prevents insurrection and riot, and subjects anyway make bad troops.

prince's military should consist of paid soldiers, since these are well-trained and reliable,[53] suplemented by select draftees incorporated in peacetimes into the shooting associations.[54] The professional soldiers, though, should in Lipsius' recommendation be raised from the monarch's own population; he rejects the argument that a monarch is better off not arming his own peaceful subjects, but buying in troops from bellicose peoples.[55]

III.2. Rational Natural Law

The legimation of feudal law and authority were based on the proposition that Pope and Emperor were jointly tasked to deliver the sanctified order of rule on earth to the Redeemer on Judgement Day. Maximilian I's 1495 *Reichsreform* marked the formal demise of the concept of Christendom unified under the secular leadership of the Holy Roman Emperor; the Reformation did the same to the spiritual leadership of the Pope. Legal scholars therefore sought new ways to found laws on a universal basis.[56]

Natural Law – particularly Rational Natural Law (*Vernunftrecht*) – was based on the Roman law[57] concept of *ius gentium*, referring to the law that applied universally among individuals regardless of nationality, a system of law stripped of the peculiar formalities prevailing among Roman citizens and so having universal application.[58] Natural Law theorists from

---

On the other hand, Fritsch (*passim*) strongly recommends that subjects also participate in training and manœuvres. The Roman law references Fritsch relies on are mainly in the *codex* and the *constitutiones novellae* sections of the Corpus Iuris, i.e. the pre-Justinian and Justinian imperial decrees, not the "traditional" Roman law from the late Republic and the Principate assembled in the *digesta*.

[53] Fritsch, *De iure lustrationis*, p. 12: "*Quod miles conductitius, ad defensionem Principatus longè utilior ac promptior sit*, [...]" (That a hired soldier is far more useful and ready for the defence of the Principality); Tlusty, *Martial Ethic*, p. 13.

[54] Fritsch, *De iure lustrationis*, p. 8: *Certam cohortem exercitorum civium, qvos* Schützen *vulgariter dicimus, elegerunt, eosq[ue] singulariter as hoc privilegiis, qvae alia in aliis locis sunt, donârunt*; Iustus Lipsius, *Politicorum doctrina*, pp. 155-158 and 161-163. This was also generally the practice in the German princely states: Mitteis/Lieberich, *Deutsche Rechtsgeschichte*, §42 I 3, pp. 335-336.

[55] Lipsius, *Politicorum doctrina*, pp. 158-161 – well officered, any people can provide useful troops: *si modò exercitati & prudentes viri Dilectui praeponantur, celeriter manum bellis aptam posse aggregari* (on p. 160).

[56] Welzel, *Naturrecht*, pp. 110-111; Meder, *Rechtsgeschichte*, pp. 261-273.

[57] Püttmann, *Elementa ivris fevdalis*, §6 and §19 (pp. 5 and 13-14). Roman law was the subsidiary common law of the Holy Roman Empire, and then of Germany, until 31st December 1899. Simler (*De republica*, ff. 139r-139v), by all due respect for Roman law, applauds the fact that the *Tagsatzung* tended to decide *ex bono et aequo*, not according to strict Roman law.

[58] In D.1.1.pr.: *Ulpianus libro primo institutionum: [...] ius naturale est, quod natura omnia animalia docuit; nam ius istud non humani generis proprium, sed omnium animalium, quae in terra, quae in mari nascuntur, auium quoque commune est. hinc descendit maris atque feminae coniunctio, quam nos matrimonium appellamus, hinc liberorum procreatio, hinc educatio: uidemus etenim cetera quoque animalia, feras etiam istius iuris peritia censeri. Ius gentium est, quo gentes humanae utuntur. quod a naturali recedere facile intellegere licet, quia illud omnibus*

the 17th C saw in Natural Law the transcendental grounding of laws that had previously been provided by universal Christianity and secular Empire. The movement had two foci, related but distinct: One was international law, for which the Dutchman Huig de Groot (known as Hugo Grotius) laid the groundwork; the other was constitutionalism, pioneered by Samuel Pufendorf.[59]

In the feudal order, relations between lord and vassal, their respective freedoms, privileges, rights and obligations, were based in the feudal "contract", which (theoretically) could be freely negotiated.[60] The governing tools of absolutism were the mandates, i.e. privy council or princely edicts: unilateral, top-down legislation through which the authorities sought to institute *gute Policey* – "good policy" or a "well-regulated commonwealth".[61] It needs to be borne in mind, though, that there was no change in the legal system; technically, feudal law still applied, and the bearers of feudal law privileges and rights resisted the authorities' overriding and ignoring them.[62]

---

animalibus, hoc solis hominibus inter se commune sit (Ulpianus in the first book of the Institutions: natural law is [the law] nature taught to all animals, because that law is not peculiar to the human race, but to all animals which are born on earth or in the sea, as well as birds. From this proceeds the union of man and woman, which we call matrimony, from this the procreation of children, and education. For we also see other animals, wild ones too, judged familiar with this law. The law of nations is [the law] used by the human peoples. One may easily see that it is narrower than the natural one, as the latter is common to all animals, the formed only to humans amongst each other); Iustinianus, *Digesta*, Vol. I.

[59] Hugo Grotius (1583-1645 - *de iure belli ac pacis* and *de mare libero*); Samuel Pufendorf (1632-1694 - *de statu imperii germanici liber unus* (published in Geneva under the pseudonym Severinus de Monzambano), *de iure naturae et gentium libri octo, de officio hominis et civis libri duo*). For an overview: Welzel, *Naturrecht*; Silvestrini, *Rousseau, Pufendorf*; Dufour, *Histoire et Droit naturel*, pp. 265-284. International law was further developed by the German polymath Christian Wolff (1679-1754) and given its modern form by the Neuchâtelois Emer de Vattel (1714-1767); Hutson, *Sister Republics*, p. 19.

A comprehensive picture can only be drawn by including the works and theories of Jean Bodin (1530-1596), which laid the foundation for Church-independent, secular absolutism – space does not allow here, but for a treatment relevant to the discussion see Brändle, *Revitalisierung*.

[60] Meder, *Rechtsgeschichte*, pp. 224-225; Weissen, *Stuer*, p. 142; Ulrich, *18. Jahrhundert*, pp. 434-437.

[61] Härter, *Gute Policey*, pp. 29-31. Authorities began unilaterally amending local community charters to unify administration across their possessions and so create a territorial government; Peyer, *Verfassungsgeschichte*, pp. 116-118; Messmer, *Luzerner Patriziat*, p. 74-76; Gmür, *Städte als Landesherren*, p. 191; Jeker, *Rechtsgeschichte Solothurn*, pp. 45-46; Schib, *Geschichte Schaffhausen*, pp. 337-338. Lipsius, *Politicorum doctrina*, pp. 69-75.

[62] Mitteis/Lieberich, *Deutsche Rechtsgeschichte*, §42 III, IV, pp. 340-347; Schib, *Geschichte Schaffhausen*, pp. 324-325; conflicts between estates and their rulers were endemic in the period, and in France culminated in the French Revolution; in my view, Tlusty's "conflict between law and custom" (*Martial Ethic*, pp. 224-232) actually describes this process.

Natural law (like feudal law) still acknowledges a transcendental anchor for legal relationships, but unlike feudal law, where relationships are specific, in natural law, there are two systems of general

In Natural Law, since the sovereign (*le Souverain*) must defend the commonwealth, the sovereign is also endowed with all the tool necessary to achieve that goal, including requiring citizens (*le Citoyen*, occasionally *le Sujet*) to render military service both in times of war and of peace, as the citizen needs to learn the military arts.[63]

III.3. Burlamaqui – a Key Swiss Exponent of Modern Natural Law

Jean Jacques Burlamaqui (1694-1748) was of a prominent Geneva family. After studying in Geneva, he spent 1720-21 in England and the Netherlands, where he stayed with Barbeyrac[64] in Groningen. Back in Geneva, he taught natural law after Samuel Pufendorf's *De officio hominis et civis* and Roman civil law, and was active in Geneva politics. He was tutor to the prince at the court of the landgrave of Hesse-Kassel 1735-1739. His book *Principes du droit naturel* (1747) was translated into several languages and was immensely popular and influential thanks to its clarity of thought and lucid prose.[65]

For Burlamaqui, Man's Creator endowed him with not just reason and physical capabilities, but also with the will to pursue his happiness (*bonheur*).[66] Unlike the writers propounding an actual social contract,[67] Burlamaqui saw man as by his nature a social

---

and abstract rules: overriding natural law, and the law as promulgated and enforced by the authorities. The potential for conflict between the two was fodder for the literature of the time, as epitomised by the plays of Heinrich von Kleist (*Prinz Friedrich von Homburg, Michael Kohlhaas*), Friedrich Schiller (*Die Räuber, Wilhelm Tell*) or Johann Wolfgang von Goethe (*Faust*), and hearkened back to the conflict already treated in Sophocles' *Antigone*.

[63] Jean Jacques Burlamaqui, *Principes du droit politique*, pp. 290-291; the inconsistency in the terminology suggests that Burlamaqui did not complete the editing of this passage. The content reflects passages in Pufendorf (*De officio hominis*, pp. 280-281 (II Cap. XIII §§1, 2) and p. 303 (II Cap. XIIX §§11, 12)); in Cap. XIII, Pufendorf refers to "*civis*", in Cap. XIIX merely to "*miles*".

[64] Silvestrini, *Rousseau, Pufendorf*. Born in Béziers (Languedoc) in 1674, the family after the revocation of the Edict of Nantes fled to Lausanne, then Geneva and Berlin, where he graduated in theology in 1693. His translations of Pufendorf's *de jure naturae et gentium* (1706) and *de officio hominis et civis iuxta legem naturalem* (1707) into French earned him a professorship in Lausanne 1711. While in Lausanne, he worked on the translation of Hugo Grotius' *de jure belli ac pacis* – the translation was not completed until 1724, by which time (from 1717) he was teaching in Groningen, where he died 1744.

[65] HLS, entry "Burlamaqui". He was not able to finish the sequel, *Principes du droit politique*, and did not want it published in the shape it was in; nevertheless, his heirs were persuaded to publish his notes in 1751.

[66] Silvestrini, *Rousseau, Pufendorf*, pp. 290-295; Burlamaqui, *Principes du droit naturel*, p. 12. The English edition of 1752 uses the term "happiness" – Burlamaqui, *Principles of Natural Law*, trans. Nugent, p. 13. Thomas Jefferson in drafting the Declaration of Independence preferred Burlamaqui's trinity of "life, liberty and the pursuit of happiness" to John Locke's "life, liberty and property" – Antieau, *Natural Rights*, p. 63.

[67] First elaborated by Thomas Hobbes (1588-1679 – *Leviathan*, 1651), the *contrat social* is now closely associated with Jean-Jacques Rousseau (1712-1778 – HLS, entry "Rousseau"; *Du contrat social*, 1762); Welzel, *Naturrecht*, pp. 156-157. Both Hobbes and Rousseau saw man's natural state as one of

beast. Society as such was therefore part and parcel of the natural state; the difference between the natural state and the civic state lay in the institution of government, the appointment of a sovereign tasked with instituting laws. This entailed a certain loss of autonomy for the individual, but not a loss of liberty, since in the natural state, an individual's autonomy was limited by his fellow man's autonomy – so any liberty an individual enjoyed was precarious, at risk of being taken away by fellow man at any time. The institution of government, which through laws limits an individual's autonomy, therefore assures the individual's liberty.

Government was vested with sovereign power, but that power could not be wielded arbitrarily. Unlike the *contrat social* theoreticians, who saw the authority of government defined, circumscribed and limited only by the social contract, Burlamaqui posited the binding provisions of natural law as not just limiting the powers of government, but imbuing government with a positive purpose, i.e. to promote the individual's happiness.

Burlamaqui's grounding of the limitations of government in natural law provides the intellectual legitimation for constitutionally limited government, i.e. the principle that the sovereign may have the power to do anything, but by law not the *right* to do just anything. In the doctrine of the *contrat social* in the mould of Rousseau, the *volonté générale* reigns supreme, there is no protection of individual liberty or minorities.[68]

III.4. Legal Philosophy and Roman Law in Switzerland

The Swiss cantons had managed to exempt themselves from the jurisdiction of Maximilian's *Reichskammergericht*, so the legal Romanisation that occurred in the Empire did not happen in Switzerland to the same extent.[69]

---

isolation, and man took the conscious step to form a society, subject to conditions set out in the social contract. Rousseau's concept of the social contract is a radically democratic one, without any recognition of individual rights or freedom from State intrusion.

[68] Silvestrini, *Rousseau, Pufendorf*, p. 291. Burlamaqui was avidly read and frequently quoted by the American Revolutionary leaders: Antieau, *Natural Rights*; Hutson, *Sister Republics*, pp. 19-22; Halbrook, *Swiss Confederation*, p. 44.

[69] Jeker, *Rechtsgeschichte Solothurn*, p. 38; Gmür, *Städte als Landesherren*, p. 189; Fehr, *Absolutismus*, p. 182; on the other hand, the ideality of the constitution, including the military constitution, of the Roman Republic was consistently extolled by writers and philosophers (e.g. Niccolò Machiavelli in his *Discorsi sopra la prima deca di Tito Livio*, pp. 270-271 and *passim*, and in *I sette libri dell'arte della guerra*, p. 50), where he likens the Swiss to the ancient Romans – Grosjean, *Kriegsgenügen*, p. 134; Halbrook, *Swiss Confederation*, pp. 38-39. Lipsius in his *Politicorum sive civilis doctrina* refers not to the *corpus iuris*, but to Greek and Latin writers of antiquity, especially Cicero, and wrote a commentary (*De militia romana* (1614)) on Polybius' work on the Roman military constitution). The ruling families saw themselves very much in the mould of the *patres*, referring to Zurich as SPQT (*Senatus Populusque Turicensis*): Ulrich, *18. Jahrhundert*, pp. 367-368; Walter, *Niederländische Einflüsse*, pp. 19 and 99-106.

The reception and development of legal philosophy in Switzerland is a more complex question; on one hand, both Lausanne (in the Vaud, Bernese subject territory) and Geneva were at the cutting edge of the European discussion – on the other hand, as influential as Burlamaqui might have been outside Switzerland, it is very hard to discern whether, and if so to what extent, the new constitutional theories informed or even influenced the ruling classes.

That the Swiss were intellectually curious about the new philosophical trends can be shown – Walter does so for the reception of Dutch thought in Zurich and Berne.[70] But it is one thing for individuals, even if in the governing councils, to be interested, and quite another for this to find reflection in the canton's constitution, especially since, as has been shown, there was no formal change to the underlying legal system.

There are several possible reasons for this: For one, there was a fundamental mismatch between the "modern" advice and Swiss practice: Firstly, legal philosophers assumed that the "sovereign" would be an individual, a monarch or prince, whereas all of the cantonal governments were collective;[71] secondly, more importantly, *all* of the cantons relied on militia – none created the professional, standing army which all writers saw as essential for the realisation of the properly governed, well regulated absolutist state.

But mainly, the members of the Swiss ruling *élites* were practical people; they considered themselves and their regiment instituted by God[72] and saw no need for additional legitimation. In good Enlightenment form, they too professed to be solicitous of their subjects' "happiness",[73] but very clearly saw it as their duty to define the nature of that happiness

---

[70] Also Eisenhut, *Tugenden*; Ulrich, *18. Jahrhundert*, pp. 443-455; the curiosity was not limited to the ruling classes – the "common man" was educated and travelled enough to participate in the discussion: Brändle, *Revitalisierung*, p. 615; Bräker, *Der arme Mann im Tockenburg*.

[71] This is not a given; with a bit of stretch, the "sovereign" can include privy councils or even just the legal conception of sovereignty divorced from any person.

[72] Ziegler, *Das Große Mandat*, pp. 37-38 and p. 3 of the *Mandat und Ordnung Herren Burgermeister kleiner und grosser Räthen der Statt S. Gallen [...]* (St. Gallen: Straub, 1611): *Ob wol, zu vermehrung der Gottforcht unnd erbaren lebens: unnd hingegen zu abschaffung der lastern und unordentlichen wesens, wir vor disem gute Christliche Mandata angestellt, und dieselben offtermals, ..., durch ein weytleüffig Edict erneüweren, unnd siderhar auch zu mehrmalen ofentlich verkünden lassen: der entlichen zuversicht, man solte, auß der pflicht, so ein jedes zuvorderst Gote im himel, und dann der ordenlichen Oberkeit schuldig ist, denselben unweigerlich gehorsam gewesen seyn* (For the benefit, and for the enhancement of the fear of God and the honourable life; and conversely for the abolition of vice and of dissolute habits; we have promulgated this Christian mandate and renewed the same ... through further edicts and have caused it to be re-published several times: in the ultimate confidence that every one, out of duty owed primarily to God in heaven, so also to the properly appointed authority, shall inevitably be obedient). Also Maissen, *Geschichte*, pp. 129-130; Weissen, *Stuer*, p. 142; Ulrich, *18. Jahrhundert*, pp. 366-371; Jeker, *Rechtsgeschichte Solothurn*, p. 43; Messmer, *Luzerner Patriziat*, pp. 68-69.

[73] In both the finality of government and in the aims, this fit with European Enlightenment constitutional and philosophical thought, e.g. Lipsius, *Politicorum doctrina*, 43: *Quis finis, quò actiones omnes*

and to guide their charges, who were not capable of doing so themselves, to that end with a firm but merciful hand. The tools were the mandates, instituting *gute Policey*, with the aim of creating a large, healthy, and wealthy populace, equally obedient to their Lord and their masters.

IV. THE 2ND AMENDMENT – A SIDEWAYS GLANCE

IV.1. "Sister Republics" – Switzerland and the US in the 18th Century

In the late 18th C, republican commonwealths in Europe were rare – apart from the small free cities dotted across Europe, only Venice and Switzerland were *bona fide* republics of any size.[74] Of the two, the Swiss legend of William Tell, the entire Swiss foundation myth of successful broad-based popular resistance against a tyrannical prince overstepping the legal boundaries of his rule, fit in very well with the ideological needs of the American revolutionary movement.[75] Besides, who could miss the serendipitous parallel between the Thirteen Cantons of the Swiss Confederacy and the Thirteen Colonies?

Also, the Swiss furnished a large contingent among the American immigrants.[76] Several prominent politicians of early America were Swiss-born, and no doubt brought their political culture with them. Two important ones were John J. Zubly and Albert Gallatin:

> John J. Zubly (born Hans Joachim Züblin 1724 St. Gallen, died 1781 Savannah, GA) was an ordained Lutheran minister who moved to Savannah, GA, in 1760. He agitated against the British Crown's tax policy in the Colonies, reminding King George III in a London-published 1775 pamphlet that a handful of Swiss had defeated and defied the might of Habsburg over just such a question. He was member of the Georgia delegation at the

---

Princeps dirigat? Bonum publicum id esse ... Nam moderatori reipub[licae] beata civium vita proposita est ... Nec rempublicam tuam esse, se te reipublicae (What is the end to which every Prince directs his action? It is the common good... For the happy life of the citizens is prescribed to the rulers of the commonwealth... For the commonwealth is not yours [i.e. the Prince's], but you are the commonwealth's).

[74] Simler, *Regiment der Eydgenoßschaft*, p. 3; Hutson, *Sister Republics*, p. 9.

[75] In 1768, Henry Miller (formerly Johann Heinrich Möller, from Basel, 1702-1782) published a William Tell songbook in Philadelphia, in German: Hutson, *Sister Republics*, pp. 14-17. The first musical written and performed by Americans opened in New York City on 18th April 1796: William Dunlap's *The Archers, or the Mountaineers of Switzerland*, essentially the William Tell story, and met with appreciative audiences: Hutson, *Sister Republics*, p. 30; Halbrook, *Swiss Confederation*, pp. 34-45.

[76] How large is impossible to determine, as Switzerland is landlocked, and US immigration records list only the immigrants' port or country of departure. Also, the Swiss have no own, identifying language: Hutson, *Sister Republics*, pp. 13-15. A sizeable number of the Revolutionary War soldiers were Swiss, and the Pennsylvania or Kentucky rifle was developed from the Swiss *Jäger* rifle by Martin Meylin, a Swiss gunsmith originally from Hedingen, Zurich – Hutson, *Sister Republics*, p. 18.

Continental Congress 1775, but could not bring himself to agree to a break with the Crown and went into exile in 1777 for two years.[77]

Albert Gallatin (born 1761 in Geneva, died 1849 Astoria, NY). Emigrated 1780, first professor at Harvard, 1789 Representative in the Pennsylvania legislature, 1790 elected to the House, 1793 the Senate; Treasury Secretary under Thomas Jefferson 1801-1813, then US ambassador in St. Petersburg, at the Congress of Ghent, Paris and London.[78]

In the constitutional discussion, the Antifederalists argued that the Swiss Confederacy "worked" and there was no need for a federal constitution, drawing on sometimes heavily romanticised descriptions of Swiss conditions.[79] For the Federalists, the reality of the Swiss Confederation showed up the inadequacies of a confederacy, and militated for a federal constitution – a position that ultimately won.[80]

IV.2. Legislative Environment of the 2nd Amendment

The leading politicians of the various States did not operate in a vacuum, but were intimately acquainted with the philosophical streams and political realities of 18th C Europe. Though the Antifederalists "lost" the argument on a Federal Constitution, by way of compromise they "won" on their main criticism: The lack of a bill of rights. Without a bill of rights, the sovereign (i.e. Congress and the President) *could* pass a valid and binding law that violated Natural Law and was therefore illegitimate.[81] This was eventually corrected by the first ten Amendments adopted in 1791, which included two clearly inspired by the Swiss tradition: The 2nd (and the 10th) Amendments.[82]

The Colonies initially followed the British example on militia. While there are again differences between the various Colonies, the militia proved ineffectual in both defence against Native attacks and in the North American theatre of Britain's wars; issues of cost

---

[77] Hutson, *Sister Republics*, pp. 17-18; Halbrook, *Swiss Confederation*, pp. 34-36 and 43-44; Cornell/DeDino, *Well Regulated Right*, p. 493; HLS, entry "Züblin, Hans Joachim".

[78] Halbrook, *Swiss Confederation*, pp. 64-66; Cornell/DeDino, *Well Regulated Right*, p. 497; HLS, entry "Gallatin, Albert de".

[79] Some of the sources were serious and legitimate, others written "in a purple prose that seems excessive even for a promoter of tourism"; John Adams, the US' minister in London, wrote to the Constitutional Convention in April 1787 with a survey of the Swiss cantons' constitutions culled from these sources – Hutson, *Sister Republics*, pp. 24-29; Halbrook, *Swiss Confederation*, pp. 45-57; Adams, *A Defence*, pp. 22-56. Adams deals with the militia only in his letter on Berne (pp. 38-39), referring to the general service obligation, the individual's duty to purchase his own arms and uniform, and the *äussere Stand* (Fn 21).

[80] … and informed the framers of the first Swiss Federal Constitution in 1848: Hutson, *Sister Republics*, pp. 29-38; Hamilton/Jay/Madison, *The Federalist*, pp. 137-139 (Federalist XIX).

[81] Cf. the section on Burlmaqui, III.3, esp. *in fine*. Anderson/Cayton, *Dominion*, p. 189.

[82] Halbrook, *Swiss Confederation*, pp. 56-57 and 69; Hutson, *Sister Republics*, p. 29 (without claiming the 2nd Amendment as Swiss).

of defence and the corresponding tax load, as well as objections to the compulsory nature of service, dogged the political discussion. When fighting troops were needed, both the Colonies and the British government recruited standing troops in the Colonies for limited terms, often from classes of the population that were not eligible to join the militia; the militia administration essentially provided muster rolls, no more.[83]

Britain itself did not have a fighting militia after the 17th C, and the British troops the Colonists encountered during King George's War (War of Austrian Succession), the French and Indian War (Seven Years' War) and the Revolutionary War were all standing army or mercenaries. Especially during the Revolutionary War, they were seen as an instrument of oppression. Therefore, Britain could not serve as model for the States.[84]

The Swiss military organisation offered a template for an effective militia without a standing army. Indeed, the State militia laws referenced by Cornell and DeDino read very much like the Swiss cantons' militia mandates,[85] and Halbrook shows the direct influence of the Swiss model on State and federal legislation, including the 1792 federal Militia Act which – just like the Swiss mandates – required all male citizens to enrol in the State militia and equip and arm themselves.[86] The right to bear arms therefore is neither a private right

---

[83] For Pennsylvania: Ward, *Army of Servants*; New England: Anderson/Cayton, *Dominion*, pp. 162-166. The militia proved ineffectual in Shays' Rebellion 1786, leading to the Militia Act of 1792: Kerby, *Militia System*, pp. 106-107; Anderson/Cayton, *Dominion*, p. 186. British mobilisation of Colony forces in the Seven Years' War – successful, in the event – depended on offering generous terms to volunteers: Anderson, *Crucible*, pp. 228-231.

[84] Anderson/Cayton, *Dominion*, p. 189. For the discussion in England (and, with differences, in Scotland) in the 17th and 18th C, in terms of a standing army being at odds with ancient freedoms, see the references in Metzger, *Milizarmee im Republikanismus*, pp. 245-337. While the militia remained as an institution, the reality was that from the 17th C onwards, Britain's fighting military was the standing army, mostly recruited or pressed from classes that were excluded from the militia. Houlding, *Fit for Service*, mentions the militia only in passing. Anderson/Cayton, *Dominion*, pp. 770-771 (n. 26): "The authorized strength of the English militia was 32,000, but the only time that more than 16,000 men actually served was at the height of the French invasion threat of 1759. Even at its theoretical maximum, the English militia would have amounted to less than 3.3 percent of the male population in the sixteen to thirty age range" (with references). For a literary reference to the British militia and the low standing of its officers, see Jane Austen's *Pride and Prejudice*: Breihan/Caplan, *Jane Austen and the Militia*.

[85] Cornell/DeDino, *Well Regulated Right*, pp. 508-510; Kerby, *Militia System*, pp. 108-109, though they do not draw any Swiss references; referring to Switzerland as model: Hummel, *American Militia*, pp. 52-53. Both Zubly and Gallatin, at different times and in different ways, contributed to the discussion on the drafting and the interpretation of these provisions.

[86] Halbrook, *Swiss Confederation*, pp. 56-57 – the link between citizenship (i.e. the right to vote), bearing of arms and military service – typical for the *Landsgemeinde* cantons (Fn 10) – is evident here. The militia concept did not endure; for its westward expansion into Native American lands, the US needed standing troops (Anderson/Cayton, *Dominion*, pp. 192-193). But George Washington, as president, in 1794 called up an army of 12,950 men from various State militias to

of individuals nor a collective right of states; it is a civic right, one exercised by citizens (and only them), acting together for a public purpose;[87] like voting, it is an act of participation in government, not one of opposition to government.

V. CONCLUSIONS

There is very little in Swiss academic literature on the philosophical grounding of the militias, both in contemporary sources as well as with modern historians, regardless of political outlook.[88] One reason may certainly be that Swiss history for the period is not particularly "sexy". It is only recently that academic interest is focussing on the 18th C in a comprehensive manner.[89]

As repeatedly stated, there was no formal change to the legal system – technically, feudal law still applied;[90] but, as a reading of e.g. Wyß demonstrates, by the late 18th C, modernising commonwealths like Zurich had achieved such a "density" of legislation that one can (as Wyß does) speak of a constitutional order that had (nearly) fully overlaid the feudal law substrate.[91]

It is clear that the cantonal oligarchies saw themselves in the mould of the kindly and wise, strict but just, father of their subjects, demanding obedience, educating and guiding but not overburdening their wards, entirely in the absolutist tradition. It is equally clear that they had neither the will nor the means to enforce the absolutist principle.

A key factor is parsimony,[92] which operates at several levels and reveals a vicious (or virtuous) circle: Enforcement required a standing force beholden *only* to the "sovereign",

---

put down the Whisky Rebellion. The effort must have been more convincing than the fiasco in confronting Shays' Rebellion, since the rebels dispersed before there was action: Anderson/Cayton, *Dominion*, pp. 197-202. Some of the militia performed dismally in the War of 1812, but as in Switzerland, the numerous successful actions carried by some militias show that the weaknesses of the militia system lay in the implementation, not in the principle: Kerby, *Militia System*, pp. 105-107, 120-124 and *passim*.

[87] Cornell/DiDino, *Well Regulated Right*, p. 491.

[88] With obvious exceptions, e.g. Brändle, Gmür, Jeker, Nussbaumer, Peyer, or Walter. Metzger's thesis over 400 pages deals with the philosophical discussion in England on the militia in the 17th C and in the US, but shows no curiosity about the Swiss or even Continental European debate; Studer Immenhauser's nearly 500 pages avoids mention of the military administration.

[89] Nussbaumer, *Zuger Militär*, pp. 11 and 23 – though much remains to be done, from the preparatory sifting of the – abundant – sources to reflections on a conceptual framework.

[90] The liquidation of feudal rights required by the secularisation of the ecclesiastical estates by Napoleon and then the dissolution of the Holy Roman Empire 1803-1806 were a massive undertaking in legal and actuarial terms.

[91] Püttmann – author of a restatement of feudal law – and Wyß were contemporary.

[92] Peyer, *Verfassungsgeschichte*, pp. 95 and 129; Nussbaumer, *Zuger Militär*, p. 27.

i.e. the privy council, which would have been expensive. Increased tax revenue would have been required, and that could only have come from oppressively higher taxes on the subjects, who would easily have realised that their taxes went to fund the instrument of their oppression.[93] And so the concept went against two fundamental principles of the feudal constitution: That the estate's military might was the responsibility of all feudatories, and that the raising of taxes required the consent of the feudatories.[94]

It cannot be said that the ruling classes were soft – they had no compunction to ruthlessly assert their power when it was threatened, as in the Peasants' War; they had no reservations about risking their subjects' lives in pursuit of their political interests, as they did in both Villmergen Wars. But clearly, there was enough wealth to go around for the rulers to come to the judgement that the marginal cost of increasing their power was greater than the benefit – the mantra-like restatements of the mandates were meant to reiterate the *claim* of authority, while at the same time the authorities made no serious effort at enforcement. On the contrary, they alleviated the economic effects a harsh enforcement of their mandates would have caused. So instead of deeply held philosophical principles or lofty ideals, there is only the realisation that properly oppressing the subjects was just too expensive and would have been too much hassle.

Statecraft does deserve its place: Since the Confederacy's birth, no single canton or alliance of cantons had the might to impose itself on the others; in the constantly shifting alliances, today's winners were quite conscious that they might be tomorrow's losers, so dispute settlements as much as possible sought to re-establish the *status quo ante*. The ruling classes had a commitment to certain principles of statecraft (collective decision-making, live-and-let-live, no standing troops, parsimony) that gave the Confederacy stability, which allowed for general prosperity and a dynamism in the creation of modern administrative structures.[95] It also created a bewildering diversity, which paradoxically was so distinctive that a Swiss identity emerged, recognised in Switzerland and outside.

Diversity meant that everyone had a special deal; this was so for the cantons among themselves, but also within the cantons. Every community had some jealously guarded *acquis* which distinguished it from its neighbour and which was implicitly or explicitly guaranteed

---

[93] So explicitly outlined by Wyß, *Politisches Handbuch*, pp. 221-222; also Brändle, *Revitalisierung*, p. 611; Grosjean, *Kriegsgenügen*, pp. 154-156. The generally low tax burden went a long way to explaining the subjects' quiescence: Ulrich, *18. Jahrhundert*, p. 369. Interestingly, none of the cantons formed anything like a Praetorian Guard, a small and therefore affordable, but professional force beholden to the privy council.

[94] Peyer, *Verfassungsgeschichte*, p. 119; Messmer, *Luzerner Patriziat*, pp. 69-70.

[95] Studer Immenhauser shows the innovative drive in successful city-states (here: Berne) already in the late Middle Ages, though unfortunately does not address the military side at all.

by the others, and could be lost if that community overplayed its hand.[96] So though such special deals went against the principles of absolutism, the authorities (true to the Roman adage *divide et impera*) used them to their advantage.[97] They didn't sweat the small stuff and chose their fights; and when they fought, they made sure they won.

The fact that the armed might of the commonwealth lay in the people, and was not beholden to the rulers, firmly anchored the constitutional structure. Though it was evidently less than ideal in terms of military effectiveness, the communities retained a key role in the military organisation. Never mind how lackadaisical and occasionally farcical the day-to-day reality was, the fact remains that both rulers and subjects in principle agreed that defence of the commonwealth was a community matter. In that, the Swiss remained resolutely rooted in feudal concepts.[98]

Regarding the military side as such, two aspects deserve to be emphasised:

- By no means did the militia organisation emerge as flawed in principle – at least since Villmergen II (where both Berne's and Zurich's forces performed well), Berne and Zurich, the two military heavyweights of the Confederacy, took pains to be up to date. The Swiss collapse in front of Napoleon was primarily political; while it is fanciful to pretend that Berne – or the Confederacy, had it managed to get its military act together – stood a chance against Napoleon's troops, its militia acquitted itself well.
- The organisation that was required in order to recruit, train, arm, equip, supply and pay for the impressive militia troop numbers was a key driver in the modernisation of the administration.

Despite the comprehensive defeat inflicted by Napoleon, Switzerland re-emerged not just in its external borders, but in its internal structure as well, and again as a Confederacy;[99]

---

[96] Gmür, *Städte als Landesherren*, p. 188; as Gmür (p. 190) points out, this also rationalised the disenfranchisement of the rural subjects by the city burghers, for if you give legal equality, why not political equality?

[97] Fehr, *Absolutismus*, pp. 188-190 – they even gave the communal institutions additional responsibilities, which reduced the authorities' financial and administrative burden; Jeker, *Rechtsgeschichte Solothurn*, pp. 45-48; Messmer, *Luzerner Patriziat*, pp. 70-71: The ruling *élites* also always set aside their internal quarrels when confronted with subject insurrection.

[98] Jeker, *Rechtsgeschichte Solothurn*, pp. 67-68. It is certainly ironic that the one country in Europe that lived off the business of providing standing *élite* troops to foreign princes, for its own military constitution followed the advice of military and constitutional philosophers alike and relied exclusively on an autochthonous military (though not, as those same philosophers recommended, *professional* troops).

[99] *Sans* subject territories or ecclesiastical principalities. Though not for want of trying – Napoleon's Helvetic constitution had dissolved the cantons and created a centralised state with new administrative districts. Despite the subject territories' initial welcome of the French troops, their high-

it did not abandon faith in the militia principle, and reverted to cantonal militia immediately after Napoleon's ouster.[100]

Ultimately, never mind how far removed the aristocratic patrician or lordly guildmaster was from his disenfranchised urban or rural subject, they all, at a very basic level, seem to have firmly believed in a common political fate. In the 19th C, the distinctiveness of Switzerland's political culture nurtured through the 17th and 18th C allowed the Swiss body politic to leverage the Swiss identity to forge a functioning democratic polity out of twenty-five cantons divided by four languages, two religions, and several cultures.[101]

VI. BIBLIOGRAPHY

VI.1. Primary sources

Regulations (Anonymous):

- *Mandat und Ordnung Herren Burgermeister kleiner und grosser Räthen der Statt S. Gallen [...]* (St. Gallen: Straub, 1611), facsimile reprint in Ziegler, *Mandat*, pp. 53-88

- *Reglement für die Herren Officiers Löbl. Grenadier-Compagnie zu Fuß, wie sie sich bey Wacht- und Feuer-Anlässen zu verhalten haben* (St. Gallen: Zollikofer, 1796)

- *Reglement vor die Land-Miliz lobl. Stands Zug* (Zug: Blunschi, 1757), facsimile reprint in Nussbaumer, pp. 281-314.

Adams, John, *A Defence of the Constitutions of Government of the United States of America* (Philadelphia: Hall and Sellers, 1787)

Bräker, Ulrich, *Lebensgeschichte und Natürliche Ebentheuer des Armen Mannes im Tockenburg*, ed. H. H. Füßli (Zurich: Orell, Geßner, Füßli, 1789)

Burlamaqui, Jean Jacques, *Principes du droit naturel* (Geneva: Barillot, 1746)

Burlamaqui, Jean Jacques, *Principles of Natural Law*, translated by Mr. Nugent (London: Nourse, 1752)

---

handedness and depredations doomed the Helvetic constitution. A federal constitution had to wait until 1848: Maissen, *Geschichte*, pp. 160-171.

[100] Nussbaumer, *Zuger Militär*, p. 205. Until the forming of national military structures, private officers' associations sought to raise technical knowledge, skill and training of both officers and troops – Eugster/Jäger/Bänziger, *Appenzellische Offiziersgesellschaft*, pp. 17-27; the *Theoretisch-practische Anleitung zum Gebrauch des Bajonets als Stoß- und Schlagwaffe, Führung des Morgensterns und Säbels [etc.]*, was put together from various sources by a Grisons officer formerly in French and Swiss service and printed by subscription in 1837 (Zürich: Schulthess, 1837).

[101] Peyer, *Verfassungsgeschichte*, pp. 145-146; Ulrich, *18. Jahrhundert*, pp. 366-367; Fehr, *Absolutismus*, p. 202.

Burlamaqui, Jean Jacques, *Principes ou élémens du droit politique* (Lausanne: Grasset, 1784)

Fritsch, Ahasverus, *De iure lustrationis et seqvelae* (Naumburg: Müller, 1670)

Hamilton, Alexander / John Jay / James Madison, *The Federalist: On the New Constitution* (New York: Williams & Whiting, 1810)

Iustinianus Augustus, *Digesta*, edited by Paul Krüger and Theodor Mommsen, re-issued by J. Triantaphyllopoulos (reprint of the 3rd Ed. Berlin 1868) Vol I (Hildesheim: Weidmann, 1997)

Lavater, Hans Conrad, *Kriegsbüchlein: Das ist die Grundliche Anleitung zum Kriegswesen* (Zurich: Bodmer, 1667)

Lipsius, Iustus, *De militia romana libri quinque: commentarius ad Polybium* (Antwerp: Plantiniana, 1614)

Lipsius, Iustus, *Politicorum sive civilis doctrina libri sex* (Antwerp: Plantiniana, 1599)

Machiavelli, Niccolò, *Discorsi sopra la prima deca di Tito Livio*, Opere di Niccolò Machiavelli: cittadino e segretario fiorentino, Vol. II (Milan: Tipografica de' Classici Italiani, 1804)

Machiavelli, Niccolò, *I sette libri dell'arte della guerra*, Opere di Niccolò Machiavelli: cittadino e segretario fiorentino, Vol. IV (n.p.: n.pub., 1796)

Pufendorf, Samuel, *De officio hominis et civis libri duo*, 5th Ed., (n.p.: Liebezeit, 1693)

Püttmann, Josias Ludwig Ernst, *Elementa ivris fevdalis qua privati qua publici* (Leipzig: Weidmann & Reich, 1781)

Simler, Josias, *De republica helvetiorum libri duo* (Zurich: Froschauer, 1577)

Simler, Josias, *Von dem Regiment der Loblichen Eydgenoßschaft Zwey Bücher, In derem Ersterem Eine kurtz-gefaßte Politische Historie der Helvetisch- und Eydgenössischen Sachen [...]; In dem Anderen aber Eine Beschreibung der Eydgenossen Friedens- und Kriegsübungen / samt der Beschaffenheit des Regiments [...]* fortgesetzt von Hans Jacob Leu, 2nd Ed. (Zurich: Geßner, 1735)

Wyß, David, *Politisches Handbuch für die erwachsene Jugend der Stadt und Landschaft Zürich* (Zurich: Orell, Geßner, Füßli, 1796)

VI.2. Secondary Literature

Anderson, Fred, *Crucible of War: The Seven Years' War and the Fate of the Empire in British North America, 1754-1766*, (London: Faber and Faber, 2000)

Anderson, Fred, Andrew Cayton, *The Dominion of War: Empire and Liberty in North America, 1500-2000* (New York NY: Viking, 2005)

Antieau, Chester James, 'Natural Rights And the Founding Fathers – The Virginians', *Washington & Lee Law Review*, Vol. 17 Issue 1 (1960), 43-79

Bischofberger, Hermann, *Rechtsarchäologie und Rechtliche Volkskunde des eidgenössischen Standes Appenzell Innerrhoden* (Diss. Freiburg i. Üe.) (Oberegg: Bischofberger, 1999)

Bosshard, Ralph, 'Militärunternehmer aus dem Thurgau gegen Ende des 15. Jahrhunderts', *Thurgauer Beiträge zur Geschichte*, 134 (1997), 7-116

Brändle, Fabian, 'Nicht "Degeneration", sondern Revitalisierung: Die Landsgemeindekonflikte des 18. Jahrhunderts und das Werden der modernen Schweiz', in: *Zeitschrift für historische Forschung*, Vol. 40 (2013), 593-621

Breihan, John, Clive Caplan, 'Jane Austen and the Militia', in: *Journal of the Jane Austen Society of North America: Persuasions*, No. 14 (1992), 16-26

Bührer, Peter, *Die auswärtige Politik der alten Stadtrepublik St. Gallen 1291-1798* (St. Gallen: Zollikofer, 1954)

Cornell, Saul / Nathan DeDino, 'A Well Regulated Right: The Early American Origins of Gun Control', *Fordham Law Review*, Vol. 73 (2004), Issue 2, 487-528

Dierauer, J., 'Das Toggenburg unter äbtischer Herrschaft', *Neujahrsblätter des historischen Vereins St. Gallen*, Vol. 14 (1875)

Dufour, Alfred, 'Les ruses de la Raison d'Etat ou Histoire et Droit naturel dans l'œuvre et la pensée des Fondateurs du Droit naturel moderne', *FS Hans Thieme zum 80. Geburtstag* (Sigmaringen: Thorbeke, 1986), p. 265-284

Eisenhut, Heidi, 'Tugenden gestern und heute', *Appenzellische Jahrbücher* 139 (2012), 50-61

Eugster, Hans / Niklaus Jäger / Markus Bänziger, *150 Jahre Appenzellische Offiziersgesellschaft* (Herisau: Appenzeller Medienhaus, 2006)

Fehr, Hans, 'Der Absolutismus in der Schweiz' *Zeitschrift der Savigny-Stiftung für Rechtsgeschichte*, Vol. 69 (1952), 182-202

Flury, Therese / Karl Schmuki / Ernst Tremp, *Von der Limmat zurück an die Steinach: St Galler Kulturgüter aus Zürich* (St Gallen: am Klosterhof, 2006)

Gmür, Rudolf, 'Städte als Landesherren vom 16. bis zum 18. Jahrhundert', *FS Hans Thieme zum 80. Geburtstag* (Sigmaringen: Thorbeke, 1986), p. 177-198

Grosjean, George, 'Miliz und Kriegsgenügen als Problem im Wehrwesen des alten Bern', *Archiv des Historischen Vereins des Kantons Bern*, 42 No. 1 (1953-1954), 129-171

Halbrook, Stephen P., 'The Swiss Confederation in the Eyes of America's Founders', *Swiss American Historical Society Review*, November 2012, 32-69

Härter, Karl, 'Sicherheit und *gute Policey* im frühneuzeitlichen Alten Reich: Konzepte, Gesetze und Instrumente', in: B. Dollinger/H. Schmidt-Semisch (Eds.), *Sicherer Alltag? Politiken und Mechanismen der Sicherheitskonstruktion im Alltag* (Wiesbaden: Springer, 2016), 29-38

Hidber, Basilius, 'Der ehemalige sog. äußere Stand der Stadt und Republik Bern', *Neujahrsblatt für die bernische Jugend*, (1858)

Houlding, J.A., *Fit for Service: The Training of the British Army 1715-1795* (Oxford: OUP, 1981)

Hummel, Jeffrey Rogers, 'The American Militia and the Origin of Conscription: A Reassessment', in: *Journal of Libertarian Studies*, Vol. 15, No. 4 (Fall 2001), 29-77

Hutson, James H., *Sister Republics: Switzerland and the United States from 1776 to the Present* (Washington: Library of Congress, 1991)

Jeker, Daniel, *Rechtsgeschichtliche Aspekte zur Verfassungs- und Wehrgeschichte des Stadtstaates Solothurn zur Zeit des Dreissigjährigen Krieges* (Solothurn: Altes Zeughaus, 2000)

Kerby, Robert L., 'The Militia System and the State Militias in the War of 1812', in: *Indiana Magazine of History*, Vol. 73, No. 2 (June 1977), 102-124

Kurz, Hans Rudolf, *Das Schweizer Heer* (Dietikon: Stocker-Schmid, 1969)

Luginbühl, Hans / Anne Barth-Gasser / Fritz Baumann / Dominique Piller, *1712: Zeitgenössische Quellen zum Zweiten Villmerger- oder Toggenburgerkrieg* (Lenzburg: Merker, 2011)

Maissen, Thomas, *Geschichte der Schweiz* (Baden: hier+jetzt, 2010)

Mantel, Alfred, 'Zürcher Wehranstalten in der Zeit zwischen den beiden Villmergerkriegen', *Jahrbücher für Schweizer Geschichte*, 36 (1911), 183-213

Meder, Stephan, *Rechtsgeschichte*, 5th Ed., (Köln/Weimar/Wien: Böhlau, 2014)

Menolfi, Ernest, 'Vom Solddienst und Militärwesen in der Fürstabtei und der Stadt St Gallen', *Sankt Galler Geschichte 2003, Band 3, Frühe Neuzeit: Territorien, Wirtschaft* (St Gallen: Amt für Kultur des Kantons St Gallen, 2003), 199-218

Messmer, Kurt, 'Zum Luzerner Patriziat im 16. Jahrhundert', in: Kurt Messmer/Peter Hoppe, *Luzerner Patriziat: Sozial- und wirtschaftsgeschichtliche Studien zur Entstehung und Entwicklung im 16. und 17. Jahrhundert* (Luzerner Historische Veröffentlichungen, Bd. 5) (Luzern/München: Rex, 1976)

Metzger, Jan, *Die Milizarmee im klassischen Republikanismus* (Diss. St Gallen) (Bern/Stuttgart/Wien: Haupt, 1999)

Mitteis, Heinrich / Heinz Lieberich, *Deutsche Rechtsgeschichte*, 16th Ed., (München: C H Beck, 1981)

von Mülinen, Wolfgang Friedrich, 'Vom Aeusseren Stand und dem Urispiegel', *Blätter für bernische Geschichte, Kunst und Altertumskunde*, 12 No. 1 (1916), 1-32

Nussbaumer, Alex, *Zuger Militär: Im Spannungsfeld von Politik, Wirtschaft und Gesellschaft: Das Zuger Militärwesen im 18. Jahrhundert* (Rotkreuz: Zürcher, 1998)

Oechsli, Wilhelm, 'Orte und Zugewandte – Eine Studie des schweizerischen Bundesstaatsrechts', *Jahrbuch für schweizerische Geschichte* Vol. 13 (1888), 3-497

Peyer, Hans Conrad, *Die Verfassungsgeschichte der alten Schweiz* (Zürich: Schulthess, 1980)

von Rodt, Emanuel, *Geschichte des Bernerischen Kriegswesens*, 2 Vols., (Bern: Jenni, 1831)

Schib, Karl, *Geschichte der Stadt und Landschaft Schaffhausen* (Schaffhausen: Meili, 1972)

Schläpfer, Walter, *Appenzell Ausserrhoden (von 1597 bis zur Gegenwart)* (Herisau: Kantonskanzlei, 1972)

Schmidt, Rudolf, *Die Entwicklung der Handfeuerwaffen* (Schaffhausen: Brodtman, 1867)

Schneider, Hugo, *Vom Brustharnisch zum Waffenrock/De la cuirasse à la tunique* (Frauenfeld: Huber, 1968)

Sigg, Marco, *"Une promenade militaire"? Der Nebenkriegsschauplatz an der zürcherisch-schwyzerischen Grenze im Zweiten Villmergerkrieg (1712)* diploma thesis Military Academy at the ETH Zurich 2005

Sigg, Otto, 'Das 17. Jahrhundert', in: *Geschichte des Kantons Zürich, Band II: Frühe Neuzeit / 16. bis 18. Jahrhundert*, various editors, (Zürich: Werd, 1996), 282-363

Silvestrini, Gabriella, 'Rousseau, Pufendorf and the eighteenth-century natural law tradition', *History of European Ideas*, Vol. 36 (2010), 280–301

Sonderegger, Stefan, *Das altappenzellische Wehrwesen im Lichte der Orts- und Flurnamen* (Trogen: Meili, 1962)

Studer Immenhauser, Barbara, *Verwaltung zwischen Innovation und Tradition: Die Stadt Bern und ihr Untertanengebiet* (Ostfildern: Thorbeke, 2006)

Tlusty, B. Ann, *The Martial Ethic in Early Modern Germany: Civic Duty and the Right of Arms*, (Chippingham and Eastbourne: Palgrave Macmillan, 2011)

Ulrich, Conrad, 'Das 18. Jahrhundert', in: *Geschichte des Kantons Zürich, Band II: Frühe Neuzeit / 16. bis 18. Jahrhundert*, various editors, (Zürich: Werd, 1996), 364-505

Walter, Frieder, *Niederländische Einflüsse auf das eidgenössische Staatsdenken im späten 16. und frühen 17. Jahrhundert: Neue Aspekte der Zürcher und Berner Geschichte im Zeitalter des werdenden Absolutismus* (Zurich: Rohr, 1979)

Ward, Matthew C., 'An Army of Servants: The Pennsylvania Regiment during the Seven Years' War', in: *The Pennsylvania Magazine of History & Biography*, Vol. 119, No. 1/2 (January/April 1995), 75-93

Weissen, Kurt, *"An der stuer ist ganz nuett bezahlt". Landesherrschaft, Wirtschaft und Verwaltung in den fürstbischöflichen Herrschaften in der Umgebung Basels (1435-1525)* (Basler Beiträge zur Geschichtswissenschaft 167) (Basel: Schwabe, 1994)

Welzel, Hans, *Naturrecht und materiale Gerechtigkeit* 4th Ed. (Göttingen: Vandenhoek & Ruprecht, 1980)

Ziegler, Ernst, *Das Große Mandat der Stadt St Gallen von 1611* (St Gallen: Verlagsgemeinschaft 1983)

Ziegler, Ernst, *Die Milizen der Stadt St. Gallen* (Rorschach: Löpfe-Benz, 1992)

VI.3. On-Line Resources

DUCANGE (et al.): *Glossarium mediæ et infimæ latinitatis* <http://ducange.enc.sorbonne.fr>

HLS: *Historisches Lexikon der Schweiz / Dictionnaire Historique de la Suisse / Dizionario storico della Svizzera* <http://www.hls-dhs-dss.ch>

DOI 10.1515/apd-2016-0003

The French staff material from Johann Georg Pasch

Olivier Dupuis,
independant researcher,
Dupuisolivier@yahoo.fr

Abstract – Johann Georg Pasch was a very prolific author who published a large number of books during the third quarter of the seventeenth century. Some of these included physical exercises with a long staff and presented by Pasch himself as coming from France. Among all the known editions, four different versions can be isolated; this offers the possibility to study the filiation of the edition process. This study is combined with a textual criticism of the material, beginning with a comprehensive biography from the author and finishing with the questioning of the French origin.

Keywords – critical edition, staff, Johann Georg Pasch

I. INTRODUCTION

The main goal of this article is to propose a critical edition of the long staff material from Johann Georg Pasch, coupled with a history of publication and the filiation of editions. The growing interest in this subject over the last few years is demonstrated notably by three distinct translations in English.[1] There are also other purposes, since this critical edition is not just a mere transcription: it has to stay faithful to the German type of scholarly edition, to analyze the text's origin and provenance.[2] This paper will thus present first a contextualization of the text, including biographical information and then a description of the content.

II. CONTEXTUALIZATION

II.1. The life of Pasch (1628 – 1678)

II.1.1. From birth to death

First, I must justify the use of the spelling *Pasch*. Johann Georg Pasch himself used the spelling *Paschen* in genitive tense and *Pascha* in other cases. In his French translations, he

---

* I am indebted to Jean Chandler for his help in translating the manuscript, as well as the anonymous peer-reviewer who provided copy-editing.
[1] Van Noort in 2014 with *Pascha's Hunting Staff* and in 2015 with *Pascha's Staff with Two Ends*, Crawley in 2013 with *The Polearm Compendium*.
[2] For an introduction to textual criticism and the differences between English and German tradition in that matter, see Gabler, *Textual Criticism*.

also used *Pasche*. The German libraries catalogs often used the modern German form *Pasch* as did also Schlöttermüller in his edition of the dance treatise.[3] The choice for this article was to use the modern form of this name instead of the historical spelling for the sake of clarity and consistency.

Despite there being a huge number of books published under his name, very little information about Johann Georg Pasch is available, except for what can be found in his own words, as recently pointed out by Wellmann.[4]

Fortunately, a valuable source of information about the life of Pasch has been found some time ago: a long sermon written and printed for his funeral, printed as was the custom at the time.[5] Some of the information from this document has not been confirmed and should be handled with caution. It states that Johann Georg was born on September 9th 1628 in Dresden. His mother, Magdalena Frauenstein was the daughter of Georg Frauenstein, a businessman and member of the city council of Dresden. His father, Johann Pasch, was a servant at the court of the Prince of Saxony and his grandfather, Joachim Pasch, first minister of the protestant church of Zittau. The sermon does not give any information about his siblings, but he was possibly one of the younger children as his parents preferred him to begin work early. Pasch, who certainly received a good education, preferred instead to continue his studies in Zittau, Berlin and finally in the Marienstift Gymnasium of Stettin, in the Pomerania, where he received a classical education in Latin.[6] The student registers stored in the city's archives are only available from 1793 onwards. Therefore it is difficult to estimate how long he stayed at this school, but it was probably until between 1643 and 1645.

The sermon further ascertains that Hugh Hamilton recruited Pasch directly from the school to serve as private tutor for his children in the city of Gdańsk, but also that Pasch went to Greifswald, and then Rostock, after staying in Gdańsk, without giving any accurate dates. Hamilton was an Irish colonel, serving in the Scottish armies of the Swedish Empire of Sweden, which at that time, controlled most of the Pomerania. Hamilton was named commander of the regiment in Riga in 1641 and took position at Greifswald in 1645.[7] It is very likely that Pasch entered Hamilton's service of Hamilton before he was recorded in Greifswald, but probably not long before that, because Pasch was only eighteen years old at the time. The funeral sermon also states that Pasch pursued his studies in both cities, Greifswald and Rostock, which each had a well-established

---

[3] Pasch, *Anleitung...*, pp. 12-21.

[4] Wellmann, *Katalog*, p. 253.

[5] I am indebted to Jan Schäfer who found this sermon. It is partially published by Hazebroucq, *La technique de la danse*, pp. 124-27. For more information about funeral sermons in Germany, see Bibza, *Die deutschsprachige Leichenpredigt*, pp. 21-24.

[6] Wehrmann, *Geschichte des Königlichen Marienstifts-Gymnasiums*, pp. 49-73.

[7] Murdoch and Grosjean, *Alexander Leslie*, pp. 151 and 162.

university.[8] He studied physical exercises such as fencing, wrestling, flag waving, and also playing the lute. It is very tempting to imagine these military studies were carried out with the help and influence of the colonel Hamilton, or at least in one of the regiments he was in charge of. Pasch informed us that his military knowledge about maneuvers with muskets came from an experienced officer, which is possibly a reference to Hamilton: *Lieber Leser, nach dem ich das sehr nützliche Exercitium mit der Mußquet von einem Exercitio erharnen Officirer erlernet.*[9]

The sermon informs us that in 1649, Pasch went back to his homeland, but stayed there only briefly before going to the University of Wittenberg in 1650, where he produced and published two legal dissertations in 1652 and 1655.[10] Anecdotally, the second dissertation is a juridical analysis of the famous kidnapping of the two sons from the prince Frederick II by Kunz von Kaufungen in 1455.[11] The sermon also states that Pasch already gave lessons in physical and rhetorical exercises, both establishing him as a local celebrity among students, professors and also the young aristocracy. In 1656, he was installed as archivist of Duke Augustus, administrator of the Archbishopric of Magdeburg. The administrator was in fact a secular prince who acted as the archbishop in the Protestant province. Augustus was therefore Prince-elector of the Holy Roman Empire and the station of archivist was certainly a good opportunity for Pasch's career.[12] At this stage, Pasch was the perfect illustration of a new class of educated men coming from the burghers and serving the aristocracy as noted by Brunt.[13]

The following year, on November 16, Pasch married Anna Margaretta Siegler, daughter of the burgomeister of Wittenberg. This is confirmed by a small printed collection of the poems and songs played during the feast.[14] The couple had four children together, Anna Margaretha, born on 03/02/1659, Ehrenfried Christian, born on 05/06/1661, Anna Catharina, born on 18/03/1663 and Augustus, born on 10/01/1666 but surviving only one month.[15]

At an unknown date, Pasch became the secretary of the chancellor of Thuringia, probably after Augustus inherited the title of Duke of Saxe-Weissenfels. Finally, in 1662, he was appointed Pagenhofmeister at a page school located in Halle (Saale). I have not been able

---

[8] Guntau, *Die frühen norddeutschen Universitätsgründungen Rostock und Greifswald.*

[9] *Deutliche Beschreibung von dem Exerciren in der Musquet und Pique*, before the last page of the musket section, the second page that received the number 35.

[10] *Dissertatio Politica de Legato Dissertatio* in 1652 and *De Plagio Kaufungiano* in 1655.

[11] This subject of historical study is still fashionable. See in particular *Der Altenburger Prinzenraub 1455*. I am also indebted to Bert Gevaert for the analysis of the Latin text.

[12] For more information about August, see *Allgemeine Deutsche Biographie*, 1, pp. 680-81.

[13] Brunt, *The Influence of the French Language*, pp. 83-84.

[14] *Festivitati Nuptiali Viri Clarissimi et Consultissimi Dni. Johannis Georgii Paschn.*

[15] It is worth mentioning that the birth dates of the children did not appear in the funeral sermon for Johann Georg, but did appear in the funeral sermon for his wife. See Christoph Schrader, *Die treue Gehülffin*, p. 7.

to find any description for this post. In his bilingual treatise of 1673, Pasch translated it into French as Gouverneur des pages. This position could have been created due to the influence of the French court,[16] but this has yet to be confirmed. However, if it is true, this post had nothing to do with sport and military training. The governor of the pages is the manager for the pages' institutions. At the French court, the pages were young boys coming from noble families who had the opportunity to serve at the court for a year or more. They also received some kind of education. The governor of the pages was responsible for the entire range of the pages' service.[17]

In 1674, Pasch was involved in a project for founding a new Academy for the young aristocracy of the court of Saxony, probably following the model of different Ritterakademien that flourished in Germany during the mid-seventeenth century.[18] Moreover, in 1675 he received a salary of 100 thalers from the Oberlausitz court for an unspecified role. However, the archive mentions him as churfürstlich sächsischen Cämmerirer which means member of the court of the Prince of Saxony.[19]

According to her funeral sermon, Pasch's wife became sick and died on August 23 1678.[20] Pasch himself had fallen ill during the summer and had to stay home because of tremors. His funeral sermon suggested a link between these tremors and a blow he received on the left side of the head. However, this is far from certain, especially since this sermon did not even mention the disease of his wife. A contagious disease is a far more likely candidate for explaining his death than a blow received two months before. Eventually, Johann Georg Pasch died 49 years old, on September 1st, 1678.

---

[16] Brunt reports that the court of Versailles was the ideal for the German aristocracy, who imitated in architecture, dress and way of life. Read in particular pp. 3-4 and pp. 27-28.
[17] For example Philibert Morin, sieur de La Touche, a French fencing master, held two positions at the queen's court in 1677: fencing master and governor of pages. He received 200 pounds a year for the first post and 300 for the second. See *L'État de la France*, p. 395.
[18] For a quick overview, see Brunt, *The Influence of the French Language*, pp. 73-75.
[19] See Müller, *Ein Versuch zur Gründung einer Ritterakademie*, pp. 47-48.
[20] Christoph Schrader, *Die treue Gehülffin*, p. 8.

Figure 1: portrait of Pasch in 1673.
Pasch, Deutliche Beschreibung unterschiedener Fahnen-Lectionen, p. 2.
Herzog August Bibliothek Wolfenbüttel: Xb 4° 157.

II.1.2. Pasch, the author

Each phase of the life of Pasch seems linked by printed books. His first contact with the literary world was the publication of two legal dissertations in 1652 and 1655 at the University of Wittenberg.[21] His second was the publication of his wedding's songbook.[22] He then produced an astonishing number of publications and re-publications between 1657 and 1673. Indeed Pasch was one of the most prolific authors on the subjects of body movements and physical exercises of that period. The number of subjects he addressed was impressive: partisan, flag waving, vaulting on horses or tables, wrestling, fencing with on the thrust and on the cut, and the long staff. He also produced books about dancing, military maneuvers with muskets and pikes, and even about the art of fortification. His books are either compilations of the subjects listed above, or monographs. And, as will be demonstrated through his work on the long staff, each

---

[21] *Dissertation Politica de Legato* and *Dissertatio de Plagio Kaufungiano*.
[22] *Festivitati Nuptiali Viri Clarissimi et Consultissimi Dni. Johannis Georgii Paschn.*

subject was continuously refined or simply evolved with each edition, in such way that a comprehensive bibliography from his entire works with classification of each content goes largely outside the scope of this paper.

It is difficult to tell which parts of his work are his own work or which are copied, translated or adapted from other works. For example, Krebs suggested that his art of carving and serving the meat is an abbreviated form of an older German book about the same subject.[23] On the other hand, Hazebroucq explained that his material about the art of dancing is unique and important in the history of that art, in particular as it is the only source giving technical details about French dances from the mid-seventeenth century.[24]

What could have been the motivations of Pasch to write so many books? In his first book, published in 1657 when he had just become archivist, he explained his reasons for producing it. He claimed that after a certain time spent studying and also teaching physical exercises (*Exercitia corporis*) to groups of people, good friends suggested that he publish these exercises. Such entourage certainly helped him in time where it was very difficult to publish in Germany without any patronage.[25]

However, it is conceivable that the production of the following books, especially between 1659 and 1661 helped him to get the job of governor of the pages in Halle. He also may have received special commissions from different patrons, which could explain why many of his books are dedicated to different people. As an example, Müller mentions a document proving that Pasch had received twenty thalers for the dedication of a book in 1670.[26] Nevertheless, unlike La Touche who addressed his book to the king of France expecting to receive the post of fencing master of the Dauphin,[27] Pasch did not dedicate any books directly to Prince August before 1670. Finally, as mentioned before, even his funeral sermon was printed.

II.2. Editions on the long staff or *baston à deux bouts*

II.2.1. The first version *A* and its partial edition *a'*

The first document from Pasch that mentioned the staff was his book entitled "Brief information about the pike, flag, partisan, hunting staff, vaulting, wrestling, fencing with thrust and cut, and finally how to carve and serve meat" (*Kurtze Unterrichtung Belangend Die Pique, die Fahne, den Jägerstock, das Voltegiren, das Ringen, das Fechten auff den Stoß und Hieb und endlich das Trinciren*). It was published for the first time in 1657 and received two re-editions under the same title in 1658 and 1659, which were printed by the same printer, Ölschlegel in Wittenberg, and distributed by the same book-seller, Christian Guths from Hamburg.

---

[23] Krebs, *Quand les allemands apprenaient à trancher*, p. 15.
[24] Hazeboucq, *La technique de la danse*, p. 11-21 and 115.
[25] Brunt, *The Influence of the French Language*, pp. 82-84.
[26] Müller, *Ein Versuch zur Gründung einer Ritterakademie*, p. 48 footnote 19.
[27] Lahaye, Le fils de Louis XIV, pp. 50-52.

I have only been able to consult the more recent edition but since all mentioned details are identical I am inclined to think that the text was likewise identical. Indeed, this last edition still contained the introduction dated from February 9th 1657. The same year, in 1659, Pasch published another book on various subjects including some from this first one. It is unlikely that Pasch would have taken time to modify an old version while working on his new book.

As noted previously, Pasch explained in the introduction of this book that he produced it for his friends and his students. He certainly worked on the printed edition before being recruited as archivist, as on the title page he stated that he was a law student (*LL. Studiosus*).[28] However, it is worth noting that he also explained clearly that teaching such exercises was not his main profession: *In Betrachtung die Exercitia niemals meine Profession gewesen.*

This first book of 132 pages contains a long selection of different subjects. The works with the pike, wrestling and the serving art all received developed and detailed sections, while the section on the hunting staff or partisan (*Jägerstock oder partisan*) is limited to the titles of the different lessons. The other sections dedicated to fencing, flag waving and vaulting received an intermediate treatment: they each had an introduction followed by the titles of the lessons.

This list of lessons, included as an appendix to this article, closely follows the program developed in the later publications, and even contains some lessons left out of the later works. However, this proves that Pasch had already organized a large part of what would be published and developed in subsequent books. This also provides further evidence to suggest that Pasch already had a written version for the lessons, even if he did not publish it in this first book.

For that reason, I believe that at least one original edition existed, probably a manuscript version of the staff material from Pasch, unknown to us, that by convention receives the *siglum A*. The partial edition in 1657 is then limited to the title of each section and will be referenced later with the *siglum a'*.

II.2.2. Variant *b*, first complete edition

In 1659 Pasch published a second compilation of different materials under the long title: "Short but thorough briefing on the pike, drilling with the pike, the flag, the hunting staff, serving art, fencing on the thrust and the cut, vaulting on horses and on tables, wrestling, and dancing" (*Kurtze doch Gründliche Unterrichtung der Pique, deß Trillens in der Pique, der Fahne, deß Jägerstocks, Trincierens, Fechtens auf den Stoß und auf den Hieb, Voltesirens auf den Pferd und auf den Tisch, deß Ringens, Tantzens*). Curiously, the bookseller and printer, Johann Georg Schwander, signed the introduction of the book, rather than its author. He dedicated the entire book to the Senate of Osnabruck after having been granted citizenship to this Free

---

[28] "*LL.studiosus*" was a common way to designate a student in law at that time. See Pasch, *Anleitung*, p. 28 footnote 15.

City. This book was certainly a commission made by this bookseller himself to Pasch, which could explain why only the initials of the author, IGP, appeared on the title page.[29]

The section on the hunting staff (*Jägerstock*) appears on folios 74 recto to 82 verso. The text is composed with an introduction of seven paragraphs followed by twenty-two lessons. This edition does not reproduce six lessons that are listed in *a'*. There is only one illustration at the beginning of the section, which is reproduced below. One should also note the presence of a staff with two points on the engraving at the beginning of the book. The engraver who produced these pictures signed his work by the monogram JHB but remains unknown at this date.

An interesting detail of the writing process of this text can be found in lessons 3, 6 and 16 of this edition. There, Pasch told us that he must himself at each time turn to the left: *muß ich mich iederzeit lincks herum kehren*. This is the only time that the first-person pronoun is used in Pasch's work on the staff. The first two of these lessons were modified in the next version, and the last in the *e* version. This could be seen as a proof that a previous version of the text existed which was written in the first-person. Pasch probably decided to modify all the pronouns to the third-person for the printed edition of the text.

Figure 2: Fighter with a hunting staff or Jägerstock. Pasch, Kurtze Unterrichtung Belangend die Pique, die Fahne, den Jägerstock, p. 156. Württembergische Landesbibliothek, Stuttgart: Sport.oct.357.

II.2.3. Variant *c*, second complete edition

In 1660, Johann George Pasch produced a small monograph called "Short introduction to the hunting staff or half-pike" (*Kurtze Anleitung des Jäger Stocks oder Halbe Pique*). It was printed in Halle (Saale) by Melchior Ölschlegel, and published by Johann Ernst Tietze without any dedication. Hence, it is difficult to know the context that justifies the publication of such a

---

[29] Pasch, *Anleitung*, pp. 8-12.

small book. The only exemplar consulted was bound with other books from Pasch printed the same year. It is actually the third document inside the book 8 ARS MIL 1106/3 from the State University Library of Lower Saxony of Goettingen. However, unlike the previous compilation, each document here is autonomous, which means that each has its own complete title page with edition date. It is thus not possible to determine whether it was distributed alone, or inside a larger compilation.

The most obvious improvement from the previous edition was the addition of a set of sixteen illustrations, with direct references to these inside the text. However, Pasch also proceeded to make minor modifications of the text, and combined the last two lessons into one. This version thus contained only 21 lessons.

II.2.4. Variant *e*, third complete edition and the hypothetical variant *d*

In 1666 Pasch published a new compilation of different works entitled "Complete Fencing, Wrestling and Vaulting Book" (*Vollständiges Fecht- Ringe und Voltigier Buch*) with Christian Vester, in Halle (Saale). Naturally, it contains material about fencing with rapier, wrestling, and vaulting, but it also contains a complete chapter about the staff. Each part has its independent title, and the one for the staff is "Short Instruction about *Baston à deux bous*, Hunting staff or half-pike or Jumping-staff" (*Kurtze Anleitung, Wie der* Baston à Deux Bous*, Jägerstock oder halbe Pique oder Springestock*). This book is dedicated to the Silesian principality of Oels.[30] This was a completely new version of the staff material, including thirteen new lessons, and a completely new set of illustrations.

Pasch re-used this last version of his staff material almost identically in two other editions. The first was another compilation entitled "Clear description of the exercises in Musket and Pike and also about the *baston à deux bous* or hunting staff" (*Deutliche Beschreibung von dem Exerciren in der Musquet und Pique, wie auch von dem* Baston a deux Bous*, Jägerstock*). This was printed in 1667, again by Christian Vester, re-using the same plates for the illustrations and the typographic pages for the staff, except for the dedication page. This time, it was dedicated to a certain Frederick, Duke of Saxony. Pasch probably anticipated a little bit as Frederick 1st was only made Duke of Saxe-Gotha-Altenburg officially in 1675.[31]

The third re-edition appeared with the title "Short instructions how the *Baston à deux bouts*, that is Hunting staff, Half Pike or Leaping Pole is actually to be used" (*Kurtze Anlejdung wie der* Baston à deux bous *das ist Jaegerstock, halbe Pique oder Springe-Stock eigentlich zu gebrauchen*). The title page informs us that this book was printed by Friedrich Arnst in Leipzig in 1670. Below, a complement of text informs us that this work was supposed to have been "mostly translated to German, with diligence, from the French language" (*Mit Fleiß meistentheils aus französicher Sprache teutsch übersetzt*). Curiously, the book contains a second and somewhat different title page. This page presents a slightly different title: "Short instructions how the *Baston à deux bouts*, the Hunting staff, Half Pike or Leaping

---

[30] For more information about this principality, see Köbler, Historisches Lexikon, p. 490.

[31] *Allgemeine Deutsche Biographie*, 8, pp. 2-3.

Pole as it is called by many, is actually to be used" (*Kurtze Anleitung wie der* Baston à deux bous, *Jägerstock, oder halbe Pique oder Springestock wie ihn etliche nennen, eigentlich zugebrauchen*), and on which Furthermore, here the printer's name is given as Christian Vester, working in Halle, as for the two previous editions, and the printing date was 1669. It should also be noted that any mention of a translation from French to German is missing. All the following pages, after the dedication pages, are identical to the two previous editions mentioned in this section. I was not able to find an independent version of the 1669 edition. Therefore, I suppose that the printing was carried out by Christian Vester, but that, for an unknown reason, the prints were not distributed, until, in 1670, Pasch re-used the printed books and asked Arnst, printer from Leipzig, to produce a new title page, and maybe the dedication section, and to perform the binding of the books. Finally, it is worth noting that this edition was dedicated directly to Augustus, administrator of Magdeburg.

Compared to the previous known versions, *b* and *c*, this version *e* adds thirteen lessons. Most of these additions are not essential to the art, and consist of variations on the existing exercises. For example, lesson 19, as added in version *e*, instructs the reader to "perform [the previous] lesson with two strikes in all four directions".[32] The only exception is lesson 31, in which Pasch introduced a new exercise, the jumping thrust. This version was also the first one to give the French name *baston à deux bouts*, meaning "staff with two ends", to the material, before the German name *jägerstock* or "hunting staff".

One great improvement was the addition of a completely new set of 33 illustrations. These illustrations were certainly produced by Johann Georg Flach, an engraver who was in business with Pasch since at least 1661, in which year Flach put his monogram in the form of his initials, "JGF made it" (*JGF Fecit*) above the engraving in two books produced by Pasch. The dictionary of monograms of Brulliot confirmed that these initials are Flach's. Brulliot even noticed sarcastically that Flach was a "poor engraver who produced engravings for subjects of little importance".[33] In the book on the musket which contains a section on the long staff, the engraving on the front page holds the unambiguous text *Johann George Flach Inven: et fecit 1667*, which proves that Flach was also the artist who created the illustrations and that he did not only engrave them. This relation between Flach and Pasch was certainly strong as Flach was mentioned in the funeral sermon as being at the side of the couple during their sickness.

Finally, in this version, lessons 27 to 29 all made erroneous references to previous chapters (20 to 22 instead of 23 to 25 as expected). There is no such mistake in the *b* and *c* versions, and the next version, though being shortened, gave the correct reference in the 27th lesson, to the previous 23 lesson. One can immediately set aside the idea of a direct copy of the known previous version as the numbers differed: the references were previously to lessons 15 to 17. Therefore, here it is possible to see a piece of evidence for the existence of an

---

[32] Translation by Van Noort.
[33] Brulliot, *Dictionnaire des monogrammes*, 1, p. 191, number 1480. The two books are *Kurtze jedoch Deutliche Beschreibung handlend von Fechten auß dem Stoss und Hieb* and *Vier und achtzig Fahnen-Lectiones*.

intermediate version between *c* and *e* where three of the new lessons have not yet been added. Without any known published versions, it should be considered as a manuscript version. I therefore suggest to refer to this hypothetical version with the *siglum* D. If such an edition had existed, its production should be estimated between 1661 and 1665.

II.2.5. Variant *f*, the bilingual version

In 1673, Pasch published a huge compilation of different subjects all described in both German and French, printed in Halle (Saale), by Melchior Ölschlegel. The title was "Separate description of the various lessons with the flag divided in eight plays; Followed by lessons with pike, partisan, and half-pike or the staff with two ends" (*Description distincte des diverses leçons au drappeau divisées en huit jeux. En suite du jeu de la pique, de la pertuisane et demy pique ou de baston à deux bouts* in French and *Deutliche Beschreibung unterschiedener Fahnen-Lectionen in acht Spiel eingetheilet, nebst dem Piquen-Spiel, Pertuisan und halben Piquen, oder Jägerstock* in German). This version does not contain any dedication.

The etched title page was certainly produced by Johann Georg Flach, even if the monogram differs a little from known examples of his work: the three letters J, G and F are superimposed. Before this title page, a sumptuous portrait of Pasch, etched by another, unknown artist, appears.

In comparison to the previous version, the text for the staff has been shortened in many places, certainly to facilitate the presentation in two columns of both versions, in German and in French. Therefore, this version, despite being the most recent, should not be taken as the ideal version for the edition of the text. However, in some parts of the text it includes some improvements as well as corrections for rare mistakes.

There are three types of differences with the version *e* :
- removal of paragraphs,
- removal of a large section of the text from the introduction but also from the lessons,
- improvements in the text and corrections of mistakes conserved in previous versions.

II.2.6. Filiation of editions

The following table summarizes the filiation of editions of the staff material from Pasch. The capital letters refer to handwritten versions, the lower case letters to printed versions.

Variant	Commentaries and dating	Set of pictures
A	unpublished, existence proved in 1657	unknown
a'	partial publication of A in 1657, 1658 and 1659	no picture
b	printed in 1659	no picture
c	printed in 1660	first set
D	hypothetical variant, should have been produced between 1661 and 1665	unknown
e	printed in 1666, 1667, 1669 and 1670	second set
f	printed in 1673	second set

Table 1: Filiation of editions

II.3. Overview of the content

II.3.1. Physical description of the staves

Pasch gives very accurate dimensions for the staff in the second paragraph of the introduction: it should have a thickness of four fingers and a length of three ells and a half: *ein starcker Stock ohngefehr 4 Finger dicke und viertehalbe Ellen*. It is difficult to translate these old measures into modern ones, especially the finger for which there is no modern estimate. Maybe it simply means that the staff is as thick as four fingers aligned? In Germany, the exact length of the ell differed from one city to another between 50 to 80cm. Pasch was probably aware of the difficulty for a German reader to interpret this size as from the *e* version he added a more flexible indication "as high as a man can reach", which probably means the height from the ground to the top of the raised hand. Pasch probably used the Saxon ell length, which is about 56.6cm.[34] This gives a 1.98m staff, which is coherent with the second indication for a man of 1.60m tall. There is one particularity for this weapon that separates it from other pole arms: the two sides have the same thickness and each is provided with the same spear head. Pasch erroneously mentioned a "big extremity" (*dicke Ende*) in all editions except the last one, where this mention disappeared (§2). This staff is thus a perfectly balanced weapon.

II.3.2. Vocabulary

Pasch seems to have used a common vocabulary shared between all the physical exercises taught. The most noticeable point is the large borrowing of French words. Brunt studied French influence on the German society in the mid-seventeenth century and the introduction of new fashions coming from France especially in the aristocracy. This influence led to a large production of technical literature, and also explains the extensive use of French vocabulary appearing in Pasch's work. Brunt concludes that from the last third of the seventeenth century, "the use of French words in German was obligatory for any German who wished to demonstrate his learning and superior social status."[35]

Some of the French words used by Pasch had already been introduced in German at the end of the sixteenth century or during the first half of the seventeenth century, certainly during the thirty years war: to advance (*marchieren*), to engage (*attaquieren*), to defend (*defendieren*), a manner (*Manier*), a parry (*Parade*) or a pike (*Pique*). The only innovation was a verb to precisely describe to gliding the hands along the shaft (*glissiren*). According to Brunt's study, Pasch was even the first author to use this word.[36]

---

[34] Scholz and Vogelsang, *Einheiten*, p. 109.
[35] Brunt, *The Influence of the French Language*, pp. 25-28 and 91.
[36] Jones, *A Lexicon of French Borrowings*, pp. 119, 321, 413, 418, 481-82 and 514. Brunt, *The Influence of the French Language*, p. 321.

II.3.3. Content

After a short introduction, Pasch proposes a set of exercises or lessons (*Lection*). The level of detail given is not specific to the staff but looks like the signature style of Pasch. This set of exercises follow the tradition of the military training of the soldier,[37] but brought to its highest point, thus leading Pasch to produce a work similar to the analytical methods of the nineteenth century.

Pasch includes many techniques for the student alone with his staff, describing movements without mentioning any target and out of the context of any opponent or opposition, like solo drills. There are also no exercises designed for a group demonstration, as typical for the pike or the flag drill. But they can be used for an individual drill before an audience, in which case Pasch asked to begin and finish the exercises with the salute (§34)[38].

He presents two types of thrusts, the Spanish-thrust and a thrust done in two times, first to the front and secondly to the back. The Spanish-thrust (§2-9) is a thrust done while walking and switching hands position after each step. This is certainly derived from the pike exercises.[39] The thrust done front and back seems more particular to the two pointed staff, thrusting from the two sides alternatively (§1 and 31). The first version mentioned a Spanish-thrust done with crossed hands, but this was left out of the later versions.

Pasch proposes a unique type of parry, twirling the staff like a canoe paddle, from below or from above (§11-12). Pasch also mentioned this parry in version *A* while turning around but this variant was not conserved in the later versions.

The lateral attacks were divided into two categories, depending on the trajectory of the staff. If the attack follows a near vertical plane, Pasch calls it a strike (*Schlag*). Otherwise, if the attack follows a near horizontal plane, it is a cut (*Hieb*).

Pasch proposed two different strikes: in one the hit is charged by passing the point of the staff above the head and switching the hands (§7-10). The second is done by slipping one hand to another to project the opposite point, either from above, or from below (§23-30).

There are three different "cuts". One is done with one hand holding the staff by its end and making it rotate. The second is a sort of moulinet done above the head or the shoulder, called a "cut all around" (*Hiebe rund herumb*) by Pasch. The third is a back and forth cut done from one side to another.

To these actions two salutes are added: one to be done in front of an audience, the other to show your prowess in front of strangers (§34).

For each lesson, Pasch proposes a specific footwork pattern inside a limited list. Three of these are rotations which are really particular and probably specific to this weapon. The first is a rotation of a quarter turn done with the front foot fixed (§1, §21-22). This could

---

[37] For a good introduction to this subject, see Sikora, *Die Mechanisierung des Kriegers*.
[38] All the numbers given here refer to the equivalent lesson in the critical edition.
[39] For example, see the lesson 43 of the pike in the book printed in 1673.

be coupled with a two steps forward to attack in such a way that rotation could be done with the same foot and in the same direction (§2, §7, §9, §23, §27). The second is a cycle of four rotations, two half turns and two quarter turns coupled with one or two steps between each rotation (§3-5, §10, §15). The third is stepping straight but turning half around at each step (§16).

The following table summarized the different type of content and gives the matching paragraphs in the *c* and *e* versions.

Manipulations	c version	e version
The three manners to carry the staff	introduction	introduction
solo drill as a manner of salute	§21	§33
Thrusts		
thrusting front and back	§1	§1
Spanish-thrusts alone	§2-4	§2-5
jumping thrust	missing	§31
Parries		
parries from above	§8	§11
parries from below	§9	§12
Strikes		
Strike above the head followed by a Spanish-thrust	§6	§7, §9
Strike above the head alone	§7	§8, §10
Strikes from above	§15-17	§23-26
Strikes from below	§18-20	§27-30
Cuts		
Cuts with one hand	§10	§13-15
moulinet moving straight while turning	§11	§16
Cuts from the elbow	§12	§17-20
moulinet in the four corners	§13-14	§21-22

Table 2: Summary of the lessons on the staff

II.4. The French staff or *baston à deux bouts*

II.4.1. The French origin

In the introduction of the *b* version, Pasch claims that "this exercise at the present does not particularly flourish in Germany, while it is only common in France." He added in the title of the edition of 1670 that this material was "mostly translated, with diligence, from the French language to German."[40] Does Pasch pretend that this material is French to make it look more prestigious? It is not impossible that the weapon was first given a German name, the hunting staff. However, I have not been able to find any other mention

---

[40] Both translations by R. van Noort.

of the use of such a weapon in a context of war or self-defense. This hunting staff could then be the closest German weapon resembling the French staff. However, Pasch also attributes the material to the partisan in the first version, and later to the half-pike and the jumping-staff and only uses directly the French name, *baston à deux bouts* in later versions. The jumping-staff is certainly the name of a small spear. Based on a dictionary from 1662, the French military weapon called *esponton*, wich was a spear for officers, could be translated in German to half-pike or jumping-staff (*eine halbe picke, ein springstock*).[41] One should also note that Pasch dedicated a specific chapter to the partisan in his 1673 publication with a largely different group of lessons. Finally, yet importantly, the illustrations delivered with the manuals unambiguously show a weapon with two similar points at each extremity. This does not fit with any half-pike or any other similar weapon. It seems to me that Pasch conserved such German terms in parallel of the French word, *bâton à deux bouts* because, despite the trend for French vocabulary, this weapon was mostly unknown to his contemporary countrymen and did not have a proper name.

In parallel, the existence of a French cultural phenomenon around the weapon is unmistakable. I have been able to trace the persistence of the practice of staff fighting in France from the late fifteenth century through the nineteenth century. This was reinforced more recently by the discovery of an ordinance from 1501 only dedicated to staff play. Two points above all must be remembered, namely on the one hand that the Parisian fencing masters had to prove their skill with the long staff during their master examination in 1634. On the other hand, in France this weapon was associated to traveling workers above all social categories, which means that it was a very low class weapon![42]

The long staff material is not the only part that has a French origin. Hazebroucq showed clearly that the dances presented by Pasch came from France, even if no other description for them exists from that period.[43] Something similar seems to have happened with the staff. There are only a few French technical sources that give details about how to fence with the French staff during the seventeenth century.

The only fencing master who mentions this weapon in his treatise is Besnard, in 1653. He presents the staff with two ends as a weapon for artisans or other people of low social condition but does not give any advice for its use.[44]

In 1678, Louys de Gaya published a military treatise in which he briefly mentions the staff with two ends in the following terms:

> We can also add to the weapons the staff, commonly called with both ends (because of iron spikes, which are at the two extremities) which is a

---

[41] Nathanael Duez, *Le vray et parfait guidon de la langue francoise*, p. 92.
[42] For the cultural history of the staff in France, see Dupuis, *L'escrime au bâton*, pp. 154-61. About the staff ordinance from Mazan, see Dupuis, *Organization and Regulation of Fencing*, p. 248.
[43] Hazebroucq, *La technique de la danse*, pp. 96-118.
[44] Charles Besnard, *Le maistre d'arme libéral*, p. 107. "*Les merciers, chaudronniers et autres de basse condition, apprenoient les uns avec les autres à bien jouer de leurs bastons à deux bouts, desquels ils faisoient merveilles aux assemblées et foires quand il y arrivoit sédition.*"

straight and smooth piece of wood. It is somewhat heavier and thicker than a pike, and its length is six and a half feet between the ferrules. These ferrules hold in place two spikes protruding four and a half inches from the staff. One wears it under the hip as a halberd, but the handling is different, because of all the variety of techniques it is possible to do with it. Half-moulinets can be used to assume a fencing guard, or during the approach. One can also use it to thrust or to beat.[45]

The physical description of the staff is very accurate and close to that given by Pasch. De Gaya also mentions moulinets similar to those in the lessons of Pasch, but he remains too vague to make a proper comparison. The description given by Jacques Collombon in 1650 in his *Traité de l'exercice militaire* contains a large list of technical vocabulary, which is a much better source to compare with Pasch's techniques. The entire section is difficult to understand, but I have attempted a partial translation given below, and a complete reproduction *in extenso* in the appendix.

The staff with two ends can be carried in two ways on the shoulder or by counterweight, the arm stretched out below. When we are in fear, one must present the tip, thrust him, do a false rising strike to force him to get back. Then one must turn the face and the staff; thrust two times front and back, turning oneself. Then follow the false rising strikes on both sides [...], then the moulinet thrusting behind, doing it twice while parrying, then moulinet with a discharge, do it twice switching hands. Then the moulinet stepping forward, [...] then stop to see which way to go and pull the four thrusts forward, backward, act as one, stay in a close place [...] That is all the play of the staff with two ends.[46]

Collombon mentions many actions that sound similar to the lessons of Pasch. For example, Pasch describes carrying the staff below the outstretched arm in his introduction. Pasch also proposes to thrust forward and backward (§1). Many variations of moulinets are presented in both works, even if it is difficult to link Collombon's passage precisely to Pasch's lessons. Collombon tells us to switch hands, stepping forward while doing moulinets, and Pasch proposes many exercises that could fit this description. The "discharges" of Collombon could possibly be linked to some of the cuts of Pasch, for example the cut done with one hand (§13) or the cuts done from the elbow (§17).

---

[45] Louis de Gaya, *Traité des armes*, pp. 38-39: *Nous pouvons encore mettre au nombre des Armes le Bâton, que nous appellons communement à deux bouts (à cause des pointes de fer qui sont aux deux extremitez) qui est d'un brin de bois bien droit & bien uny, quelque peu plus pesant & plus gros que celuy d'une Pique, dont la longueur est de six pieds & demy entre les viroles, qui accolent les deux pointes saillantes hors du Baston de quatre pouces & demy. On le porte sous hanche comme la Hallebarde ; mais le maniement en est different : parce que de toutes les manieres on en peut faire le demy-moulinet pour se mettre en garde, & se servir aux approches, ou de la pointe ou de l'estramaçon.*

[46] Collombon, pp. 15-16.

However, it is difficult to link some techniques mentioned by Collombon to lessons of Pasch. For example the false rising strikes do not exactly match the strikes from below of Pasch (§27), and Pasch proposes only two types of thrusts in comparison to the four thrusts mentioned by Collombon. The French author also proposes many combinations with the moulinets, which do not match Pasch's lessons, such as combining a moulinet with a thrust when Pasch only combines thrusts with vertical strikes. Furthermore, nothing in the short text of Collombon can be understood as working on the four faces or corners, though this seems to be fundamental in Pasch's exercises.

Ultimately, there are many kindred techniques that argue for confirming the assertion of a French origin to the staff material of Pasch.

However, it is very unlikely that this staff material has been translated directly from French to German. The style, the pedagogy, and the organization of the text are similar in many points to those used in the other sections of Pasch's works. There are also no known French works that could be compared in size and content. Finally but significantly, this assertion appears in the title of only one of the three known editions of the version *e*. One should also remember that this book was dedicated to duke Augustus himself. Hence, it seems that Pasch tried to give more value to his work by attributing a French origin not only for the material but also for the text.

II.4.2. Posterity

It seems that the works produced by Pasch have garnered more attention from historians for the series of engravings than for their content.[47] Even Anglo, in his excellent essay on representations of movement in fencing, war and dance, forgot to mention Pasch, although he was probably the only author who produced a technical treatise for each of them![48]

This also concerns the French staff material from Pasch, which was never republished in German after Pasch. At this stage, there is no evidence that the stick Pasch has been emulated in Germany. However, this apparent disaffection has also been the case in France. The French military books seem to have forgotten this weapon by the end of the seventeenth century. Neither Mannesson in 1684 nor Giffart in 1696 mention it in their books.[49] Moreover, during the eighteenth century, the staff with two ends disappeared not only from the French military scene, but also from the common vocabulary. This does not mean that the practice of staff fighting disappeared in France, but it seems to have been overshadowed in this country by the walking stick. One must wait until the second half of the nineteenth century to find technical manuals on the French staff, mostly from military contexts. However, there are many similarities between the military staff techniques from the nineteenth century and those presented by Pasch. In both the movements consist of large circles and moulinets to provide a security area around the fighter. Thrusts can be provided front and back, the fighter is invited to work facing four directions, using

---

[47] Anglo, *Martial Arts*, pp. 48-60. Wellmann, *Hand und Leib*, pp. 20-22.
[48] Anglo, *L'escrime, la danse et l'art de la guerre*.
[49] Allain Manesson Mallet, *Les travaux de Mars*. Pierre Giffart, *L'Art militaire françois*.

alternatively wide horizontal and vertical cuts. These specificities can also be found in French walking sticks techniques dedicated to face many opponents.[50] It would require a more detailed study, but it is very tempting to see one of the ancestors of the French walking stick of the nineteenth century in the staff techniques presented by Pasch.

II.5. Conclusion

Johann Georg Pasch was the perfect example of the educated German middle-class that rose up after the Thirty-Year Wars. After having studied in renowned Universities, he entered into the service of the Duke of Saxe-Weissenfels. He then took the opportunity to publish books with the help of different patrons. However, the subjects differed drastically from those of other authors of his time: all of his books are pedagogical manuals dedicated to the physical instruction of the young aristocracy.

Thanks to the French cultural influence on the German court, Pasch was inclined to include the French staff in his teachings and publications. It is paradoxical to see a weapon relegated in France to the lower-class people and ignored in the French fencing treatises, being exported to the German court. The French origin adorned it with a virtue such that in 1670 this weapon received an edition dedicated directly to a Prince-Elector.

This allows us to have a technical source of great value over two hundred years before the first French technical treatise dealing with this weapon appeared.

The existence of several known editions gives the opportunity to study in detail the evolution of a technical treatise. From a presumed preliminary manuscript version of which we only know the chapter titles, Pasch published an educational treatise, then enriched it with both illustrations and text improvements. Finally, he amply supplemented the text and renewed the illustrations.

III. EDITION OF THE STAFF MATERIAL

III.1. Transcription rules

I have followed most of the transcription rules adopted by Schlottermüller in his edition of the dance manual.

The syntax and the grammar from the original text have been strictly respected, in particular the inversions between dative and accusative.

The symbol "e" above a vowel in the original texts means a diphthong and is transcribed with a dieresis following the modern custom in German. The long and short "s" have all been transcribed with the letter "s". When the two letters "sz" are ligatured, they are transcribed using the letter "ß". In one unique case, the letter "v" that has the value of

---

[50] Dupuis, *L'escrime au bâton*, especially pp. 171 and 175-76.

"u" is transcribed with "u" (*attaquiret*). The numbers are all emphasized with a final point in the original editions, as was the custom in that time (for example *10. 20. und 30.*). These points have not been reproduced here.

All versions contained a large number of contracted forms for right and left (*rechts* and *lincks*) or their derivative forms. All these contracted forms have been developed in this edition. There are some rare contraction marks. The most common contraction is the nasal mark, a tilde above a letter. For example above the "n" in *weñ* which means *wenn* (§1). Otherwise, some words have been shortened like *erstl.* (§7) and *neml.* (§12). These have also all been developed without mention here as *erstlich* and *nemlich*.

All historical editions followed similar rules about the fonts used. The standard text was in Fractur, and Latin, French or Italian words were written in italic Roman. In the following edition, the standard German text is in standard Roman and the Latin or French words are emphasized in italic.

Except for rare interrogation and exclamation points, the original editions used the point to mark the end of a paragraph. Inside the paragraphs, the editor used only the slash. The following edition does not follow this old use of punctuation and commas and points have been introduced following modern rules.

Finally, the capitals above the names have been generalized in the modern manner for a German text. This rule is only partially applied inside the original editions.

III.2. Organization of the edition

I made the choice to present two different versions in a two columns presentation. The *c* version from 1660 appears in the left column. The right column contains the critical edition, in other words an ideal version, based on the *e* version with some improvements using the *f* version.

The variation of underlining informs the reader of differences between the versions, with the help of additional notes. The meaning of each underlined section is explained below for each edition. It is important to note that only the significant modifications are emphasized and the spelling differences for a specific word have been neglected.

III.2.1. Version *c*

"Was das Fechten" this emphasizes a difference with the version *b*. An edition note gives the text from the previous version. If there is no such note, it means that it is an addition of version *c* without any matching text in version *b*.

"bekand" this emphasizes a difference between version *c* and the critical edition.

III.2.2. Critical edition

"*floriret*" this emphasizes a modification from version *c*, or an improvement taken from version *f*. In the latter case, an edition note has been added.

"*Baston à deux bous*, Jägerstock, halbe Pique oder der Springestock" this emphasizes a difference between version *e* and version *f*, where the ideal version kept version *e*.

"viertehalbe Ellen" this emphasizes parts that have been deleted in version *f*.

III.2.3. Revision Notes
The revision notes for each edition are located in a dedicated column beside the text. Most of these notes give the reader the text from another version for a specific passage. In some specific cases, the discussion is too long and requires a specific paragraph. In such cases, the note refers to its dedicated paragraph inside the following section.

III.3. Specific notes
To avoid confusion, the lesson number used in the following discussion is always that of the critical edition.

III.3.1. Lesson 3
The sentence *In diesen Stockaden mustu dich jederzeit lincks herum kehren. Es wird aber glißiret und zugetreten wie in der vorhergehenden andern Lection* is missing in version f and was replaced by two indications for the direction of rotation: lincks herumb hernach halbe herumb and ferner halb lincks herumb. These indications are less accurate than the text of the previous version. In my opinion, Pasch made these modifications to reduce the size of the paragraph.

III.3.2. Lessons 14, 15, 18, 19, 20
In these lessons, first added in version *e*, Pasch used the word *Schlag* instead of *Hieb* to refer to the strikes done. However, these lessons are all variants of lessons on the horizontal strikes, which are normally called *Hiebe* by Pasch.

These paragraphs have all been added in a late version and maybe Pasch used the word *Schlag* in its generic meaning here. To avoid any confusion, in these lessons I chose to substitute *Hieb* -or its plural form *Hieben* when convenient- for *Schlag* or *Schläge*.

III.3.3. Lesson 16
Version *f* differs from all other versions in the footwork. However, it appears to be a correction made by Pasch. The first foot position in the text is at the beginning: *Wann nun zuletzt dein L. Fuß hinten stehet*. Version *f* differs and indicates instead R. *Fuß*. Actually, picture 12 in version *c* or picture 21 in the later versions depicts this position, and clearly shows the left foot forward.

This is also not coherent with the second part of the lesson, which begins with *wenn nun dein rechten Fuß vorstehet*. It explains how to do the movement backward, beginning with the right foot forward. To my understanding of the lesson, version *f* is the correct one and I used this in the critical edition.

III.3.4. Lesson 25

Version *c* substitutes the sentence *weiter auff deine lincke Seite lincks herum und trit mit deinem rechten Fuß, folgends auff* with the homeoteleuton *folgends auff auff*, which was likely an edition mistake. The following known edition, *e*, does not correct the mistake but removes one of the *auff*.

This mistake combines with another mistake, which appears also in version *c*: an inversion from *rechten Fuß* to *lincken Fuß* just before the previous mistake. The lesson became very confused, which could explain why Pasch chose to rewrite the paragraph entirely in his bilingual version *f*.

For all these reasons, I chose to publish the text from the last version *f* instead of a corrected version in the style of the previous versions.

III.4. Edition

Version *c* from 1660	Notes
Was das Fechten auff den Hieb und Stoß ist^a, solches ist gnugsam bekand, weiln aber dieses *Exercitium* noch zur Zeit in Teutschland nicht sonderlich bekand, sondern in Franckreich nur bräuchlich. Als habe ich die Nothturfft zu seyn erachtet, zuvorhero ehe die Lectiones gesetzet werden, etwas davon zu melden: Was es für ein Instrument, wie lang es seyn muß, und was es für ein Nutzen hat.	a) *b: Was daß Pickspielen, trillen in der Pique und Fahnschwingen ist*
Der Jägerstock oder halbe Pique an sich selber nun, ist ein starcker Stock ohngefehr 4 Finger dicke und viertehalbe Ellen lang. Auf beyden Enden Spitzen, wordurch man sich im fall der Noth gegen 10, 20 und 30 Mann welche blosse Degen haben wehren kan. Es scheinet zwar fast unmüglich zu seyn, wer aber desselben Wissenschafft hat, wird solches bekräfftigen müssen, doch muß solches nur geschehen im Nothfall.	
Wann einer^a etwan in einem Hause von vielen mit blossen Degen ümbringet und sich befürchten müste, daß das Hauß gestürmet würde, so thete er besser. Er schlüge sich durch und reterirte sich an einen sichern Ort, als daß er wartete biß sie ins Hauß kämen, und er als dann den Stock in der Enge nicht gebrauchen könte. Oder wann er auff offener Gassen von vielen mit Degen attaquiret würde, so kan er sich ebenfalß auffhalten und auff den raumen Platze^b so lange wehren, biß Leute darzu kommen, wie denn in diesen *Exercitio* dergleichen Lectiones seyn, daß man sich über eine Viertelstunde auff einer Stelle wo Raum ist, gegen 20 oder 30 wehren kan, daß muß aber alles im Nothfall geschehen dann keinen zu rathen! Daß er sich muthwillig in Gefahr gebe wie dann auch andere *Exercitia* als Fechten, Ringen und dergleichen in der Noth und zur *Defension* nur sollen gebrauchet werden.	a) *b: er* b) *b: und sich auff den raumen Platze*
Ist also erstlich zu wissen nöthig das der Stock auff dreyerley Manier getragen werden kan.	

Critical edition	Notes
Was das Fechten auff den Hieb und Stoß sey, solches ist gnugsam bekandt, weiln aber dieses *Exercitium* noch zur Zeit in Teutschland nicht sonderlich *floriret*, sondern in Franckreich nur bräuchlich. Als habe ich die Nothdurfft zuseyn erachtet, zuvorhero ehe die Lectiones gesetzet werden, etwas davon zu melden: Was es für ein Instrument? Wie lang es seyn muß? Und was es vor ein Nutzen hat.[a]	a) *f*: this entire paragraph is missing in this edition.
Der *Baston à deux bous*, Jägerstock, halbe Pique oder Springestock[a] wie selbigen etzliche nennen an sich selber nun, ist ein starcker Stock ohngefehr 4 Finger dicke und viertehalbe Ellen lang oder so lang als ein Mann, welcher ihn brauchen wil, reichen kan[b]. Auff beyden Enden Spitzen mit Schneiden, wie Num. 1 weiset, wordurch man sich im fall der Noth gegen viele[c] Mann welche blosse Degen haben wehren kan. Es scheinet zwar fast unmüglich zuseyn, wer aber desselben Wissenschafft hat, wird es bekräfftigen müssen, doch muß solches nur geschehen im Nothfall.	a) *f: Die halbe Pique oder Jägerstock* b) *e: als ein Mensch reichen kan, welcher ihn brauchen will* c) *e: 10, 20, und 30*
Wann einer etwan in einem Hause von vielen mit blossen Degen umbringet und sich befurchten müste, das das Hauß gestürmet würde, so thät er besser. Er schlüge sich durch und reterirte sich an einen sichern Ort, als daß er wartete biß sie ins Hauß kämen, und er als dann den Stock in der Enge nicht gebrauchen könte. Oder wann er auf offener Gassen von vielen mit Degen attaquiret würde, so kan er sich ebenfalß aufhalten und auf den raumen-Platze so lange wehren, biß Leute darzukommen wie denn in diesen *Exercitio* dergleichen Lectiones seyn, daß man sich über eine halbe Viertelstunde auff einer Stelle wo Raum ist, gegen 20 oder 30 wehren kan, daß muß aber alles im Nothfall geschehen dann keinen zu rathen! Daß er sich muthwillig in Gefahr gebe wie dann auch andere *Exercitia* als Fechten, Ringen und dergleichen in der Noth und zur *Defension* nur sollen gebrauchet werden.	
Ist also erstlich zu wissen nöthig das der Stock auff dreyerley Manier getragen werden kan.	

Version *c* from 1660	Notes
Die erste Manier ist, wann du den Stock in der mitten mit rechter Hand fassest, nimbst denselben unter deinen rechten Arm, daß die eine Spitze hinten hoch, die andere aber forne niedrig ist, wie N. 1 zeiget.	
Die ander Manier. Hälstu den Stock eben unter deinen rechten Arm, wie vor, nur daß du deine rechte Hand in der Mitten des Stocks verkehrest, das die Finger oben liegen wie N. 2 weiset.	
Bey der dritten Manier komt der Stock eben so unter deinen rechten Arm, nur daß du deine lincke Hand auf den Stock und deine rechte Hand auff deinen lincken Arm legest, wie N. 3 weiset. Und auff solche Manieren kan der Stock in Marchieren getragen werden, dafern du nun diese Lectiones vor Leuten spielest so mache einen Reverentz wie N. 4 zeiget.[a]	a) *b : diese Lectiones nach einander machen wilst, so mache erstlich in dem du den Stock unter deiner rechten Arm hast, daß die forderste Spitze niedrig und die hinderste hoch ist, mit deinen rechten Fuß und Stock einen Reverentz.*
Nun folgen die Lectiones	
1. Stelle[a] deinen lincken Fuß vor und den rechten zurück. Fasse den Stock zwey Spannen von der einen Spitze mit deiner lincken Hand und zwey Spannen von der andern Spitze mit deiner rechten Hand, wie N. 5 zeiget, und wenn dich nun etliche wollen vorn angreiffen, so glissire vor durch beyde Hände und geschwinde wiederum zurück. Wann du auf die lincke Seite vor und zurück glissiren wilst,[b] so mustu mit deinen rechten Fuß fort treten, doch daß dein lincker Fuß vor bleibet und dein rechter hinten kömbt, und also in alle vier Ecken. Und zu ieden mahl mit deine rechten Fuß fort getreten, du must dich aber allezeit ümbsehen, bald hinder dich, bald auff die Seiten, wo sie dich wollen angreiffen, dann an selbigen Ort must du dich auch defendiren. Wann du nun diese Lection in alle vier Ecken gemachet hast und also wiederumb so stehest, allwo du angefangen, so glissire vorauß[c] daß du mit deiner rechten Hand den Stock an der einen Spitzen hast und mit der lincken den Stock ohngefehr drey Spannen von selbiger Spitzen.	a) *b: Die Stellung. Als Stelle...* b) *b: und geschwinde zurück was in another place of the sentence, after zurürck glißiren wilst.* c) *b: vorn raus*

Critical edition	Notes
Die erste Manier ist, wann du den Stock in der mitten mit rechter Hand fassest, nimbst denselben unter deinen rechten Arm, daß die eine Spitze hinten hoch, die andere aber forne niedrig ist,[a] wie N. 2 zeiget.	a) f : replaced by *unter deinen rechten Arm nimbst*
Die ander Manier. Hälstu den Stock eben unter deinen rechten Arm, wie vor, nur daß du deine rechte Hand in der Mitten des Stocks verkehrest, das die Finger oben liegen wie N. 3 weiset.	
Bey der dritten Manier kompt der Stock eben so unter deinen rechten Arm, nur daß du deine lincke Hand auf den Stock und deine rechte Hand auf deinen lincken Arm legest, wie N. 4 weiset. Und auff solche Manieren kan der Stock in Marchieren[a] getragen werden dafern du nun diese Lectiones vor jemanden *Exerciren* wilst so mache einen Reverentz wie N. 5 zeiget.	a) *e*: *Margiren*, corrected using the version c as this part was missing in the verson f.
Nun folgen die Lectiones	
1. Stelle deinen lincken Fusz vor und den rechten zurück. Fasse den Stock zwey Spannen von der einen Spitze mit deiner lincken Hand und zwey Spannen von der andern Spitze mit deiner rechten Hand, wie N. 6 zeiget, und wenn dich nun jemand wil forn angreiffen, so glißire vor durch beyde Hände wie N. 7 weiset, und geschwinde wiedrum zurück wie N. 8 zuersehen. Wann du auf die lincke Seite vor und zurück glißiren wilst, so mustu mit deinen rechten Fuß fort treten, doch das dein lincker Fuß vor bleibet und dein rechter hinten kömt, und also in alle vier Ecken. Und zu jedenmahl mit deine rechten Fuß fort getreten, du must dich aber allezeit umbsehen, bald hinter dich, bald auf die Seiten, wo sie dich wollen angreiffen, dann an selbigen Ort mustu dich auch *defendiren.* Wann du nun diese Lection in alle vier Ecken gemachet hast und also wiedrumb so stehest, alwo du angefangen, so glißire vorauß daß du mit deiner rechten Hand den Stock an der einen Spitzen und mit der lincken den Stock ohngefehr drey Spannen von selbiger Spitzen hast,[a] wie N. 7 geshehen.	a) *e*: *Hast* was placed in a similar way than b and c versions. The actual place is an improvement of f.

Version *c* from 1660	Notes
2. Die zwey Spaniol-Stockaden in alle vier Ecken, als glissire die lincke an die rechte Hand biß ans dicke Ende und mit der rechten Hand glissire nauß biß ans Ort wo die lincke Hand gewesen ist und trit mit deinen rechten Fuß vor, wie N. 6. zeiget. Glissire die rechte Hand an die lincke Hand biß ans dicke Ende und mit der lincken Hand glissire nauß biß ans Ort wo die rechte Hand gewesen ist und trit mit deinen lincken Fuß vor und also mache es in alle vier Ecken biß du wiederum zustehen kombst wo du angefangen hast und zwar iederzeit lincks herumb.	
3.ª Mache die zwey Spaniol-Stockaden halb herum als erstlich hinder dich, hernach halb herumb wiederum an selbigen[b] Ort wo du erstlich gestanden dann auff deine lincke Seite ferner halb herum auff deine rechte Seite zuletzt wiederum an den Ort wo du zum Anfange gestanden. In diesen Stockaden mustu dich[c] iederzeit lincks herum kehren. Es wird aber glissiret und zugetreten wie in der vorhergehenden andern Lection.ᵉ	a) the version *c* is erroneous and indicates the number *8*. b) *b: selben* c) *b: muß ich mich*
4. Mache nur eine Spaniol-Stockade halb herumb als in dem du stehest wie du hast angefangen. So mache eine Stockade hinder dich lincks halb herum und trit mit deinem rechten Fuß vor wie N. 7. zeiget. Hernach eine Spaniol-Stockade wiederum an den Ort wo du erstlich gestanden halb rechts herum und trit mit deinem lincken Fuß vor, weiter auff deine lincke Seite Lincks herum und trit mit deinem rechten Fuß vor folgends auff deine rechte Seite halb rechts herum und trit mit deinem lincken Fusz vor und zuletzt lincks herum an den Ort alwo du angefangen hast und trit mit deinem rechten Fuß vor und mache noch eine Stockade. Esª muß zu iedem Trit eine Spaniol-Stockade gemacht werden. Zu dieser Spaniol-Stockade glissirestu mit rechten und lincken Hand wie in den vorhergehenden Lectionibus gedacht worden.	a) *b: rechten Fuß vor und*

Critical edition	Notes
2. Die zwey Spaniol-Stockaden in allen vier Ecken, als glißire die lincke an die rechte Hand biß an die Spitze[a] und mit der rechten Hand glißire naus biß ans Ort wo die lincke Hand gewesen ist und tritt mit deinen rechten Fuß vor, wie N. 9. zeiget. Glißire die rechte Hand an die lincke Hand biß an die Spitze[n] und mit der lincken Hand glißire naus biß ans Ort wo die rechte Hand gewesen ist und tritt mit deinen lincken Fuß vor und also mache es in alle vier Ecken biß du wiedrumb zustehen kombst wo du angefangen hast und zwar jederzeit lincks herumb.	a) *e: ans dicke Ende*.
3. Mache die zwey Spaniol-Stockaden halb herum als erstlich hinter dich hernach halb herumb wiedrumb an selbigen Ort wo du erst gestanden dann auff deine lincke Seiten ferner halb herumb auf deine rechte Seite zuletzt wiederum an den Ort wo du zum Anfange gestanden. In diesen Stockaden mustu dich jederzeit lincks herum kehren. Es wird aber glißiret und zugetreten wie in der vorhergehenden andern Lection.[a]	a) See III.3.1.
4. Mache nur eine Spaniol-Stockade halb herumb als in dem du stehest wie du hast angefangen. So mache eine Stockade hinter dich lincks halb herum und trit mit deinen rechten Fuß vor wie N. 10 zeiget. Hernach eine Spaniol-Stockade wiedrum an den Ort wo du erstlichen gestanden halb rechts herumb und tritt mit deinen lincken Fuß vor, weiter auf deine lincke Seite lincks herumb, und tritt mit deinen rechten Fuß vor folgends auf deine rechte Seite halb rechts herum und tritt mit deinen lincken Fuß vor und zuletzt lincks herumb an den Ort allwo du angefangen hast und trit mit deinen rechten Fuß vor und mache noch eine Stockade. Es muß zu jeden Tritt eine Spaniol-Stockade gemacht werden. Zu dieser Spaniol-Stockade glißirest du mit rechten und lincken Hand wie in den vorhergehenden *Lectionibus* gedacht worden.	
5. Gleich wie die zwey Spaniol-Stockaden in alle vier Ecken gemacht werden, also kan es auch etzliche mahl vor und hinter sich geschehen.	

80   The French staff material from Johann Georg Pasch

Version *c* from 1660	Notes
5. Mache die Schläge über den Kopff und Spaniol-Stockade darzu, nehmlich in dem du stehest wo du angefangen hast und dein lincken Fuß vor, so glissire deine rechte Hand biß an deine lincke^a. Greiff mit deiner lincken Hand unter deine Rechte und glissire die lincke Hand biß an die Spitze des Stocks und trit mit deinem lincken^b Fuß vor wie N. 8 zeiget und schlage also zu. Mache eine Spaniol-stockade und trit mit deinem lincken Fuß vor, wie in der andern Lection gemeldet und also mache es in alle vier Ecken biß du zustehen kömst wo du angefangen hast und zwar iederzeit lincks herumb.	a) *b: lincke Hand* b) this indication is a mistake corrected in the version *e*.
6.ª Mache die Schläge über den Kopff und Spaniol-stockade halb darzu halb herum wie du sie in alle vier Ecken gemacht hast, als erstlich hinder dich halb herum. Hernach wiederum an selbig Ort, wo du erstlich gestanden halb herum dann auff deine lincke Seite ferner halb herumb auf deine rechte Seiten. Zuletzt wiederum an deinen Ort wo du zum Anfang gestanden. In dieser Lection mustu dich^b iederzeit lincks herumb kehren. Es wird aber glissiret und zugetreten wie in der vorhergehenden Lection.	a) This paragraph has been reproduced twice in the version *c*. b) *b: muß ich mich*
7. Mache die Schläge über den Kopff ohne Spaniol-Stockaden halb herumb als in dem du stehest wo du angefangen. So glissire deine rechte Hand biß an deine lincke. Greiff mit deiner lincken Hand unter deine rechte^a und glissire die Lincke biß an die Spitze des Stockes. Trit mit deinem rechten Fuß halb lincks herum und schlage also zu wie N. 9 weiset. Glissire deine lincke Hand biß an deine rechte.ª Greiff mit deiner rechten Hand unter deine lincke Hand und glissire die rechte Hand biß an die Spitze des Stockes. Trit mit deinen lincken Fuß halb rechts herum, daß du an den Ort kombst alwo du angefangen hast und schlage also zu. Glissire wiederum deine rechte Hand biß an deine lincke. Und greiff mit deiner lincken Hand unter deine rechte und glissire die lincke Hand biß an die Spitze des Stocks. Tritt mit deinen rechten Fuß Lincks herumb auff deine lincke Seite und schlage also zu. Glissire ferner deine lincke Hand biß an deine rechte. Greiff mit deiner rechten Hand unter deine lincke und glissire die rechte Hand biß an die Spitze des Stockes. Tritt mit deinem lincken Fuß	a) *b: rechte Hand*

Critical edition	Notes
6. Mache die Schläge über den Kopff und Spaniol-Stockade darzu, nehmlich in dem du stehest wo du angefangen hast und dein lincken Fuß vor, so glißire deine rechte Hand biß an deine Lincke wie N. 11 weiset. Greiff mit deiner lincken Hand unter deine Rechte und glißire die lincke Hand biß an die Spitze des Stocks und tritt mit deinem rechten Fuß vor wie N. 12 zeiget und schlage also zu. Mache eine Spaniol-Stockade und trit mit deinem lincken Fuß vor wie in der andern Lection gemeldet und also mache es in alle vier Ecken biß du zu stehen kömst wo du angefangen hast und zwar jederzeit lincks herumb.	
7. Mache die Schläge über den Kopff und Spaniol-Stockade darzu halb herum wie du sie in alle vier Ecken gemacht hast, als erstlich hinter dich halb herum. Hernach wiederum an selbigen Ort, wo du erstlich gestanden halb herum dann auf deine lincke Seiten ferner halb herum auf deine rechte Seiten. Zuletzt wiederum an deinen Ort wo du zum Anfange gestanden. In dieser Lection mustu dich jederzeit lincks herum kehren. Es wird aber glißiret und zugetreten wie in der vorhergehenden Lection.	
8. Mache die Schläge über den Kopff ohne Spaniol-Stockaden halb herum als in dem du stehest wo du angefangen. So glißire deine rechte Hand biß an deine Lincke. Greiff mit deiner lincken Hand unter deine rechte und glißire die lincke biß an die Spitze des Stockes. Tritt mit deinen rechten Fuß halb lincks herum und schlage also zu wie N. 13 weiset. Glißire deine lincke Hand biß an deine rechte. Greiff mit deiner rechten Hand unter deine lincke Hand und glißire die rechte Hand biß an die Spitze des Stockes. Trit mit deinen lincken Fuß halb rechts herum, das du an den Ort kompst alwo du angefangen hast und schlage also zu. Glißire wiederum deine rechte Hand biß an deine lincke. Greiff mit deiner lincken Hand unter deine rechte und glißire die lincke biß an die Spitze des Stocks. Trit mit deinen rechten Fuß lincks herumb auf deine lincke Seite und schlage also zu. Glißire ferner deine lincke Hand biß an deine rechte. Greif mit deiner rechten Hand unter deine lincke und glißire die rechte Hand biß an die Spitze des Stockes. Tritt	

Version c from 1660	Notes
halb rechts herumb und schlage also zu. Glissire zuletzt deine rechte Hand biß an deine lincke und greiff mit deiner lincken Hand unter deine rechte Hand und glissire die lincke Hand biß an die Spitze des Stocks. Tritt mit deinem rechten Fuß Lincks herum auff deine lincke Seite, daß du an den Ort zustehen komst alwo du angefangen und schlage also zu.	
8. Mache die Paraden von oben vor und zurück. Alß setze die Füsse gleich und fasse den Stock mit rechter und lincker Hand in die mitten doch daß deine Finger in der rechten Hand oben und in der lincken Hand unten kommen. Halt den Stock vor dir,[b] daß die eine Spitze bey deiner lincken Hand und die ander bey deiner rechten Hand ist, wie N. 10 zeiget. Laß die Spitze welche bey deiner lincken Hand ist von oben von dir warts bey deinen lincken Fuß vorbey gehen, hernach eben selbige Spitze bey deinem rechten Fuße vorbey und so weiter und gehe etzliche Schritte vor und zurück.	a) *b: gerade vor dir*
9. Mache die Paraden von unten vor und zurück. Nemlich in dem du mit deinen Füssen gleich stehest und den Stock in den Händen wie im vorigen Paraden helst. So lasse die Spitze welche bey deiner lincken Hand ist von unten hinter dir warts bey deinen lincken Fusz vorbey gehen, hernach eben selbige Spitze bey deinen rechten Fuß vorbey. Und gehe etzliche Schritt vor und zurück wie vorhin.	

Critical edition	Notes
mit deinen lincken Fuß halb rechts herumb und schlage also zu. Glißire zuletzt deine rechte Hand biß an deine lincke und greiff mit deiner lincken Hand unter deine rechte Hand und glißire die lincke Hand biß an die Spitze des Stocks. Tritt mit deinen rechten Fuß lincks herum auf deine lincke Seite, das du an den Ort zustehen komst allwo du angefangen und schlage also zu. Und mache eine Spaniol-Stockade.	
9. Wie du die Schläge über den Kopff und Spaniol-Stockade in Quadrat machest. Also kan es auch etliche mahl vor und hinter sich geschehn.	
10. Gleich wie die Schläge über den Kopff ohne Spaniol-Stockaden in alle vier Ecken gemachet werden. Also kan auch solches vor und hinter sich geschehen.	
11. Mache die Paraden von oben vor und zurück. Alß setze die Füsse gleich und fasse den Stock mit rechter und lincker Hand in die mitten doch das deine Finger in der rechten Hand oben und in der lincken Hand unten kommen. Halt den Stock vor dir, das die eine Spitze bey deiner lincken Hand und die ander bey deiner rechten Hand ist, wie N. 14 zeiget. Laß die Spitze welche bey deiner lincken Hand ist von oben von dir warts bey deinen lincken Fuß vorbey gehn, wie N. 15 weiset, hernach eben selbige Spitze bey deinen rechten Fuß vorbey wie N. 16 zuersehen und so weiter und gehe etzliche Schritt vor und zurück.	
12. Mache die Paraden von unten vor und zurück. Nemlich in dem du mit deinen Füssen gleich stehest und den Stock in den Händen wie in vorigen Paraden hälst. So lasse die Spitze welche bey deiner lincken Hand ist von unten hinter dir warts bey deinen lincken Fusz vorbey gehen, wie N. 17 zeiget, hernach eben selbige Spitze bey deinen rechten Fuß vorbey wie N. 18 weiset und so weiter. Und gehe etzliche Schrit vor und zurück wie vorhin.	

Version *c* from 1660	Notes
10. Tritt mit deinem lincken Fuß zurück und verkehre deine rechte Hand. Glissire eine Spitze hinter dich bey deiner lincken Seiten vorbey wie N. 11. weiset und mache die Hiebe auff beyden Seiten vor und zurück als in dem du so stehest. So haue einen gantzen Circkel mit deiner rechten Hand rechts herumb und tritt mit deinen lincken Fuß vor. Fasse den Stock mit deiner lincken Hand daß die Finger unten kommen und glissire eine Spitze wiederum hinter dich bey deiner rechten Seiten vorbey und haue mit deiner lincken Hand Lincks herumb einen gantzen Circkel. Tritt mit deinen rechten Fuß vor und fasse den Stock mit deiner rechten Hand daß die Finger unten kommen und glissire nochmahls eine Spitze hinter dich bey deiner lincken Seiten vorbey und mache noch <u>solche vier</u> Hiebe. Wann nun zuletzt dein rechter Fuß vor komt und du wiederum die Spitze des Stocks bey deiner lincken Seiten vorbey glissiret hast. So haue einen gantzen Circkel mit rechten Hand rechts herum und tritt mit deinem rechten Fuß zurück. Fasse den Stock mit deiner lincken Hand daß die Finger unten kommen und glissire eine Spitze hinter dich bey deiner rechten Seiten vorbey. Haue einen gantzen Circkel mit lincker Hand lincks herum und tritt mit deinen lincken Fuß zurück. Fasse den Stock mit deiner rechten Hand das die Finger unten kommen und glissire eine Spitze hinter dich bey deiner lincken Seiten vorbey und mache noch <u>solche vier</u> Hiebe.	

Critical edition	Notes
13. Tritt mit deinen lincken Fuß zurück und verkehre deine rechte Hand. Glißire eine Spitze hinter dich bey deiner lincken Seiten vorbey wie N. 19 weiset und mache die Hiebe auf beyden Seiten vor und zurück als in dem du so stehest. So haue einen gantzen Circkel mit deiner rechten Hand rechts herum und trit mit deinen lincken Fuß vor. Fasse den Stock mit deiner lincken Hand das die Finger unten kommen und glißire eine Spitze wiederum hinter dich bey deiner rechten Seiten vorbey wie N. 20 zuersehen, und haue mit deiner lincken Hand Lincks herum einen gantzen Circkel. Tritt mit deinen rechten Fuß vor und fasse den Stock mit deiner rechten Hand das die Finger unten kommen und glißire nochmahls eine Spitze hinter dich bey deiner lincken Seiten vorbey und mache noch etzliche solche Hiebe. Wann nun zuletzt dein rechter Fuß vor kommt und du wiederumb die Spitze des Stocks bey deiner lincken Seiten vorbey glissiret hast. So haue einen gantzen Circkel mit rechten Hand rechts herumb und tritt mit deinen rechten Fuß zurück. Fasse den Stock mit deiner lincken Hand das die Finger unten kommen und glissire eine Spitze hinter dich bey deiner rechten Seiten vorbey. Haue einen gantzen Circkel mit lincker Hand lincks herum und tritt mit deinen lincken Fuß zurück. Fasse den Stock mit deiner rechten Hand das die Finger unten kommen und glißire eine Spitze hinter dich bey deiner lincken Seiten vorbey und mache noch etzliche solche Hiebe.	
14. Diese Lection kan in alle vier Ecken jederzeit halb herumb mit zwey[a] Hiebe[b] gemachet werden.	a) *f. einen* which is a mistake. b) See III.3.2.
15 Diese Lection kan in alle vier Ecken jederzeit halb herumb mit einen Hiebe[a] gemachet werden.	a) See III.3.2.

Version *c* from 1660	Notes
11. Wann nun zuletzt dein lincker Fuß hinten stehet so fasse den Stock mit rechten Hand daß die Finger oben kommen eine Spanne von der lincken Hand in dem der Stock lincks herumb gehet und du deine lincke Hand bey der Spitze hast, das die Finger unten kommen wie N. 12 zeiget, und mache die Hiebe mit beyden Händen vor und zurück als in dem dein lincken Fuß hinten stehet. So wirff deinen rechten Fuß nach deiner lincken Seiten hinter deinen rechten Fuß herumb, daß du dein Gesichte auff die andre Seite kehrest und mit den Füssen gleich stehest und haue mit beyden Händen einen gantzen Circkel lincks umb den Kopff. Wirff deinen rechten Fuß uber deinen lincken herum daß deine Füsse gleich zu stehen kommen und du zu stehen komst wie du erst gestanden und haue mit beyden Händen einen gantzen Circkel Lincks umb den Kopff. Mache noch vier solche Hiebe und trit zu ieden zu wie gemeldet worden. Wenn nun dein rechten Fuß vorstehet, so mache diese Hiebe zurück als würff deinen rechten Fuß übern lincken Fuß[h] nach deiner lincken Seiten zurück[i] daß du dein Gesichte auff die andere Seite wendest und haue mit beyden Händen einen gantzen Circkel lincks umb den Kopff. Wirff ferner deinen lincken Fuß nach deiner lincken Seiten hinter deinen rechten Fuß herumb und haue mit beyden Händen einen gantzen Circkul Lincks umb den Kopff. Mache noch solche vier Hiebe biß du an den Ort kommest alwo du angefangen und tritt zu ieden Hieb zurück wie albereit gemeldet worden. Bey diesen Hieben kehrestu dich allezeit auff deine rechte oder lincke Seiten und stehest mit deinen Füssen gleich.	

Critical edition	Notes
16. Wann nun zuletzt dein rechter[a] Fuß hinten stehet so fasse den Stock mit rechten Hand daß die Finger oben kommen eine Spanne von der lincken Handen in dem der Stock lincks herumb gehet und du deine lincke Hand bey der Spitze hast, das die Finger unten kommen wie N. 21 zeiget, und mache die Hiebe mit beyden Händen vor und zurück als in dem dein lincken Fuß hinten stehet. So wirf deinen rechten[a] Fuß nach deiner lincken Seiten vor[c], daß du dein Gesichte auff die andre Seite kehrest und mit den Füssen gleich stehest und haue mit beyden Händen einen gantzen Circkel lincks ümb den Kopf. Wirff deinen lincken Fuß hinter deinen rechten[d] herum daß deine Füsse gleich zustehen kommen und du zustehen kompst wie du erst gestanden und haue mit beyden Händen einen gantzen Circkel Lincks umb den Kopff. Mache noch etzliche solche Hiebe und tritt zu jeden zu wie gemeldet worden. Wenn nun dein rechten Fuß vorstehet, so mache diese Hiebe zurück als wirff deinen rechten Fuß übern lincken Fuß nach deiner lincken Seiten zurück[i] daß du dein Gesichte auf die andre Seite wendest und haue mit beyden Händen einen gantzen Circkel lincks umb den Kopff. Wirff ferner deinen lincken Fuß nach deiner lincken Seiten hinter deinen rechten Fuß herumb und haue mit beyden Händen einen gantzen Circkel Lincks umb den Kopff. Mache noch etzliche solche Hiebe biß du an den Ort kommest alwo du angefangen und tritt zu jeden Hieb zurück wie albereit gemeldet worden. Bey diesen Hieben kehrestu dich allezeit auff deine rechte oder lincke Seiten und stehest mit deinen Füssen gleich.	a) See III.3.3 c) *e: hinter deinen rechten Fuß herumb* This is not coherent with the initial foot position, see notes *a* and *d*. d) *e: deinen rechten Fuß über deinen lincken.* i) *f: zu*

Version *c* from 1660	Notes
12. Wenn nun dein lincker Fuß hinten kombt, so laß den Stock an deinen lincken Arm lauffen daß du also stehest [a] wie N. 13 zeiget und haue auff beyde Seiten vor und zurück. Nehmlich[b] haue mit beyden Händen von dir nach deiner rechten Seiten zu, daß der Stock an deinen rechten Arm zu liegen kömt und tritt mit deinem lincken Fuß vor.	a) *b: daß du also stehest* was placed below, see the following note.
Haue wiederumb mit bey den Händen von dir nach deiner lincken Seite zu daß der Stock an deinen lincken Arm zu liegen kombt und tritt mit deinem rechten Fuß vor und mache noch solche vier Hiebe und tritt zu ieden zu wie gemeldet.	b) *b: in dem du also stehest so* is insterted here.
Wenn nun zuletzt dein rechter Fuß vorkomt und der Stock an deinen lincken Arm lieget, so mache diese Lection wiederum zurück. Als haue mit beyden Händen von dir nach deiner rechten Seiten zu, daß der Stock an deinen rechten Arm leufft und tritt mit deinem rechten Fuß zurück. Haue ferner mit beyden Händen von dir nach deiner lincken Seiten zu daß der Stock an deinen lincken Arm läufft und tritt mit deinem lincken Fuß zurück und mache also noch solche vier Hiebe biß du an den Ort komst alwo du angefangen und tritt zu ieden Hieb zurück wie in dieser Lection gemeldet worden.	

Critical edition	Notes
17. Wenn nun dein lincker Fuß hinten kompt, so laß den Stock an deinen lincken Arm lauffen daß du also stehest[a] wie N. 22 zeiget und haue auff beyde Seiten vor und zurück. Nehmlich[b] haue mit beyden Händen von dir nach deiner rechten Seiten zu, das der Stock an deinen rechten Arm zu liegen kommt und tritt mit deinen lincken Fuß vor wie N. 23 weiset. Haue wiederumb mit bey den Händen von dir nach deiner lincken Seite zu das der Stock an deinen lincken Arm zu liegen kommt und tritt mit deinem rechten Fuß vor und mache noch etzliche solche Hiebe und tritt zu jeden zu wie gemeldet. Wann nun zuletzt dein rechter Fuß vorkommt und der Stock an deinen lincken Arm lieget, so mache diese Lection wiederum zurück. Als haue mit beyden Händen von dir nach deiner rechten Seiten zu das der Stock an deinen rechten Arm läufft und tritt mit deinen rechten Fuß zurück. Haue ferner mit beyden Händen von dir nach deiner lincken Seiten zu das der Stock an deinen lincken Arm läufft und tritt mit deinen lincken Fuß zurück und mache also noch etzliche solche Hiebe biß du an den Ort komst alwo du angefangen und tritt zu jeden Hieb zurück wie in dieser Lection gemeldet worden.	
18. Diese Lection kanstu in alle vier Ecken mit zwey Hiebe[a] machen.	a) See III.3.2.
19. Diese Lection kanstu auch in alle vier Ecken iederzeit halb herum mit zwey Hiebe[a] machen.	a) See III.3.2.
20. Diese Lection kan auch in alle vier Ecken iederzeit halb herum mit einem Hieb[a] gemachet werden, zuletzt mache ich zwey Hiebe[a].	a) See III.3.2.

Version *c* from 1660	Notes
13. Nun folgen die Hiebe rund herumb Rechts. Als in dem dein rechter Fuß vorstehet, so tritt mit deinem lincken Fuß auff deine rechte Seite in einem Winckel und haue einen gantzen Circkel Rechts umb den Kopff wie <u>in der vorgehenden Lection geschehen</u>. Tritt ferner mit deinen lincken Fuß in den andern Winckel und haue einen gantzen Cirkul Rechts ümb den Kopff auf diese Art in den dritten und vierten Winckel und tritt zu ieden Hiebe welchen du Rechts ümb den Kopff thust. <u>Trit</u> mit deinen lincken Fuß fort biß dein Lincker vor zu stehen kömbt und du an den Ort stehest alwo du angefangen.ᶜ	
14. Mache diese Hiebe Lincks rund herum in alle <u>Seite oder Ecken</u> wie du sie recht gemacht hast nur daß dieses Lincks geschicht. Auch Lincks herum hauest und mit deinem rechten Fuß allezeit fort tritst. Wenn du nun zuletzt dein Gesichte hinwendest und stehest wo du hast angefangen dein rechter Fuß auch vorstehet, so setze deinen rechten Fuß zurück und glissire den Stock bey deiner rechten Seiten vorbey, daß deine lincke Hand an der Spitze und deine rechte Hand zwey Spannen darvon ist.	
15. <u>Wenn nun dein rechter Fuß zurück stehet und du den Stock bey deiner rechten Seiten vorbey glissiret hast,</u> so mache die Schläge von oben herunter in aller vier Ecken. Alß in dem dein lincker Fuß vorstehet. So schlage von oben herunter und trit mit deinem rechten Fuß vor <u>wie N. 14. zeiget</u>. Glissire bey deiner lincken Seiten vorbey, daß deine rechte Hand an die Spitze und die lincke Hand zwey Spannen von der Spitze kömt, und schlage wiederum von oben herunter und trit mit deinem lincken Fuß vor und also in alle vier Ecken biß du an den Ort wiederum kommest, allwo du angefangen und zwar iederzeit lincks herum. Wenn du nun so stehest wie du diese Lection angefangenᵃ und bey deiner rechten Seiten vorbey glissiret hast, daß deine lincke Hand an der Spitze des Stocks und deine rechte Hand zwey Spannen darvon.	a) *b*: *nemlich dein rechter Fuß vor* was inserted here

Critical edition	Notes
21. Nun folgen die Hiebe rund herumb Rechts. Als in dem dein rechter Fuß vorstehet, so tritt mit deinem lincken Fus auff deine rechte Seiten in einem Winckel und haue einen gantzen Circkel Rechts umb den Kopff wie N. 24 zeiget. Tritt ferner mit deinem lincken Fus in den andern Winckel und haue einen gantzen Cirkel Rechts umb den Kopff auf diese Art in den dritten und vierdten Winckel und tritt zu jeden Hiebe welchen du Rechts ümb den Kopff thust. Zu tritt mit deinem lincken Fus fort bis dein lincker vor zustehen kömbt und du an den Ort stehest allwo du angefangen.ᵃ	a) *f* : shortened and replaced by *und also in alle vier Winckel*.
22. Mache diese Hiebe lincks rund herum in alle vier Winckel wie du sie Recht gemacht hast nur dasz dieses Lincks geschicht. Auch Lincks herum hauest und mit deinem rechten Fusz allezeit fort tritestᵇ wie N. 25 weiset. Wenn du nun zuletzt dein Gesichte hinwendest und stehest wo du hast angefangen dein rechter Fuß auch vorstehet, so setze deinen rechten Fuß zurück und glißire den Stock bey deiner rechten Seiten vorbey, daß deine lincke Hand an der Spitze und deine rechte Hand zwey Spannen darvon ist, wie N. 26 zu ersehen.	
23. Wenn nun dein rechter Fuß zurücke stehet und du den Stock bey deiner rechten Seiten vorbey glißiret hast so mache die Schläge von oben herunter in aller vier Ecken. Alß in dem dein lincker Fuß vorstehet. So schlage von oben herunter und tritt mit deinem rechten Fuß vor wie N. 27 zeiget. Glißire bey deiner lincken Seiten vorbey daß deine rechte Hand an die Spitze und die lincke Hand zwey Spannen von der Spitze komt wie N. 28 weiset, und schlage wiederum von oben herunter und tritt mit deinem lincken Fuß vor wie N. 29 zuersehen und also in alle vier Ecken biß du an den Ort wiederumb kömmest, allwo du angefangen und zwar jederzeit lincks herum. Wenn du nun so stehest wie du diese Lection angefangen und bey deiner rechten Seiten vorbey glißiret hast, das deine lincke Hand an der Spitze des Stocks und deine rechte Hand zwey Spannen darvon.	

Version *c* from 1660	Notes
16. So mache diese Schläge von oben herunter in alle vier Ecken halb herum. Alß erstlich hinter dich hernach wiederum an selbigen Ort wo du erstlich gestanden. Dann auff deine lincke Seite hernach halb herum auff deine rechte Seiten zuletzt wiederum an den Ort wo du anfangs gestanden in diesen Schlägen muß ich mich iederzeit lincks herum kehren. Es wird aber glissiret und zugetreten wie in der vorhergehenden Lection. Wann nun dein lincker Fuß vorstehet und du bey deiner rechten Seiten vorbey glissiret hast.	
17. So mache nur einen Schlag von oben herunter in alle vier Ecken, alß erstlich hinter dich lincks halb herum und tritt mit deinem rechten Fuß vor, hernach wiederum an den Ort wo du erstlich angefangen rechts herum und tritt mit deinem lincken[a] Fuß vor, folgends[b] auff deine lincke Seite lincks herum und tritt mit deinem rechten Fuß, folgends auff[c] deine rechte Seite halb Rechts herum und tritt mit deinem lincken Fuß vor und zuletzt Lincks herum an den Ort, allwo du angefangen hast. Und trit mit deinem rechten Fuß vor. In dieser lection wird glissiret wie in der[d] vorhergehenden lection.	a) *rechten* in *c* and *e* version *rechten*, which seems to be a mistake. See III.3.4. b) *b: weiter* c) See III.3.4 x) *b: wie die*
18. Mache die Schläge von unten herauff in alle vier Ecken wie N. 15 zeiget. In dieser Lection wird glissiret und zugetreten wie in der funffzehenden lection, nur daß du von unten herauff nach des Adversarii Ellenbogen schlägest.	
19. Mache die Schläge von unten herauff in alle vier Ecken halb herum. In dieser Lection wird glissiret und zugetreten wie in der sechzehenden Lection. Nur daß du von unten herauff nach des Adversarii Ellenbogen wie in voriger Lection schlägest.[b]	
20. Mache nur einen Schlag von oben herunter in alle vier Ecken. In dieser Lection wird glissiret und zugetreten wie in der siebenzehenden Lection. Nur daß du von unten herauff nach der Adversarii Ellenbogen schlägest.	

Critical edition	Notes
24. So mache diese Schläge von oben herunter in alle vier Ecken halb herum. Als erstlich hinter dich[a] hernach wiederum an selbigen Ort wo du erstlich gestanden.[a] Dann auf deine lincke Seite hernach halb herum[b] auf deine rechte Seiten zuletzt wiederum an den Ort wo du anfangs gestanden in diesen Schlägen must du dich jederzeit lincks herum kehren. Es wird aber glißiret und zugetreten wie in der vorhergehenden Lection. Wann nun dein lincker Fuß vorstehet und du bey deiner rechten Seiten vorbey glißiret hast.	a) f: *halb lincks* was inserted here b) *f: hernach halb lincks herumb*.
25.[a] So mache nur einen Schlag von oben herunter in alle vier Ecken. Als erstlich halb lincks hinter dich, hernach wiederumb an den Ort wo du erstlich angefangen halb rechts. Folgends auff deine lincke Seite dann halb Rechts herumb nach deiner rechten Seiten und zuletzt lincks herumb an den Ort allwo du angefangen hast und machest zuletzt zwey Schläge.	a) See III.3.4
26. Gleich wie die schläge von oben herunter in alle vier Ecken gemacht werden. Also kan auch solches[a] vor und hinter sich gemacht geschehen.[b]	a) *e: können sie auch.* b) *e: werden.*
27. Mache die Schläge von unten herauff in alle vier Ecken wie N. 30 zeiget. In dieser Lection wird glißiret und getreten wie in der drey und zwanzigsten Lection, nur daß du von unten herauff nach des *Adversarii* Ellebogen schlägest.	a) *e: zwantzigsten Lection*, mistake corrected in *f*.
28. Mache die Schläge von unten herauff in alle vier Ecken halb herum. In dieser Lection wird glißiret und zugetreten wie in der vier und zwantzigsten[a] Lection. Nur daß du von unten herauff nach des *Adversarii* Ellebogen wie in voriger Lection schlägest	a) *e: ein und zwantzigsten.*
29. Mache nur einen Schlag von unten herauff in alle vier Ecken. In dieser Lection wird glißiret und zugetreten wie in der fünf und zwantzigsten[a] Lection. Nur daß du von unten herauff nach der *Adversarii* Ellebogen schlägest.	a) *e: zwey und zwantzigsten.*

Version c from 1660	Notes
21. Lege den Stock auff die rechte Achsel, daß du die eine Spitze in der rechten Hand hast wie N. 16ª weiset und laß den Stock über deine lincke Achsel lauffen, daß du den Stock mitten mit deiner rechten Hand fangest. Laß den Stock umb deine rechte Hand lauffen, daß du selbigen wiederum inwendig in deiner rechten Hand bekomst. Nimb^b den Stock unter deinen rechten Arm daß die forderste Spitze niedrig ist und die hinderste hoch und mache wenn du diese Lectiones vor vornehmen Leuten gemachet^c einen Reverentz wie N. 4 geschehen. Dann sonsten wenn du mit deinen Adversariis zuthun hättest, so verstehet sichs daß keines Reverentz von nöthen und so viel von dem Jägerstock oder halber Piquen.	a) c: the number is 61 which is wrong. b) b: beginning of the 22th paragraph. c) b: *mit deinen rechten Fuß und Stock.*

Critical edition	Notes
30. Wie die Schläge von unten herauff in alle vier Ecken gemacht werden. Also mache selbige auch vor und hinter sich.	
31. Mache die gesprungene Stockade[a] als mache eine Stockade und springe mit beyden Füssen fort wir N. 31 zeiget. Glißire mit der Rechten an die Lincke. Greiff mit der Lincken unter die Reche und rutsche mit der Lincken biß ans Ende und schlage hinter dich wie N. 31[b] weiset. Mache eine Spaniol-stockade halb Rechts herumb wie N.32 weiset und solches mache in alle vier Ecken.	a) e: *Spaniol-stockade*. b) f: gives the number 32 which is a mistake. Since now each number of picture in f version are wrong.
32.[a] Mache diese Spanier-stockade in alle vier Ecken halb herumb.	a) Only in version *e*
33.[a] Diese Lection kanstu auch vor und hinter sich machen. Wann du diese Lection aber zurück machest, so mustu mit deinen Füssen zurücke springen.	a) 32 in *f* version.
34.[a] Lege den Stock auff die rechte Achsel, daß du die eine Spitze in der rechten Hand hast, wie N. 33 weiset und laß den Stock über deine lincke Achsel lauffen das du den Stock mitten mit deiner rechten Hand fangest wie N. 34 zuersehn. Laß den Stock umb deine rechte Hand lauffen das du selbigen wiedrum inwendig in deiner rechten Hand bekomst. Nimb den Stock unter deinen rechten Arm das die forderste Spitze niedrig ist und die hinderste hoch[c] und mache wann du diese Lectiones vor vornehmen Leuten *exercirest* einen Reverentz wie N. 5 geschehen. Dann sonsten wenn du mit deinen *Adversariis* zu thun hättest, so verstehet sichs das keine Reverentz von nöthen und so viel von dem *Baston à deux bous*, Jägerstock oder halber Piquen.	a) 33 in *f* version.

IV. APPENDIX

IV.1. Edition of the partial version a'

The following table gives the complete text of the hunting staff part of the first publication a' in the left column. The right column gives the matching paragraph number in the ideal version.

Text	Paragraph
Jägerstock oder Partisan	title
Der Stock wird auff dreyerley manier getragen	beginning of introduction
Reverentz	end of introduction
Wie man sich stellet.	beginning of §1
Vor und hinden glisirt in alle vier Ecken	end of §1
Spaniol-Stockaden in alle vier Ecken und darzu gestossen	§2
Spaniol-Stockaden halb herumb und dazu gestossen in alle vier Ecken	§3
Spaniol-Stockaden halb rumb ohnen stossen	§4
Uber den Kopf gedrehet und dazu gestossen in alle vier Ecken	§6
Diese Lection halb rumb und dazu gestossen in alle vier Ecken	§7
Diese Lection halb rumb ohne stossen	§8
Paraden von oben vor und zurück	§11
Paraden von unten vor und zurück	§12
Paraden von oben rechts rund rumb	abandoned
Paraden von unten rechts rund rumb	abandoned
Zurück glisirt und gehauen vor und zurück	§13
Mit beyden Händen gehauen vor und zurück	§16
Auff beyden seiten gehauen vor und zurück daß der Stock allezeit an die Arme kommt	§17
Rund rumb gehauen rechts	§21
Rund rumb gehauen links	§22
Zurück glisirt und nieder geschlagen zweymahl in alle vier Ecken	§23
Diese Lection halb rumb mit zween Schlägen	§24
Diese Lection halb rumb mit einem Schlag	§25
Diese Lection halb rumb mit zween Schlägen nach dem Ellebogen in alle vier Ecken	§27
Diese Lection halb rumb mit zween Schlägen	§28
Diese Lection nach dem Ellebogen halb rumb mit einem Schlag	§29
Spaniol-Stockaden mit verkehrer Hand in alle vier Ecken und darzu gestossen	abandoned
Diese Lection halb rumb und darzu gestossen	abandoned
Diese Lection halb rumb ohne stossen	abandoned
Den Stock hinter gestossen und geschlagen	abandoned
Den Stock auff die rechte Achsel gelegt und herumb lauffen lassen daß er in die rechte Hand kommt	beginning of §34
Den Stock umb die rechte Hand lauffen lassen	middle of §34
Reverentz	end of §34

Table 3: Edition of the partial version a'

IV.2. Collombon's text about *baston à deux bouts*

This extract comes from the book of Collombon, pages 15 to 16. It is the most detailed technical source on the French staff of the seventeenth century, though the extensive use of technical terms without any explanations makes it difficult to understand.

Le jeu du Baston à deux bout.

Le baston à deux bout se porte de deux façons sur l'épaule ou bien en contrepoids, le bras estendu en bas, lors qu'on est en crainte, faut presenter la pointe, luy envoyer une estocade, faire un faut montant pour le faire retirer, puis tourner visage, faire virer le baston, tirer deux estocades devant & dernier[51] en se tournant. Puis les faux montans de deux costez, puis les passées en tournant le corps, les faire deux fois, puis le moulinet, envoyant une estocade dernier, le faire deux fois en parant, puis le point en dernier, le faire deux fois, puis le moulinet en déchargeant, le faire deux fois en changeant de main, puis le moulinet passant par devant, puis les décharges, passant dessous le baston, les faire deux fois, puis les doubler, décharger deux fois puis les largir, tourner le corps, les faire deux fois, puis s'arrester pour voir dequel costé faut aller, puis tirer les quatre pointes devant, dernier, faire comme estant en lieu estroit, & ce qui est necessaire de faire ; Car il ne faut pas chercher le commencement ny la fin, mais se servir des tours qui vous puissent servir. Voila tout le jeu du baston à deux bout.

---

[51] The word « *dernier* » (« last ») was systematically used in this book with the meaning of « behind » or « back ».

V. BIBLIOGRAPHY

V.1. Primary sources

Allain Manesson Mallet, *Les travaux de Mars ou l'art de la guerre*, 3, Paris, Denys Thierry, 1684.

Charles Besnard, *Le maistre d'arme libéral*, Rennes, Julien Herbert, 1653.

Christoph Schrader, *Die treue Gehülffin eines Ehemannes an der Wohl erbarn, Hoch-Ehr und Tugendreichen Frauen Annen Margarethen gebohrnen Sieglerin, des Edlen Großachtbaren und Wohlgelahrten Herrn Johann Georg Paschn...* Halle, Salfeld, 1678. Exemplary consulted: Berlin, state library, 710-257, 43. <http://resolver.staatsbibliothek-berlin.de/SBB0000905100000000>, accessed 15 November 2015.

Christoph Schrader, *Wohlanständige Exercitia Eines Christen Dem Weiland Edlen Großachtbaren und Wohlgelahrten Herrn Johann Georg Paschn...* Halle, Salfel, 1678. Exemplary consulted: Erfurt, University and research library Erfurt/Gotha, LP D 8° III, 00007 (11).

Festivitati Nuptiali Viri Clarissimi et Consultissimi Dni. Johannis Georgii Paschn, Serenissimi, Principis Magdeb. Secretarii Digniss. Sponsi Cum Virgine Anna Margarita Sieglerin, bonis omnibus prosequuntur Fautores et Amici Wittebergernses, Wittenberg, Hake, 1657. Exemplary consulted: Halle, University and Federal Library from Sachsen-Anhalt, an Pon Zd 198 (4). <http://nbn-resolving.de/urn:nbn:de:gbv:3:1-89363>, accessed 15 November 2015.

Jacques Collombon, *Traité de l'exercice militaire, où est l'instruction des jeux de toutes sortes d'armes, et celuy du drapeau, avec une méthode très facile pour faire faire l'exercice aux soldats et dresser toutes sortes de bataillons*, Lyon, Pierre Anard, 1650.

Johann Georg Pasch, *Anleitung sich bei grossen Herrn, Höfen und andern beliebt zu machen*, ed. by Uwe W. Schlottermüller (Freiburg: fa-gisis, 2000).

Johann Georg Pasch, *Deutliche Beschreibung unterschiedener Fahnen-Lectionen in acht Spiel eingetheilet, nebst dem Piquen-Spiel, Pertuisan und halben Piquen, oder Jägerstock*, Halle, Melchior Ölschlegel, 1673. Exemplary consulted: Wolfenbüttel: Herzog August Bibliothek, Xb 4° 157. <http://diglib.hab.de/drucke/xb-4f-157/start.htm>, accessed 29 January 2016.

Johann Georg Pasch, *Deutliche Beschreibung von dem Exerciren in der Musquet und Pique, wie auch von dem Baston a deux Bous, Jägerstock*, Halle, Christian Vester, 1667. Exemplary consulted: Forschungsbibliothek Gotha, Math 2° 00326/01 (01) <http://nbn-resolving.de/urn/resolver.pl?urn=urn:nbn:de:urmel-99313174-0a07-4f3c-8487-06d9b0ff51671>, accessed 15 November 2015.

Johann Georg Pasch, *Dissertatio De Plagio Kaufungiano Anno MCCCCLV. Commisso...* Wittenberg, Johann Röhner, 1655. Exemplary consulted: Dresden, State Library, Hist.Sax.C.623,19 <http://nbn-resolving.de/urn:nbn:de:gbv:3:1-17851>, accessed 15 November 2015.

Johann Georg Pasch *Dissertatio Politica de Legato / Quam praeside Dn. Michaele Wendelero ... Johannes Georgius Pascha, Dresd. A. & R. in Auditorio Majori, die XVII. Martii*, Wittenberg, Johann Röhner, 1652.

Johann Georg Pasch, *Kurtze Anleitung Wie der Jägerstock oder halbe Pique eigentlich zugebrauchen und was vor Lectiones darauff seyn*, Halle, Melchior Ölschlegel, 1660. Exemplary consulted: Göttingen, Niedersaechsische Staats- und Universitätsbibliothek, 8 ARS MIL 1106/3 (3). <http://resolver.sub.uni-goettingen.de/purl?PPN591440717>, accessed 14 December 2015.

Johann Georg Pasch, *Kurtze Anlejdung wie der Baston à deux bous das ist Jaegerstock, halbe Pique oder Springe-Stock eigentlich zu gebrauchen*, Leipzig, Friedrich Arnst, 1670. Exemplary consulted: Wolfenbüttel : Herzog August Bibliothek, H: N 223.2° Helmst. <http://nbn-resolving.de/urn:nbn:de:gbv:23-drucke/n-223-2f-helmst6>, accessed 10 March 2016.

Johann Georg Pasch, *Kurtze doch Gründliche Unterrichtung der Pique, deß Trillens in der Pique, der Fahne, deß Jägerstocks, Trincierens, Fechtens auf den Stoß und auf den Hieb, Voltesirens auf den Pferd und auf den Tisch, deß Ringens, Tantzens*, Osnabrück, Johann Georg Schwander, 1659. Exemplary consulted: Stuttgart, Federal Library, Sport.oct.357. <http://digital.wlb-stuttgart.de/purl/bsz371927072>, accessed 15 November 2015.

Johann Georg Pasch, *Kurtze jedoch Deutliche Beschreibung handlend von Fechten auß dem Stoss und Hieb*, Halle, Melchior Ölschlegel, 1661. Exemplary consulted: Stuttgart, Federal Library, MC Sport.qt.52.

Johann Georg Pasch, *Kurtze Unterrichtung Belangend Die Pique, die Fahne, den Jägerstock, das Voltegiren, das Ringen, das Fechten auff den Stoß und Hieb und endlich das Trinciren*, Wittenberg, Ölschlegel, 1657 (ré-ed. 1658, 1659). Exemplary consulted: Wolfenbüttel, Herzog-August-Bibliothek, Hn 198 <http://nbn-resolving.de/urn:nbn:de:gbv:23-drucke/hn-1988>, accessed 15 November 2015.

Johann Georg Pasch, *Vier und achtzig Fahnen-Lectiones*, Halle, Melchior Ölschlegel, 1661. Exemplary consulted: Göttingen, Niedersaechsische Staats- und Universitätsbibliothek, 8 ARS MIL 908/15. <http://resolver.sub.uni-goettingen.de/purl?PPN59394447X>, accessed 14 December 2015.

Johann Georg Pasch, *Vollständiges Fecht- Ringe und Voltigier Buch*, Halle, Christian Vester, 1666. Exemplary consulted: Vienna, Austrian National Library, 72.C.38. <http://data.onb.ac.at/ABO/%2BZ184136601>, accessed 08 December 2015.

L'État de la France où l'on voit tous les Princes, Ducs et Pairs, Marêchaux de France, et autres Officiers de la Courone... Paris, A. Besongne, 1677.

Louis de Gaya, *Traité des armes, des machines de guerre, des feux d'artifice, des enseignes et des instrumens militaires*, Paris, Sébastien Cramoisy, 1678.

Nathanael Duez, *Le vray et parfait guidon de la langue francoise*, Amsterdam, Ludwig and Daniel Elzevier, 1662.

Pierre Giffart, *L'Art militaire françois pour l'infanterie contenant l'exercice et le maniement des armes, tant des officiers que des soldats*, Paris, Pierre Giffart, 1696.

V.2. Secondary sources

Anglo, Sydney, *L'escrime, la danse et l'art de la guerre, le livre et la représentation du mouvement* (Paris: Bibliothèque nationale de France, 2011).

Anglo Sydney, *Martial Arts of Renaissance Europe* (New Haven: Yale University Press, 2000).

Bibza, Gábor, *Die deutschsprachige Leichenpredigt der frühen Neuzeit in Ungarn (1571 - 1711)* (Berlin: Lit Verlag, 2010).

Brulliot, François, *Dictionnaire des monogrammes, marques figurées, lettres initiales, noms abrégés, etc.*, 3 vols. (Munich: J.G. Cotta, 1832-34).

Brunt, Richard J., *The Influence of the French Language on the German Vocabulary (1649-1735)*, Studia Linguistica Germanica 18 (Berlin, New York: De Gruyter, 1983).

Crawley, T. Philip, *The Polearm Compendium* <http://www.lulu.com/shop/philip-t-crawley/the-polearm-compendium/ebook/product-20700660.html>, accessed 15 November 2015.

Der Altenburger Prinzenraub 1455: Strukturen und Mentalitäten eines spätmittelalterlichen Konflikts, ed. by Joachim Emig (Beucha: Sax-Verlag, 2007).

Dupuis, Olivier, 'L'escrime au bâton et à la canne en France, du XVIe au XIXe siècle', *Arts de combat, Théorie & pratique en Europe - XIVe-XXe siècle*, ed. by Fabrice Cognot (Dijon: AEDEH, 2011), pp. 153-82.

Dupuis, Olivier. 'Organization and Regulation of Fencing in the Realm of France in the Renaissance', *Acta Periodica Duellatorum*, 2 (2014), 233-54.

Gabler, Hans Walter, 'Textual Criticism and Theory in Modern German Editing', *Contemporary German Editorial Theory*, ed. by Hans Walter Gabler, George Bornstein and Gillian Borland Pierce (Ann Arbor: The University of Michigan Press, 1995), pp. 1-16.

Guntau, Martin, 'Die frühen norddeutschen Universitätsgründungen Rostock und Greifswald', *Ein Jahrtausend Mecklenburg und Vorpommern : Biographie einer norddeutschen Region in Einzeldarstellungen*, ed. by Wolf Karge (Rostock: Hinstorff, 1995), pp. 97-102.

Hazebroucq, Hubert, *La technique de la danse de bal vers 1660 : nouvelles perspectives*, master 2 dissertation (University of Reims 2013), <http://dumas.ccsd.cnrs.fr/dumas-00994362>, accessed 15 November 2015.

Jones, William Jervis, *A Lexicon of French Borrowings in the German Vocabulary (1575-1648)*, (Berlin, New York: De Gruyter, 1976).

Kathe, Heinz, *Die Wittenberger Philosophische Fakultät 1502 - 1817* (Köln, Weimar, Wien: Böhlau, 2002).

Köbler Gerhard, *Historisches Lexikon der Deutschen Länder: die deutschen Territorien vom Mittelalter bis zur Gegenwart* (Munich: Beck, 2007).

Krebs, Jean-Daniel, 'Quand les allemands apprenaient à trancher', *Études Germaniques*, 41 (1986), 8-23.

Lahaye, Matthieu, *Le fils de Louis XIV : monseigneur le Grand Dauphin, 1661-1711* (Seyssel : Champ vallon, 2013).

Müller, Georg, 'Ein Versuch zur Gründung einer Ritterakademie zu Dresden (1674)', *Neues Archiv für Sächsische Geschichte und Altertumskunde*, 10 (1889), 43-57.

Murdoch, Steve and Grosjean, Alexia, *Alexander Leslie and the Scottish Generals of the Thirty Years' War, 1618–1648* (London: Pickering & Chatto, 2014).

Scholz, Günter and Vogelsang, Klaus, *Einheiten, Formelzeichen, Größen* (Leipzig: Fachbuchverlag, 1991).

Sikora, Michael, 'Die Mechanisierung des Kriegers', *Bewegtes Leben, Körpertechniken in der Frühen Neuzeit*, ed. by Rebekka von Mallinckrodt (Wiesbaden: Harrassowitz, 2008), pp. 143-166.

Van Noort, Reinier, *Pascha's Hunting Staff*, <http://www.bruchius.com/docs/Pascha%20Hunting%20Staff%20by%20RvN.pdf>, accessed 8 March 2016.

Van Noort, Reinier, *Pascha's Staff with Two Ends*, <http://www.bruchius.com/docs/Pascha%20Hunting%20Staff%20by%20RvN.pdf>, accessed 8 March 2016.

Wehrmann, Martin, 'Geschichte des Königlichen Marienstifts-Gymnasiums 1544–1894', *Festschrift zum dreihundertfünfzigjährigen Jubiläum des Königlichen Marienstifts-Gymnasiums zu Stettin am 24 und 25 September 1894* (Herrcke & Lebeling: Stettin 1894). pp. 1-164.

Wellmann, Janina, 'Hand und Leib, Arbeiten und Üben. Instruktionsgraphiken der Bewegung im 17. und 18. Jahrhunder', in *Bewegtes Leben Körpertechniken in der frühen Neuzeit*, ed. by Rebekka von Mallinckrodt (Wiesbaden: Harrassowitz, 2008), pp. 15-38.

Wellmann, Janina, 'Katalog, Hand und Leib, Arbeiten und Üben', in *Bewegtes Leben Körpertechniken in der frühen Neuzeit*, ed. by Rebekka von Mallinckrodt (Wiesbaden: Harrassowitz, 2008), pp. 249-59.

DOI 10.1515/apd-2016-0004

The use of the saber in the army of Napoleon

Bert Gevaert
Katholieke Universiteit Leuven (Belgium)
Hallebardiers / Sint Michielsgilde Brugge (Belgium)
Bert.gevaert@sint-lodewijkscollege.be

Abstract – Though Napoleonic warfare is usually associated with guns and cannons, edged weapons still played an important role on the battlefield. Swords and sabers could dominate battles and this was certainly the case in the hands of experienced cavalrymen. In contrast to gunshot wounds, wounds caused by the saber could be treated quite easily and caused fewer casualties. In 18th and 19th century France, not only manuals about the use of foil and epee were published, but also some important works on the military saber: de Saint Martin, Alexandre Muller... The saber was not only used in individual fights against the enemy, but also as a duelling weapon in the French army.

Keywords – saber; Napoleonic warfare; Napoleon; duelling; Material culture; Historical European Martial Arts (HEMA); History

"The sword is the weapon in which you should have most confidence, because it rarely fails you by breaking in your hands. Its blows are the more certain, accordingly as you direct them coolly; and hold it properly."
Antoine Fortuné de Brack, Light Cavalry Exercises, 1876[1]

I. INTRODUCTION

Though Napoleon (1769-1821) started his own military career as an artillery officer and achieved several victories by clever use of cannons, edged weapons still played an important role on the Napoleonic battlefield. Swords and sabers could dominate battles and this was certainly the case in the hands of experienced cavalrymen. The general image, although, is that Napoleonic warfare was dominated by firepower.

Smoothbore flintlock muskets indeed caused most of the wounds, but the accuracy of the weapon was strongly limited at ranges greater than 100 m.[2] An individual infantryman

---

*In writing this article I received valuable information from Matt Easton and Marcus Hampel. Special thanks go to La famille Bonaparte, Ken Broeders, illustrator, graphic novel artist/writer, and expert on Napoleonic matter.

[1] de Brack, *Light cavalry out-posts*, p. 51.

[2] Westwood, 'rifle', p. 375.

would be very lucky if he could hit something at more than 80 m and at 200 m only a concentrated mass of soldiers could be effective, so firing muskets en masse had to be used as a military tactic.³

Some calculations estimate that only 5% of the casualties in war were caused by bullets fired at a range of about 100 m and that this number was reduced to 2% when the bullets were fired from up to 200 m.⁴ Alessandro Barbero gives us other interesting numbers about the accuracy of musket fire in the Napoleonic era: only one bullet out of 459 actually hit the target at which iat was aimed. At Waterloo, where many shots were fired at close range, only one bullet out of 162 hit its target.⁵

In combination, however, with the bayonet, it became an important weapon in close quarter fights. Whole, well trained, divisions of soldiers armed with bayonets could even stop cavalry charges as proven at the Battle of Waterloo (18 June 1815).

Though Fortuné de Brack (see below) is quite positive about the French firearms, which he considers as "the best in Europe",⁶ he nevertheless puts a lot of attention to the technical problems which can arise when using these weapons: flintstones can get lost, the barrel can get dirty, the cock can fall down without you wanting it (e.g. when you are at rest), the cartridges can get wet by rain or damp,... ⁷ Louis Rilliet, second lieutenant in a cuirassiers division (1804-1814) writes about a small battle near Janowitz, known as the Battle of Katzbach (26 August 1813) where infantry soldiers could not use their muskets because of the heavy rain.⁸

It is also important to consider that pistols and muskets caused a lot of smoke so sometimes soldiers had the feeling that they where shooting blindfolded. This is also the reason why uniforms in the Napoleonic era had very bright colours, so soldiers could easily recognize their own regiments and certainly not shoot at them... Besides muskets, pistols were also used, but these had the huge disadvantage that they are only certain when they are fired very close to the target, but not too close because when the muzzle of the pistol touches the enemy, "the pistol may burst and wound the man firing."⁹ Thus pistols were best used in combination with the saber and to make sure you don't waste time, it was best to fasten the lanyard of the pistol so you can throw it to your left and immediately use the saber.¹⁰

---

³ Westwood, 'musket', p. 669.

⁴ Hughes, *Firepower: weapons effectiveness on the battlefield 1630-1850*, p. 127.

⁵ Barbero, *Waterloo. Het verhaal van de veldslag*, p. 159.

⁶ de Brack, *Light cavalry out-posts*, p. 46.

⁷ Ibid., pp. 46-51.

⁸ Rilliet, *Journal d'un sous-lieutenant de cuirassiers*, p. 81.

⁹ de Brack, *Light cavalry out-posts*, p. 48.

¹⁰ Ibid., p. 50.

Rifles, which had grooved barrels, had a longer range and better accuracy, but the weapon was too costly and therefore it was seldom used in the French army. In contrast, the British and their allies made wide use of this weapon at the Battle of Waterloo, so their shots were more successful.[11]

Firearms did play a significant role on the Napoleonic battlefield (only to be surpassed by artillery) but they were not always reliable and didn't guarantee success in personal combat. It is therefore no surprise that Fortuné de Brack says that a cavalry soldier should have most confidence in his saber.[12] Even modern scholars agree on this:

> The cavalry's principal purpose was to attack the enemy and engange hand-to-hand. To that end, the most important part of a cavalryman's equipment was his sword.[13]

Almost every soldier in the army of Napoleon carried a saber; not only the cavalry but also the infantry had their own shorter sabers. The purpose of this article is to shed some light on the use of the saber in the army of Napoleon, especially because this year the bicentenary of the Battle of Waterloo was celebrated. Thousands of people have visited the huge reenactment (about 5000 reenactors and at least 300 horses) which took place at Waterloo on the 19th and 20th of June 2015.

II. TRAINING WITH THE SABER

II.1. Prequel: Fencing with the smallsword and epee

By the end of the 18th century France had a long fencing tradition: not only was it here that the most famous Italian fencer and smallsword master Domenico Angelo Tremamondo (1716-1802) studied fencing under the wing of the French master Teillagory,[14] but it was also the place of origin of several fencing treatises.

Between 1623 and 1801 about 38 fencing manuals were published in France,[15] most of them dealing with the smallsword – to mention only the ones published in the 18th century - Labat (*Questions sur l'art en fait d'armes ou de l'épee*, Toulouse, 1701), Jean de Brye (*L'art de tirer les armes*, Paris, 1721), Jean Jamin de Beaupré (*Méthode très facile pour former la noblesse dans l'art de l'épée*, 1721), Basnières (*De la beauté de l'escrime*, 1732), Martin (*Le maistre d'armes ou l'abrégé de l'exercice de lépée*, Strassbourg, 1737), Louis Charpentier (*Les vrais principes de l'épee*, 1742), François Bas (*Nouvelles et utiles observations pour bien tirer les armes*, Basles, 1749),

---

[11] Westwood, 'Musket', pp. 818-819.

[12] de Brack, *Light cavalry out-posts*, p. 51.

[13] Haythornthwaite, *Napoleonic cavalry*, p. 29.

[14] Loades, *Swords and swordsmen*, p. 342.

[15] Briost, Drévillon, and Serna, *Croiser le fer*, pp. 202 and 497.

Jean-Baptiste Le Perche du Coudray (*L'exercice des armes ou le maniement du fleuret pour aider la mémoire de ceux qui sont amateurs de cet art*, 1750), Gérard Gordine (*Principes et quintessences des armes*, Liège, 1754), Guillaume Danet (*L'art des armes ou la manière la plus certaine de se servir utilement de l'épée soit pour attaquer, soit pour se défendre, simplifiée et démontrée dans toute son étendue et sa perfection, suivant les meilleurs principes de théorie et de pratique adoptées actuellement en France*, Paris, 1766),...

In the 19th century one of the best known French treatises was published by Antoine Texier La Boëssière (1766-1818), son of Texier la Boessière: *Traité de l'art des armes, a l'usage des professeurs et des amateurs* (Paris, 1818).

Figure 1: Fencing with the smallsword, followed by smallsword versus saber. Below: Basket hilt foil, heavily padded glove, plastron, fencing slipper, and fencing mask.
Detail from "Fencing," Diderot and d'Alambert: Encyclopédie méthodique ou dictionnaire raisonné des sciences, des arts, et des métiers (1765), plate XV.

The importance of France as nation of fencing also explains why Angelo (Domenico Angelo Tremamondo), the "Angel of fencing" published his very influential work *L'ecole des Armes* (1763) in French, though he lived in England. It was he who put an emphasis on fencing as a sport and not as a martial art.[16]

That fencing became more and more a sport and not a deadly art, can also be explained by the use of the foil (*fleuret*), depicted for the first time in Philibert de la Touche, *Les vrays principes de l'épée* (1667)[17]

Figure 2 : Philibert de la Touche, Les vrays principes de l'épée (1667), plate 4.

Another French invention was the fencing mask, invented by Texier La Boessière (1723-1803). He introduced a mask with wire mesh and this replaced the old masks, which were made of leather or tinplate with small holes to see or with a horizontal eye slit (see illustration in the *Encyclopédie* of Diderot and d'Alambert). Though the new mask of Boessière offered better visibility, wearing a mask was still seen as an act of cowardice and of lack of trust in the capacities of the opponent. Here the philosophy was that a skilled fencer would not thrust his opponent in the eyes.[18]

France also had some brilliant fencers, including the Chevalier de Saint Georges (1745-1799), who was a student of Texier La Boessière, and the famous Chevalier d'Eon (1728-1810).

---

[16] Ibid., p. 186.

[17] Amberger, *The secret history of the sword*, p 243.

[18] Cohen, *By the sword*, p. 75.

The contemporaries of d'Eon didn't know for sure if she was actually a he, but nevertheless d'Eon was not only a secret agent for France, an officer in the French army, but also a brilliant fencer. He – or she? - gave lessons in fencing and sometimes fenced for huge audiences. The most famous of these demonstrations was the bout against, the Chevalier de Saint Georges, who had the reputation of being the best fencer of his generation. All newspapers wrote about the outcome of the bout: d'Eon won with seven hits to one,[19] which is a very surprising result, especially because Angelo had written about him:

> (…) he surpassed all his contemporaries and predecessors. No professor or amateur ever showed so much accuracy or so much strength, such length of lunge and such quickness; his attacks were a perpetual series of hits, his parade (parries) were so closed that it was in vain to attempt to touch him – in short, he was all nerve.[20]

II.2. The rise of the saber and saber manuals

But French fencing also had a very important martial and military side and fencing with the foil and epee is certainly not enough to use on the battlefield. In the 18th century a new weapon was introduced in the French world of fencing: the saber! Because of the curved blade, the prime object of this weapon was to slice and not to thrust. In its longer version it was popular in the cavalry (though they also used "sabers" with straight blades, so it's better to call these "swords"), in its shorter version it became known as the cutlass. The saber was much more durable than the epee and smallsword and also better to use against the bayonet. Quite soon, and in line with the literary tradition of Europe, the first manuals were published.

It is not my intention to provide a full list and detailed description or analyse of all French saber manuals or manuals written by soldiers who served in the army of Napoleon, but I only want to give the reader an idea of the richness of some saber treatises with a Napoleonic or French connection. Here I will present you the writings of de Saint Martin (1804), Alexandre Muller (1816), Fortuné de Brack (1831) and F.C. Cristmann (1838). I have selected these four works for the following reasons: de Saint Martin has without doubt published one of the most elaborate French treatises on saber fencing and can be situated in the middle of the reign of Napoleon (though he was not fighting or working under his command), while Muller was a soldier under Napoleon but published one of the shortest and most practical saber treatises. The work of Fortuné de Brack is not a real saber manual, but a military handbook which also contains a very short but interesting section on the use of the saber. Finally I end with Christmann, who fought in the French army, but wrote his work in German. Nevertheless, his experiences are those of a French

---

[19] Ibid., pp. 84-91.

[20] Ibid., p. 94.

cavalryman so, in my opinion, it is a valuable source for saber fencing connected to or influenced by the army of Napoleon.

Further, it is important to note that soldiers using the saber primarily also had to be excellent horsemen, and that many manuals were also published on horsemanship. Though horsemanship was also taught by the use of manuals[21] and it was in combination with the horse that the saber became most effective, I have more or less neglected this in this article because my focus is on the use of the saber on foot.

To my knowledge, French manuals didn't make much difference between extremely curved, lightly curved (*demi-courbé*) or even straight blades, as De La Roche-Aymon writes:

> Whether a saber is straight or curved, the use of it is almost the same, with the only exception that the straight blade, independent even from the use of the edge, must use its point more, not only for the attack, but also for the riposte.[22]

One of the first 18th century French fencing manuals where a saber-like weapon can be seen is written by Pierre Jacques François Girard (1736), *Nouveau traité de la perfection sur le fait des armes*. It focusses on fencing with the smallsword (*épée de pointe seule*), not only against another smallsword but also against the rapier, flail, pike and saber (*espadon*).[23]

Figure 3: Girard, Nouveau traité de la perfection sur le fait des armes (1736), plate 74.

---

[21] For more info see: ≤http://fonds-ancien.equestre.info>.

[22] *Que le sabre soit droit ou courbé, l'usage en est à peu près le même; à cette exception qu'avec la lame droite, indépendamment même de l'usage du taillant, on doit encore plus souvent employer la pointe, soit pour l'attaque, soit pour la riposte.* de la Roche-Aymon, *Troupes Légères, ou réflexions sur l'organisation, l'instruction et la tactique de l'infanterie et de la cavalerie légères*, p. 301.

[23] Girard, *Nouveau traité de la perfection sur le fait des armes*.

II.2.1. De Saint Martin: L'art de faire des armes réduit à ses vrais principes (1804)

The only information about M.J. de Saint Martin can be found in his own work, *L'art de faire des armes réduit à ses vrais principes* (The Art of Fencing Reduced to its true principles) (Vienna, 1804). He was a student of Guillaume Danet and calls himself '*ancien officier de cavallerie et Maitre d'armes Imperial*' (ancient cavalry officer and imperial master of arms) and elsewhere *professeur imperial de L'Académie Thérésienne* (Imperial professor in the Theresian Academy, this is the Austrian Academy named after empress Marie Thérèse). When his work was published he had already been in Austria for seven years, so he actually didn't serve under Napoleon.[24] He states that he had about 30 years of experience before he published his treatise. For the use of the saber, he claims that he wrote his own theories, after he had put his ideas in practice in real combat situations.[25]

His work actually consists of two parts, but with one long and very interesting introduction to both parts. In part one he discusses the use of the smallsword, but more relevant for us is the second part *traité de l'espadron* (treatise on the spadroon/saber)

According to de Saint Martin, the saber can be used against multiple opponents, cavalry against cavalry by the use of the moulinet including the *coup de Jarnac, que l'ennemi ne peut guere parer que par le plus grand hazard* (which the enemy can hardly parry, only by the greatest coincidence).[26]

Figure 4 : de Saint Martin: L 'art de faire des armes réduit à ses vrais principes, L'art de l'espadon (1804), plate 7. The coup de Jarnac *after a feint to the head.*

---

[24] de Saint Martin, *L'art de faire des armes réduit à ses vrais principes*, p. II.

[25] Ibid., pp. III and IX.

[26] Ibid., pp. IX-X.

He also teaches how to use the saber against the bayonet and is against using sticks as training tools.[27] It is interesting to see that after these brief general remarks, de Saint Martin offers a list of twenty rules – quite similar to the rules presented by Girard - regarding respect in the *salle d'armes:* don't curse (rule 1), don't speak evil about those who are or are not in the room (rule 2), don't smoke or drink in the salle (rule 10), when one walks on the feet of another, one has to apologize (rule 16.), don't blow your nose too loudly (rule 17),…

After the section on the smallsword, section two starts, again with a brief introduction. De Saint Martin explicitly says that this section is meant for the cavalry,[28] though he always makes a distinction between saber techniques on foot and on horseback. After a short praise of the Hungarian nation (for their brave spirit and military talents), he explains the intention of his section on the saber and then his lessons start…

Figure 5 : de Saint Martin: L 'art de faire des armes réduit à ses vrais principes, L'art de l'espadon (1804), plate 1. In fencing on foot, the nails of the hand have to be hold upwards, on horse the nails have to be hold downwards.

De Saint Martin prefers the head and right arm as important targets (but other areas such as the belly are also targets) and strongly suggests the use of many feints.

---

[27] Ibid., pp. XII.

[28] de Saint Martin, *L'art de faire des armes réduit à ses vrais principes, L'art de l'Espadon*, p. II.

Figure 6 : de Saint Martin: L 'art de faire des armes réduit à ses vrais principes, L'art de l'espadon (1804), plate 6.

Other advice he gives is not to hold the saber too firmly, because this makes the swordsman tired,[29] it is also interesting to look the enemy in the eyes, to read the lines of his attack.[30]

De Saint Martin warns his readers about barbarians (Turks, Tartars and other people) with shorter and more curved swords who try to behead ther enemies. But because these people have to turn their saber to make it easier to cut off the head, they frequently miss their cut.[31] Nevertheless, de Saint Martin also tells how to fight against these ferocious people.

---

[29] Ibid., p. 34.

[30] Ibid., p. 34.

[31] Ibid., p. 35.

Figure 7 : de Saint Martin: L 'art de faire des armes réduit à ses vrais principes, L'art de l'espadon (1804), plate 23.

Finally the work ends with some advice on (using the saber in) naval warfare and a violent attack against duels with the pistol: having the notion to duel with pistols can only arise in the head of a fool. Who would ever want to fight like this is nothing but a vicious animal.[32]

II.2.2. Alexandre Muller: Théorie sur l'escrime à cheval (1816)

Not much information about the life of Alexandre Muller can be found. We know for sure that he served as captain under Marshall Claude-Victor Perrin (1764-1841) in the French cavalry and that he obtained a serious wound during his military career. At the end of the Empire he became instructor in Lunéville and later he worked in a military school in Saumur. In this school his task was to instruct other instructors for cavalry regiments. After following the lessons of Muller, these officers had to go back to their regiments to teach what they had learned from the school in Saumur.

Alexandre Muller wrote three treatises on the use of weapons: two on the use of the bayonet (*Le maniement de la baïonette*), published for the first time in 1815 and republished (and updated) in 1828, 1835 and 1845.[33]

In 1816 he published his third treatise, this time dedicated to the use of the saber: *Théorie sur l'escrime à cheval, pour se défendre avec avantage contre toute espèce d'arme blanches* (Theory on

---

[32] Ibid., pp. 53-54.

[33] Muller, *La baïonette et son maniement*, pp. 2-3.

mounted fencing to defend oneself with advantage against any kind of edged weapon.). This work was published with 51 images of very high quality and was an attempt to satisfy the need for good instructors after the terrible loss of many experienced French soldiers during to the war in Russia (1812).[34]

It is surprising to see that saber fencing is reduced to 'easy' principles without much theory, probably to make the instruction of saber fencing as efficient as possible. Muller only presents two guards: the *quarte* and the *tierce* and, in general, the instructions are very brief, easy to understand especially because of the clear images.

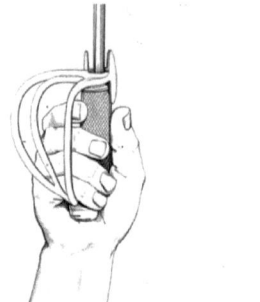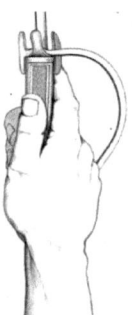

Figure 8 and 9 : Muller, Théorie sur l'escrime à cheval, pour se défendre avec avantage contre toute espèce d'arme blanches *(1816), plate 3 and 4. In the quarte the edge is turned towards the left shoulder or inwards; in the tierce the the edge is turned towards the right shoulder or outwards.*

---

[34] Muller, *Le sabre et l'escrime du cavalier,* pp. 1 and 8.

Figure 10 : Muller, Théorie sur l'escrime à cheval, pour se défendre avec avantage contre toute espèce d'arme blanches *(1816), plate 8.*

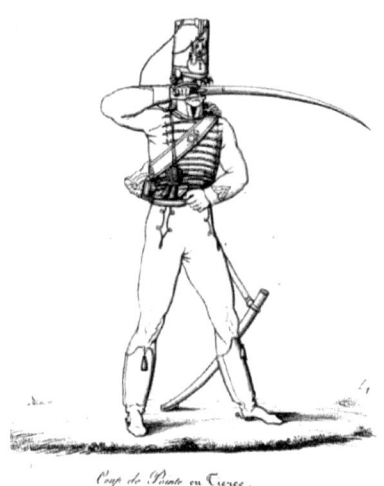

Figure 11 : Muller, Théorie sur l'escrime à cheval, pour se défendre avec avantage contre toute espèce d'arme blanches *(1816), plate 11.*

Figure 12 : Muller, Théorie sur l'escrime à cheval, pour se défendre avec avantage contre toute espèce d'arme blanches *(1816), plate 28.*

Muller gives instructions on how to fight with the saber against other sabers, but also against lances and bayonets. Generally, Muller advises to aim, as much as possible, at the face by cutting and by thrusting. This is certainly the case when one fights against cuirassiers who are better protected than other cavalry soldiers.

Hitting the reins of the horse is also advised by Muller,[35] as Flemish carabinier Joseph Abbeel experienced in the battle of Borodino (7 September 1812):

> After we had executed several charges on the cavalry of the enemy, I finally got wounded – at half past two in the afternoon – for the first time. In a charge on the dragoons of the Tsar, I moved myself a little bit to the side to make it easier for me to follow them. But one of them came to me and cut off the reins that I held in my hand. Without the leather of those bridles I would certainly have lost a thumb and a finger of my left hand. Immediately I took the watering rein [bridle strap used to bring the horse to a river and let it drink] in my bloody hand and I used my spurs. My attacker thought he could escape me, but he didn't get far because he didn't have a copper or iron jacket as we have, which could protect him against the thrust of my sword. After this was done, I returned to my regiment with my sword full of blood. When my lieutenant saw that I was wounded and that I could not use my reins anymore, he wanted to send me to the infirmary, but I told him that I

---

[35] Ibid., pp. 28 and 34.

was not seriously wounded and that I would soon be able to put my hands on another pair of reins.³⁶

It is also interesting to note that Muller gives techniques to protect the head of the horse, because when a horse is hit on the head, the ranks of the cavalry can be disrupted, making it easier for the enemy to break them.³⁷

Figure 13 : Muller, Théorie sur l'escrime à cheval, pour se défendre avec avantage contre toute espèce d'arme blanches *(1816), plate 50.*

It is interesting to see that Muller also sheds some light on how the instruction with the saber was done, here we can see small protective tips on the points of the sabers, lances and bayonet. The soldier on the table illustrates the case where a cavalry soldier is attacked by a bayonet from below.

---

³⁶ My translation from the original Dutch text: Abbeel, *Met Napoleon naar Moskou,* p. 78.

³⁷ Muller, *Le sabre et l'escrime du cavalier,* pp. 32-33.

II.2.3. Antoine Fortuné de Brack: Avant-postes de cavalerie légère' (1831)

De Brack was a French officer who participated in several military campaigns with Napoleon and who obtained the Legion of Honor for his conduct in the battle of Wagram (5-6 July 1809). From 1807 until 1812 he was member of the 7th Hussars and from 1812 till 1815 he served in the 2nd Lancers of the Guard (the famous Red Lancers). After the defeat of Napoleon, he went to Brazil and returned to France in 1830. In 1831 he published his *Avant-postes de cavalerie légère*, translated into English by Major Lonsdale A. Hale and Captain F.T. Hobson as *Light cavalry out-posts*. This work, a real treasure trove on various kind of military subjects, was reprinted several times and was still in use during the Second World War.[38]

His famous book is written in the Platonic tradition of question and answer, though it is certainly not a theoretical consideration on the art of war, because de Brack himself was a man of action who knew what he was writing about.

In the use of the saber, de Brack generally advises:

> Thrust, thrust, as much as you can; you will throw to the ground all you touch; you will demoralize the enemy who has escaped your cuts, and you will add to these advantages that of never exposing yourself and being always on guard. In the first wars in Spain our dragoons achieved by their thrusts a reputation which demoralized the Spanish and English troops.[39]

In the Battle of Regensburg/Ratisbon (23 April 1809) the French cavalry confronted the Austrian cavalry and tried to wound as many of them by thrusting, while the Austrians put their confidence in the cut. This was certainly to the advantage of the French cuirassiers who were better protected by their cuirass which covered their front and backsides, while the Austrian cuirass only protected the front of the chest.[40]

Thrusting does not mean that a soldier has to omit cutting, "as a general rule only deliver cuts when the enemy is in front of or alongside you."[41]

A swordsman should strike his opponent

> at the level of the neck, because it is natural for a horseman attacked to lower his head, and thus you strike him in the face; if your blow fails, it hits the shoulder or forearm, and places him *hors de combat*.[42]

---

[38] Roucaud, 'Etude des Avant-postes de cavalerie légère par le général de Brack', pp. 110-113.

[39] de Brack, *Light cavalry out-posts*, p. 51.

[40] Op de Beeck, *Napoleons nachtmerrie.*, p. 75.

[41] de Brack, *Light cavalry out-posts*, p. 51.

[42] Ibid., p. 51.

Further:

> Every cutting edge is a saw, more or less fine, which produces its effect only by moving horizontally on the object it is used against. To produce this effect at the moment you strike, draw back the hand to the rear; therein lies the secret of the terrible sabre cuts of the Mamelukes.[43]

De Brack even writes about how to sharpen a sword (here he laments that soldiers don't take enough effort to sharpen their blades before combat), which file to use for this job, how to clean and dry the scabbard (and to put the sword gently in the scabbard, because otherwise you can cause edge damage!), how to avoid rust and even provides us with a very interesting anecdote:

> Under the Empire, the cavalry did not carry a hatchet, and the sword was used instead of it, for purposes of the bivouac; the blade and edge consequently were soon in a bad condition; but the troopers, who understood their business, soon found a remedy for this unavoidable abuse of their weapon: 1st, by only using the lower part of the blade in cutting wood, pickets, etc. and thus keeping the upper part in good order for the fight; 2nd, by always carrying with them a small very soft file, with which they sharpened the blade when it had lost its edge.[44]

De Brack also critizes soldiers using their blades to roast meat, which is ruining the temper of the blade, nevertheless sergeant Bourgogne refers several times to this practice.[45]

De Brack concludes his section on the sword with the "General rule; take as much care of the blade of your sword as of the blade of your razor."[46]

II.2.4. F.C. Christmann (and G. Pfeffinger): Theoretisch-Praktische Anleitung des Hau und Stossfechtens (1838)

To conclude this brief description of four valuable works concerning the use of the saber in the army of Napoleon, I have added the treatise of Christmann and Pfeffinger: *Theoretisch-Praktische Anleitung des Hau und Stossfechtens und des Schwadronhauens nach einer ganz neuen Methode bearbeitet* (Theoretical-practical instructions for fencing with cuts and thrusts and against multiple opponents according to a completely new method).

The only biographical information about Christmann can be found in the introduction of his book, written by Pfeffinger. Christmann was born in Germany (*ein geborner Mainzer*), professor in the art of fencing (*professor der fechtkunst*), member of the French fencing

---

[43] Ibid., p. 52.

[44] Ibid., p. 53.

[45] Bourgogne, *Mémoires du sergent Bourgogne (1812-1813)*, ed. by Cottin and Hénault, pp. 63, 102, 108, 261 and 284.

[46] de Brack, *Light cavalry out-posts*, p. 55.

academy in Boulogne and several other German academies. He fought in the *Garde Impérial* (the elite corps of Napoleon) and participated in many battles (*viele Feldzüge*).[47] Unfortunately this is the only information we have about the military career of Christmann. Pfeffinger also adds that Christmann has a lot of experience and taught his method to many students.

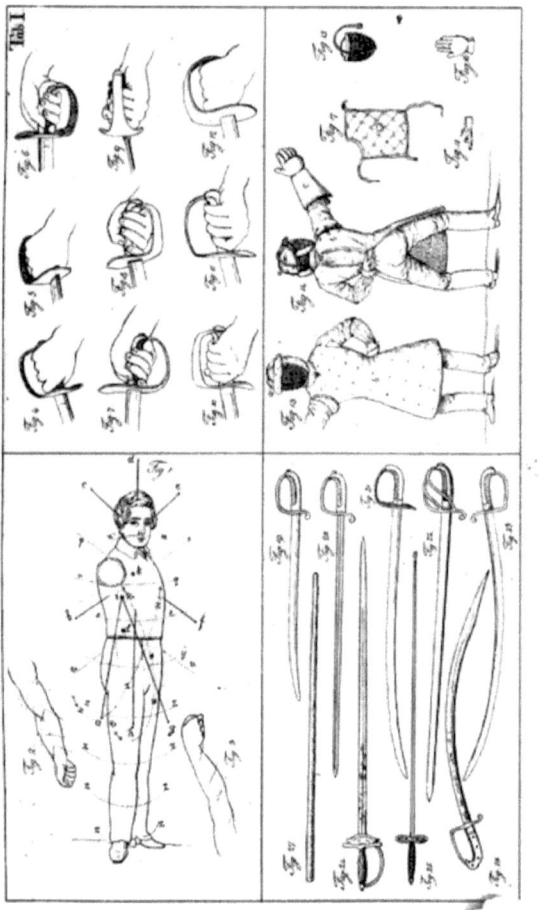

Figure 14: *Christmann,* Theoretisch-Praktische Anleitung des Hau und Stossfechtens *(1838), plate 1.*

Christmann gives a description of the different hilts, the protective gear, the target zones and also of the different kind of sabers.

---

[47] Christmann and Pfeffinger, *Theoretisch-Praktische Anleitung des Hau und Stossfechtens und des Schwadronhauens nach einer ganz neuen Methode bearbeitet,* p. III.

After studying from many masters, Christmann developped his own method (in collaboration with Pfeffinger) and according to Christopher Amberger, the centerpiece of this method is "the changing of the line of attack"[48]

In the introduction to the book, Pfeffinger writes that their system is primarily meant for soldiers of the German army,[49] whether they have to face one or multiple opponents.[50] In the work of Christmann, we see different combat situations where the saber is facing other weapons such as the bayonet and even the lance of a mounted cavalryman. He also adds some interesting 'Bartitsu-like' situations where civilians, armed with sticks or unarmed, have to defend themselves against (un)armed ruffians.

Figure 15: Christmann, Theoretisch-Praktische Anleitung des Hau und Stossfechtens *(1838), plate 10.*

---

[48] Amberger, *Saber fencing: Germany,* 1838.

[49] Christmann and Pfeffinger, *Theoretisch-Praktische Anleitung des Hau und Stossfechtens,* p. V.

[50] Ibid., pp. V-VI.

Figure 16: Christmann, Theoretisch-Praktische Anleitung des Hau und Stossfechtens *(1838), plate 9.*

The treatise of Christmann is not only written for combat, it also deals with the use of the saber as a a way of physical exercise. According to Christman, training with the saber is very helpful for young people to make them healthier and stronger. It takes away theirapathy to turn them in people who are proud on their nation and who have self confidence.[51] These ideas about the physical advantage of training with the saber are elaborated on in the introduction.[52] In this way, Christmann puts a huge emphasis on the sportive aspect of the saber. For people who only want to focus on the sportive aspect, it is possible to fence only with the so called 'legal' techniques, but Christmann adds that he has also included illegal techniques for the soldier who wishes to hit his opponent by all possible means. Of course it is possible for people who only want to use legal techniques to skip the illegal ones, however it is good to know both illegal and legal techniques. Further, Christmann gives advice for people who want to fence without protection to use only cuts and no thrusts.[53]

---

[51] Ibid., pp. VII-IX.

[52] Ibid., pp. 1-25.

[53] Ibid., pp. 26-27.

Figure 17: Christmann, Theoretisch-Praktische Anleitung des Hau und Stossfechtens *(1838), plate 6.*

After this second introduction, the reader still has to wait awhile beforelessons in the art of the saber begin. First he has to go through another theoretical part (Chapter 2) on the kind of sabers, the parts of the saber, protective gear, fencing with the stick, the position of the body, distance between fencers, target zones,… and even how to salute with the saber. After this introduction, the actual lessons start, which are remarkable because of their very systematical approach to fencing.

Without a doubt, Christmann's book is one of the most systematic and elaborate treatises on saber fencing, combining both the sportive and the martial aspect of fencing with the saber.

II.3. Schools

In Napoleonic France, students could go to several specialized military schools, such as the most prestigious *Ecole Militaire Impériale de Saint-Cyr* at Fontainebleau (Paris), where they learned horse riding, fencing, mathematics, military drawing, fortification, geography, history, military administration and human sciences. In another military school, the *Prytanée Militaire* in La Flèche (in the valley of the Loire) several masters were active in dancing, fencing, drawing, French grammar, German, English,…[54]

To become cavalry officer, Louis Rilliet went to the cavalry school of Saint Germain-en-Laye (near Paris), where he studied for three to four years with about 600 students. The

---

[54] *Histoire de la guerre d'Espagne contre Napoléon Buonaparte,* tome I, pp. 96-97.

teaching staff included four teachers of mathematics, four of history-geography, two teachers of literature, two of military administration,... and two fencing masters.[55]

II.4. Masters-at-arms

Most soldiers in the army of Napoleon, however, didn't go to military schools, but learned how to deal with edged weapons from their master-at-arms (*maître d'armes*). This was a soldier or lower officer who was skilled in the use of bladed weapons. Sometimes he was even known as fencing master (*maître d'escrime*) and assisted by provosts (*prévot d'armes*). He was the instructor at the regimental fencing school and could represent the regiment in tournaments against other units. He taught swordmanship and could even provide private lessons for an extra fee. Since the master-at-arms was not an official function in the army, Crowdy adds:

> Perhaps the only formal instruction given to the master and his provosts was to withdraw lessons if the men became stormy and querulous rather than reserved and polite.[56]

It is not clear how frequent these lessons were and probably most of the soldiers learned how to deal with their sabers from the experience they obtained during military campaigns. Joseph Abbeel, who had some experience with horses in his homeland, became member of the carabiniers and is very brief in describing his military training. When he arrived in the military barracks of Lunéville (France) in September of 1806, he received his uniform and learned to walk in military parades on foot and on horseback. On the fourth day he was already challenged to a duel and though he had never had a saber in his hands, he didn't refuse the challenge. This was enough for his adversary who claimed he only wanted to test the bravery of Abbeel. In February 1807 (so after nearly three months of training) the carabineers had to leave to go on campaign, because they "now already had some experience in horseriding and using weapons".[57] When he and his comrades arrived in Bad-Freienwalde (near Berlin) he received some more instruction and that is the last thing Abbeel writes about his training in the use of weapons.

III. TYPES OF SABERS

III.1. Cavalry

As mentioned before, the saber (or sword) was the ultimate weapon of the French cavalry during the Napoleonic wars, but they were also used by the infantry. (The French navy also made use of cutlasses, but because the French were never involved in close quarter

---

[55] Rilliet, *Journal d'un sous-lieutenant de cuirassiers*, p. 6.

[56] Crowdy, *Napoleon's infantry handbook*, p. 48.

[57] My translation from the original Dutch text: Abbeel, *Met Napoleon naar Moskou*, p. 13.

fighting and because the French navy during the Napoleonic era was not succesful, I have omitted the use of the cutlass in the French navy)

Many different types of cavalry sabers were used, but they can generally be divided into three groups: straight sabers (swords), slightly curved sabers and very curved sabers. The straighter the saber, the better it is for thrusting and the deadlier the wound. If needed, it can be used to cut with and it can also be used to hit an enemy who is situated at a lower position or even lying on the ground. Nevertheless, the thrust is more difficult to make than the cut and there is a risk of losing the sword in a thrust because it is difficult to withdraw it.[58] Another risk is that the soldier damages his wrist, as De Brack mentions:

> I have often seen troopers sprain their wrist, and be disabled for a whole campaing from having given a thrust awkwardly; it is easy to understand this, since they oppose only their fore arm to the whole force of the weight and speed of a mounted man. If they had drawn back the arm they would not have been hurt and would have been ready either to renew the attack or to return to the guard.[59]

In this way, the *dragonne* (lanyard or wrist strap) was very handy: a soldier could release his sword after the impact after it had done its deadly work, without actually losing the weapon. The straight blade was advised for the heavy cavalry (cuirassiers and carabiniers), while the lighter cavalry used the curved saber.[60]

---

[58] Reinhard, *The book of swords*, p. 149.

[59] de Brack, *Light cavalry out-posts*, p. 52.

[60] Haythornthwaite, *Napoleonic cavalry*, p. 28.

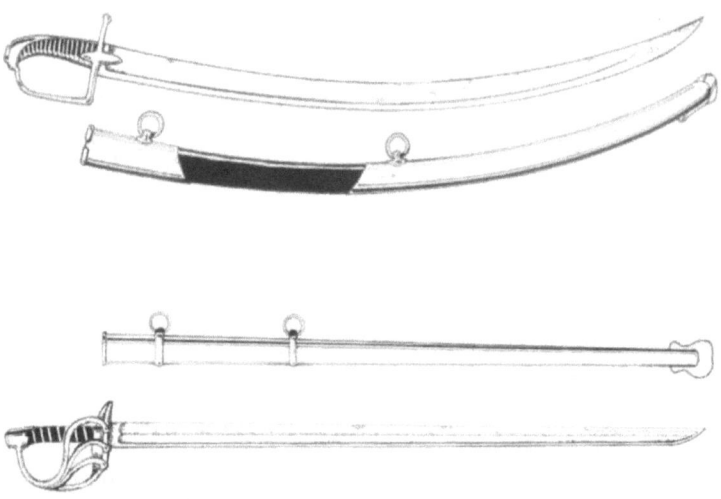

Figure 18: Above: An. IV pattern Hussar saber (model 1795-1796), which inspired the British 1788 light cavalry saber. Below: heavy cavalry saber (sword), an XIII pattern. Both of these weapons were carried in an iron scabbard. Haythornthwaite, Napoleonic cavalry, p. 31.

The curved blade was perhaps easier to use, and with some training it could also be used to thrust. On the other hand, and as illustrated by several examples further in this text, it was much easier to survive a cutting wound.

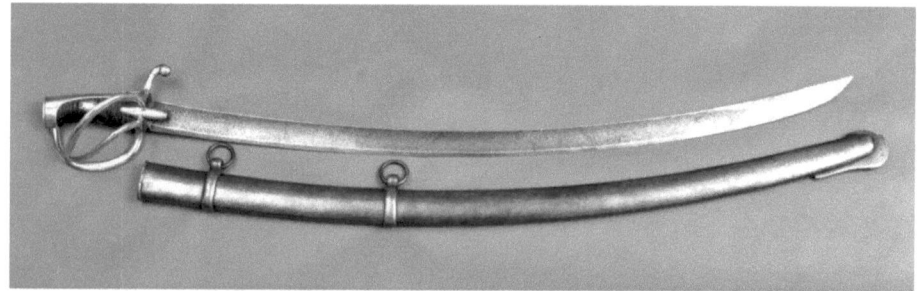

Figure 19: Light cavalry saber (An. XI-pattern, known as the 'chasseur-sabre') and iron scabbard, made at Klingenthal: this was the weapon of the light cavalry, Hussars, Lancers, Chasseurs à Cheval. This saber has a weight of 1,21 kg (the scabbard weights about 1,3 kg) and a blade of 87 cm.
Source: http://swordscollection.blogspot.com.ar (accessed 5 May 2015).
Reproduced with permission of the owner.

Most cavalry blades were kept in iron scabbards, which had a bad influence on the sharpness of the edge and could even cause rusting. On the other hand: leather scabbards were too expensive to make and less sturdy.[61]

Probably most edges were not sharp enough to cut off limbs as a whole and they were certainly not razor sharp. Still, they could have a terrible power, as sergeant Bourgogne tells about his sergeant-major who was involved in a duel and whose head was cut from front to chin.[62]

Cutting off heads (and other body parts) was the the "speciality" of Mamelukes as Dominique Larrey described in his writings (see below) and which is also recorded in other texts. When French soldier Jean-Roch Coignet participated in the Battle of Austerlitz (2 December 1805), he also saw the devastating power of the curved saber of the 48 mamelukes who were involved in the battle

> These mamelukes are excellent horsemen, they can do with their horses whatever they want. With their curved saber, they can cut off a head in just one blow, and with their sharp stirrups they cut the flanks of soldiers.[63]

Though the Mamelukes in the Battle of Austerlitz served under the French flag, they originally were fearsome enemies of the French when they fought them in the Egyptian campaign of Napoleon (1798-1799). The French were so impressed by them, that they made them a small but impressive part of their army. They never actually numbered more than 150 soldiers, though later even Europeans could become member of their regiment, so their numbers increased. The French admired the flamboyant clothing of the mamelukes, their bravery in battle and imitated the Mameluke way of oriental clothing and… sabers.[64]

---

[61] Ibid., p. 28.

[62] Bourgogne, *Mémoires du sergent Bourgogne*, p. 334.

[63] *Ces mamelucks étaient de merveilleux cavaliers; ils faisaient de leur cheval ce qu'ils voulaient. Avec leur sabre recourbé, ils enlevaient une tête d'un seul coup, et avec leurs étriers tranchants ils coupaient les reins d'un soldat.* Coignet, *Les cahiers du capitaine Coignet (1799-1815)*, ed. by Larchey, p. 473.

[64] Pawly and Courcelle, *Napoleon's mamelukes*, pp. p. 8-9 and 15-16.

Figure 20: Reconstruction of French Mameluke Saber, made by Miran Krsticic. Reproduced with permission of the owner.

III.2. Infantry: grenadiers and officers

Even the infantry of Napoleon's army carried sabers (called a *briquet*), in the beginning it was worn by all grenadiers and light infantry, but later it was limited to sub-officers, grenadiers, carabineers and rummers by the imperial decree of 7 October 1807. The weapon was 75 cm long, including 15 cm for the hilt.[65] Similar to the cavalry sabers the briquet was also decorated with a dragonne.

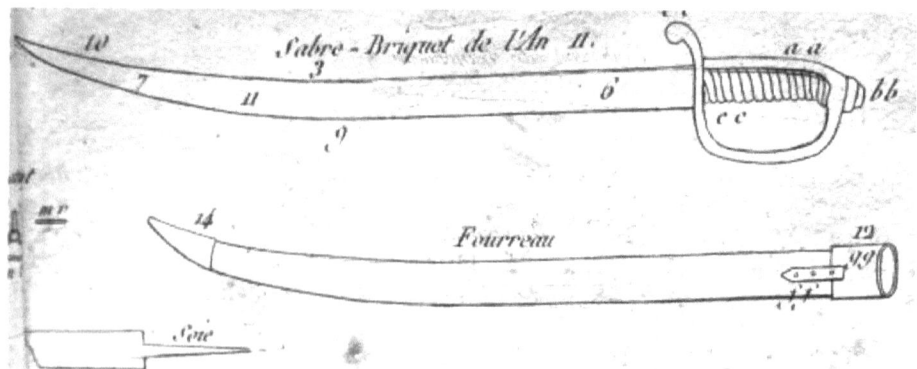

Figure 21: The rounded hand guard made the saber very similar to a tinder striker, hence it was mockingly called 'briquet' (a sort of metal blade to strike against flints to make fire). Crowdy, Napoleon's infantry handbook, p. 101.

---

[65] Crowdy, *Napoleon's infantry handbook*, p. 101.

A special saber was carried by the sappers (*sapeur d'infanterie*) who specialized in performing assault demolitions. They were usuallly much stronger than the common infantrymen and also wore special uniforms (e.g. a leather apron). They were equipped with an axe, heavy gauntlets and a sawtooth saber.[66]

The usual weapon for infantry officers was the spontoon (or espontoon). In regulations from 1779, one can read that this weapon had a blade of about 70 cm, not meant for cutting or parrying but mainly for thrusting. From 1790 onwards, the saber became more popular, probably because the officers wanted to imitate the light cavalry officers.[67]

IV. DUELLING IN THE FRENCH ARMY

Officially, duelling was not permitted in the French army, but in reality it was also not really forbidden and even extremely popular. In 1792 an edict stated that it was forbidden to draw swords within the walls of a fortress, so actually it was acceptable to fight outside of the walls of the garrison or encampment.[68] The example of the 5th Hussars regiment clearly shows why the army staff didn't encourage duelling: in this regiment about eleven soldiers and sub officers died as a result of duelling between 1793 and 1810, in the period between 1796 and 1813 duelling wounds caused 19 soldiers and sub officers to be unable to perform their duties.[69] Nevertheless, and in spite of strong moral condemnations against duelling (as by Barrère in the *Moniteur* 183 of 2 July 1791), duelling wasn't even mentioned in the French national law and there was certainly no specific law against it.[70] According to Cohen "courts tended to act only when a fatality resulted from a breach of established etiquette."[71]

Duels between soldiers indeed had certain rules of etiquette: after an official challenge, the details were arranged between the offended parties with the assistance of 'seconds'. These seconds agreed on time and place and they could even act as mediators when one of the parties wanted a way of reconciliation. It was also the seconds who determined the choice of weapons: pistols or sabers. The choice for pistols was usually influenced by an injury to one or both of the duellists, which caused him not to be able to fight with an edged weapon (so he had to choose a distance weapon such as the pistol).[72] Usually duellists fought naked to the waist (or with open shirt), so they were unable to wear hidden

---

[66] Ibid., p. 47.

[67] Ibid., p. 102.

[68] Ibid., p. 155.

[69] Massoni, *Histoire d'un régiment de cavalerie légère*, p. 229.

[70] Briost, Drévillon and Serna, *Croiser le fer*, pp. 462-463.

[71] Cohen, *By the sword*, p. 97.

[72] Crowdy, *Napoleon's infantry handbook*, p. 155.

protective mail under their shirts. This mail was sometimes even coloured in flesh colour (called *supersticerie*), to hide it even better.[73]

A fine example of etiquette between duellists can be found in the memoires of captain Parquin (1786-1845) who was involved in a duel with smallswords: his first thrust was deflected by the buckle of the suspenders of Malet, his opponent, and made him bleed slightly. For Parquin's opponent, this was not a real wound, so he wanted to continue the fight. After several exchanges and driving back his adversary, Parquin managed to give him a thrust in the right side, which caused Malet to fall down. Immediately Parquin ran to Malet to help him and even asked his own seconds to help his brave adversary. Together they brought Malet to the army surgeon who told them that the wounded Malet was going to survive his wound without any problem.[74]

Figure 22: Parquin and Malet are about to duel.
Parquin, Récits de guerre ([1842], 1892), p. 107.

Dominique Larrey (see below) mentions several cases of soldiers whom he treated after they had fought in duels. One soldier had his forearm amputated because Larrey feared the soldier would get infected with gangrene.[75] In one case Larrey dedicated several pages to describe the treatment and healing process of the arm wound of Pierre Cadrieux, who was injured in a duel. Not one bad word is said about the origin of the wound, Larrey

---

[73] Cohen, *By the sword,* p. 97.

[74] Parquin, *Récits de guerre: Souvenirs du capitaine Parquin,* pp. 106-108.

[75] Larrey, *Mémoires de chirurgie militaire et campagnes,* p. 455.

seems very enthusiastic to describe the complex arm wound and how he could heal it, it is even used as an interesting case in the Medical School of Paris.[76]

Several French officers had a history of duelling: Pierre Augereau (1757-1816), son of a Parisian fruit-seller, fencing master, officer of Napoleon who started as a common soldier was a famous duellist. He had the reputation of a champion swordsman and had to flee the army after killing an officer in a quarrel. During this travelling life, he worked as a fencing master and even taught dancing, until he returned to the army in 1792 when deserters received amnesty from the government. In the army of Napoleon, he became a famous commander, known for his bravery and meticulous clothing and apperance.[77]

The most famous duel between two Frenchmen during the Napoleontic era was the duel between Fournier Sarlovèze (1773-1827) and an officer named Dupont. Sarlovèze was known as the "demon of the Grande Armée" and loved challenging civilians to duel with him, but he became legendary because of a long series of duels which lasted from 1794 to 1813. Finally, Dupont wanted to stop this stupid behaviour – he was about to marry- and challenged Fournier to a pistol duel. Fournier wasted his two shots and was delivered to the mercy of Dupont who still had two bullets left which made Fournier eternally in debt to Dupont and thus a long series of duelling (lasting almost 20 years) was ended.[78]

The story of the duel between these two men was the source of inspiration for Joseph Conrad's story *The Duel*, which was the basis of the movie by Ridley Scott, *The Duellists* (1977).

V. INDIVIDUAL MARTIAL PROWESS ON THE BATTLEFIELD

Stories about individual swordsmen are the most fascinating ones and in this chapter I will briefly present some spectacular stories of individual sword or saber wielding bravery on the battlefield. The power of the cavalry lay in its massed force of thousands of armed men, augmented by the speed and weight of their horses, which made them into a huge and heavy hammer designed to smash the enemy, as the most famous cavalry charge of the army of Napoleon demonstrated at Eylau (7-8 February 1807). Here the cavalry of Murat sabred down the Russian artillery and made a difficult battle into a questionable and bloody French victory.

Nevertheless, there are several stories of individual martial bravery and skill. Sometimes individual soldiers even challenged their enemies to a personal duel in the empty space between the opposing lines of battle.[79]

---

[76] Ibid., pp. 896-901.

[77] Haythornthwaitj and Courcelle, *Napoleon's commanders*, pp. 10-11.

[78] Elting, *Swords around a throne: Napoleon's Grande Armée*, pp. 174 and 694.

[79] Ibid., p. 602.

V.1. Jean-Louis Michel (1785-1865)

The best swordsman ever in the army of Napoleon was without doubt the mulatto Jean-Louis Michel (1785-1865), who was born in Haiti and came to France in 1796 as *un pupille de régiment*. Only eleven years old, probably a war orphan, looking fragile, he learned to fence from the fencing master of the regiment, the Flemishman M. d'Erape. His talents were soon discovered and soon Jean-Louis was known for his omitting of everything in fencing that he saw as superfluous: saluting, contre-coups, pauses,... In 1804 he was insulted for being a mulatto swordsmen and Jean-Louis was forced to duel. His opponent could use a normal sword, but Jean-Louis preferred a buttoned foil by which he gave his opponent a terrible punishment. He smashed him so hard in the face that he was knocked over and left bleeding on the floor. But his greatest achievement had yet to come. In 1812 the Italians who were fighting under Napoleon in Spain, refused to support their French colleagues and started to fight against them. It didn't take long for the first victims to fall, so the officers had to find a solution: it was decided that fifteen fencing masters and provosts from the Italians and Frenchmen had to fight in succession until only one regiment didn't have any man left. The two quarrelling teams went outside Madrid and some thousand men (and their families) watched the 30 people fighting for their lives. Jean-Louis fought on the French side against his first opponent, the Italian Giacomo Ferari, a tall man with a lot of combat experience. Jean-Louis defeated him without any problem, waited two minutes for the next opponent and kept on fighting until someone would injure him fatally... but that was not so easy. No less than 13 Italians were dead or seriously wounded and Jean-Louis was still standing. Though he was also bleeding, he wanted to defeat the last two Italians, who were full of fear. Then it was decided to stop the fight and the army shouted *"Vive Jean-Louis!"* *"Vive le 32ième"* (the regiment of the French)! *Vive le 1er* (the regiment of the Italians)! Jean-Louis shouted back: *"We are all one and the same family. Vive l'Armée!"* Jean-Louis retired to Metz, where he opened a fencing school, which later moved to Montpellier. Until his death, and even blind - so he had to do everything by touch- Jean-Louis kept on teaching.[80]

V.2. Jean-Baptiste Guindey/Guindet (1785-1813)

One of the most famous stories about martial skill, mentioned in several Napoleonic memoirs, is told about sergeant Jean-Baptiste Guindey/Guindet (1785-1813), quartermaster of the 10th Hussars. During the Battle of Saalfeld (10 October 1806) Guindey was confronted with the Prussian prince Louis (Lewis) Ferdinand. Baron de Marbot (1782-1854) gives us a detailled description of the fight:

> Prince Lewis might yet have fallen back on the Prussian force which was occupying Jena, but having been the prime instigator of the war it seemed to him unseemly to retire without fighting. He was cruelly punished for his temerity. Marshal Lannes, cleverly taking advantage of

---

[80] Cohen, *By the sword*, pp. 97-99.

the high ground under which Prince Lewis had so imprudently deployed his troops, first played upon them with artillery, and when they were shaken sent forward his masses of infantry, who, rapidly descending from the high ground, poured like a torrent on the Prussian battalions and broke them up in a moment. Prince Lewis, losing his head, and probably seeing the mistake he had made, tried to repair it by putting himself at the head of his cavalry, with which he impetuously charged the 9th and 10th Hussars. At first he gained a slight advantage, but our hussars, returning to the charge with fury, threw back the Prussian cavalry into the marshes, their infantry at the same time flying in confusion before ours. In the middle of the scuffle Prince Lewis found himself engaged hand-to-hand with a sergeant of the 10th Hussars, named Guindet. Being summoned to surrender, he answered with a sword-stroke which laid open the Frenchman's face, whereupon the other ran the prince through the body, killing him on the spot.[81]

Even de Brack mentions this fight:

> As soon as you have delivered the thrust, if the enemy does not surrender, deal him a backhanded blow; it was thus that Guindet killed the Prince of Prussia at Saalfield.[82]

For his action Guindey received the cross of honour, though Napoleon regretted that the prince was not taken alive. When Guindey heard about this – he was in the hospital when Napoleon uttered his regrets – he replied that Louis-Ferdinand was not really in the mood to surrender…[83] Unfortunately, Guindey lost his own life in the Battle of Hanau (20 October 1813): his body was entirely covered with saber wounds and he was surrounded by several dead Bavarian horsemen, whom he made pay terribly for his death.[84]

---

[81] de Marbot, *The memoirs of Baron de Late*, ed. by Butler, p. 178.

[82] de Brack, *Light cavalry out-posts*, p. 52.

[83] Parquin, *Récits de guerre*, p. 45.

[84] Ibid., p. 142.

*Figure 23: The fatal duel between Louis-Ferdinand and Guindey
Parquin,* Récits de guerre *([1842], 1892), plate 4.*

V.3. Jean Baptiste Antoine Marcellin de Marbot (1782-1854)

Marbot, who provided us the story of Guindey, was also involved in a very serious saber fight, when he was fighting in Spain (1811) under general Masséna.

> So, being sure that the orders had been conveyed, I was about to return, when a young English light infantry officer trotted up on his pony, crying, 'Stop, Mr. Frenchman; I should like to have a little fight with you!' I saw no need to reply to this bluster, and was making my way towards our outposts, 500 yards in arrear, while the Englishman followed me, heaping insults on me. At first I took no notice, but presently he called out, 'I can see by your uniform that you are on the staff of a marshal, and I will put in the London papers that the sight of me was enough to frighten away one of Massena's or Ney's cowardly aides-de-camp!' I admit that it was a serious error on my part, but I could no longer endure this impudent challenge coolly, so, drawing my sword, I dashed furiously at my adversary. But just as I was about to meet him, I heard a rustling in the wood, and out came two English hussars, galloping to cut off my retreat. I was caught in a trap, and understood that only a most energetic defence could save me from the disgrace of being taken prisoner, through my own fault, in sight of the whole French army, which was witness to this unequal combat. So I

flew upon the English officer; we met; he gave me a slash across the face, I ran my sword into his throat. His blood spurted over me, and the wretch fell from his horse to the ground, which he bit in his rage. Meanwhile, the two hussars were hitting me all over, chiefly on the head. In a few seconds my shako, my wallet, and my pelisse were in strips, though I was not myself wounded by any of their blows. At length, however, the elder of the two hussars, a grizzled old soldier, let me have more than an inch of his point in my right side. I replied with a vigorous backhander; my blade struck his teeth and passed between his jaws, as he was in the act of shouting, slitting his mouth to the ears. He made off promptly, to my lively satisfaction for he was by far the braver and more energetic of the two. When the younger man found himself left alone with me, he hesitated for a moment, because as our horses' heads were touching, he saw that to turn his back to me was to expose himself to be hit. However, on seeing several soldiers coming to my aid, he made up his mind, but he did not escape the dreaded wound, for in my anger I pursued him for some paces and gave him a thrust in the shoulder, which quickened his speed. During this fight, which lasted less time than it has taken to tell it, our scouts had come up quickly to set me free, and on the other side the English soldiers had marched towards the place where their officer had fallen. The two groups were firing at each other, and I was very near getting in the way of the bullets from both sides. But my brother and Ligniville, who had seen me engaged with the English officer and his two men, had hastened up to me, and I was badly in want of their help, for I was losing so much blood from the wound in my side that was growing faint, and I could not have stayed on my horse if they had not held me up. As soon as I rejoined the staff, Masséna said, taking my hand, 'Well done; rather too well done! A field officer has no business to expose himself in fighting at the outposts.' The wound in my cheek was not important; in a month's time it had healed over, and you can scarcely see the mark of it along my left whisker.[85]

V.4. Grenadier Hennin (died 1805)

Marbot managed to defeat three cavalry men in one fight, but what about grenadier Hennin, who killed seven Austrians with his saber in the Battle of Ulm (16-19 October 1805) as recorded by Nicolas Devout (1770-1823) in one of his letters to marshal Berthier (1753-1815). Hennin, who was fighting in the 108th line, was standing in the middle of an Austrian troop of soldiers and tried to grab their flag. His own musket was broken so only his saber was left to fight with. With success, he killed seven enemies and maybe he

---

[85] Marbot, *The memoirs of Baron de Late,* II, pp. 146-147.

could have killed more but his weapon broke and he was killed... Davout adds: *cette mort est digne d'un grenadier français* (this death is suitable for a French grenadier).[86]

V.5. Leaulteur

Sometimes the name of the individual swordsman is lost, as is the case of an anonymous French officer (or is he called M. Lealteur?) who defended the emperor the day after the Battle of Maloyaroslavets (24 October 1812). Sergeant Bourgogne records how this officer was defending Napoleon when he was surrounded by cossacks. Using his saber, the Frenchman killed one Cossack and wounded several of them but lost his weapon and military hat. Because he didn't have any weapon left, he took a lance of the enemy and kept on fighting. A grenadier à cheval saw what was happening and took his comrade for a Russian and pierced him with his saber. The grenadier realized what he had done and wanted to kill himself by taking as many enemies with him as possible, but didn't succeed. Now he became a hero and killed many of them with his saber. He was covered with blood and when there was no enemy left he went to his own men to ask about the officer he wounded. Luckily the officer survived his wound and could return to France.[87]

V.6. Marie-Thérèse Figueur (1774-1861)

Most of the deeds of arms were performed by men, but sometimes remarkable women appear. One of them was Mademoiselle Marie-Thérèse Figueur (1774-1861), also known as Madame Sans-Gêne (the lady without shame), who served as a women dragoon in the army of Napoleon. She dictated her memories to a certain Saint Germain, so we are well – but maybe not neutrally- informed about her life. When she was soldier in the revolutionary Army of the Eastern Pyrenees, she had to flee the enemy and rallied her comrades to follow her. Suddenly someone pointed a gun at her, but Madame Sans-Gêne was not afraid: she rushed to her opponent and hit him in the throat with her saber, in her words: *c'est ce qu'en langage militaire nous appelons le coup du cochon* (this is what we call in military language: the cut of the pig[88]). Marie-Thérèse didn't even notice that his bullet hit her helmet and messed up her hair on the left side. Later, in a battle against the Austrians (1799: Battle of Savigliano), she received four sword blows on her back, but she was only lightly wounded. When she was taken away as prisoner, some farmers tried to take off her wet boots and this caused her, in combination with the four wounds on her back, the most terrible pain of her entire life: "it was as if the ruffian was skinning my legs".[89]

During her career, several of her horses were shot from under her and she was also taken prisoner, twice by Austrian and twice by Spanish soldiers.

---

[86] Davout, *Le Maréchal Davout, Prince d'Eckmühl*, ed. by d' Eckmühl de Blocqueville, pp. 70-71.

[87] Bourgogne, *Mémoires du sergent Bourgogne*, pp. 59-60.

[88] Figueur, *Les campagnes de mademoiselle Thérèse Figueur, aujourd'hui Madame Veuve Sutter*, p. 63.

[89] Ibid., p. 96.

V.7. Madeleine Kintelberger

The last example of martial prowess is a truly exceptional story but almost forgotten in history. In 1805 a detachment of the French Seventh Hussar Regiment was attacked by a much larger group of Russian soldiers and was about to collapse. One of the fighters was Madeleine Kintelberger who lost her husband Joseph Kintelberger in the fight and who was now hopelessly trying to protect her six children. While her children were sheltering behind the ammuniton of the regiment, her husband dying in front of her eyes after he was struck by a cannon ball, and being pregnant for about six months, Madeleine was also hit by a cannon ball which almost tore away her right arm below the shoulder. Nevertheless Madeleine took up a sword, wielded it expertly and fought off several mounted attackers. Meanwhile she was bleeding from her arm and got injured again by saber cuts and lance wounds. The cossacks wanted to take this exceptional woman alive and shot her in the leg, but this didn't stop the brave lady from fighting, so they shot her in the other leg. Then the cossacks captured her and her wounded children and escaped from the battelfield. In captivity her arm was amputated, her other thirteen wounds were taken care of and, in prison, she gave birth to a twin. In 1806 she could return to her homeland, because of the temporary peace between France and Russia. General Jean Rapp provided a luxury coach to transport Madeleine and her children back to France where she received an extraordinary pension by Napoleon himelf, who never saw such an act of bravery.[90] Thomas Cardoza, who writes about this story, adds:

> Nevertheless, despite her almost unbelievable courage and suffering, today Madeleine Kintelberger is totally forgotten. She appears in no history books, no monument reminds us of her deeds, and even in her own country she remains completely unknown.[91]

VI. WOUNDS CAUSED BY THE SABER

VI.1. Introduction

Soldiers and officers in the army of Napoleon lead a life full of risks and sometimes the list of injuries a soldier could have during his entire life was absolutely impressive. Marshall Nicolas-Charles Oudinot (1767-1847) was injured about 25 times during his military career:[92]

- 1793: ball in the head (Haguenau)
- 1794: leg broken by ball (Trèves)
- 1795: five saber cuts, one ball (Neckarau)

---

[90] Cardoza, *Intrepid women*, pp. 1-2.

[91] Ibid. p. 2.

[92] Haythornthwaite and Courcelle, *Napoleon's commanders*, p. 47.

- 1796: four saber cuts, one ball (Ingolstadt)
- 1799: ball in chest (Rosenberg), ball in shoulder blade (Schwyz), ball in chest (Zürich)
- 1805: ball in thigh (Hollabrunn)
- 1807: leg broken when horse fell (Danzig)
- 1809: saber cut (Essling), ear nearly shot off (Wagram)
- 1812: grapeshot in shoulder (Polotsk), ball through body and dragged (Berezina)
- 1814: cannon ball grazes both thighs (Brienne), ball in chest (Arcis-sur Aube): Of particular interest is that this last wound was less serious because it was deflected by his decoration of the Legion of Honor

Maybe receiving 10 saber cuts during your entire military career sounds like a lot, but not one soldier probably received more saber cuts than colonel Chipault of the 4th Cuirassiers who had received 52 sabre cuts in the battle of Heilsberg (10 June 1807). He fainted from bloodloss but, after recovering, continued to serve his country.[93]

VI.2. Saber wounds treated and cured by Dominique Larrey (1766-1842)

In his famous work *Mémoires de chirurgie militaire et campagnes* (Memories on military surgery and campaigns) Dominique Larrey (1766-1842) describes many of his operations on wounded soldiers. Most of the wounds Larrey and his assistants had to treat were caused by guns, but we can also find many references to wounds caused by sabers. Larrey himself was even wounded twice (on the head) and on the left shoulder by a saber at the battle of Waterloo, when he was trying to flee and even defended himself with his own two pistols and saber.[94]

It is interesting to note that the wounds caused by edged weapons, even on the head, usually healed without problems and also quite quickly.

---

[93] Nougaret, *Anecdotes militaires, anciennes et modernes, des Français*, p. 305.

[94] Larrey, *Mémoires de chirurgie militaire et campagnes*, II p. 974.

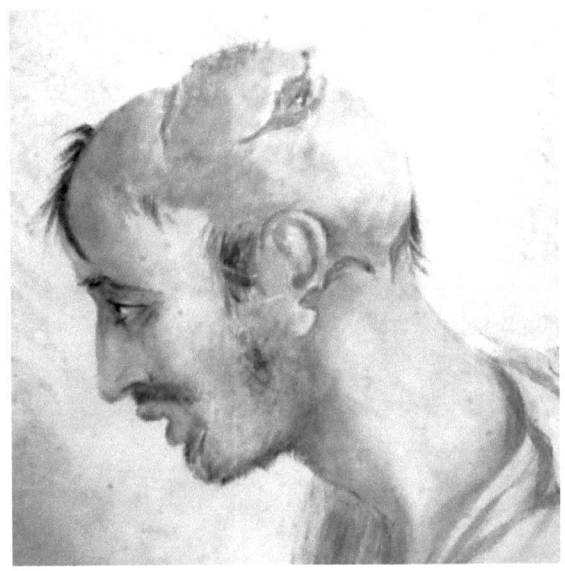

Figure 24: Soldier suffering from head and facial injuries, profile inscribed "Waterloo".
Sabre wound to head,
Hospital de la Gendarmerie, 5 July 1815.
On the image can been seen that the head is shaven to make the treatment,
usually suturing and bandaging, more easy.
Watercolour 1836 by Charles Bell
The RAMC Muniment Collection in the care of the Wellcome Library, Wellcome Images

In 1799, during the Egyptian campaign, lieutenant-colonel Paultre received several saber cuts and the thrust of a lance but he recovered after six weeks.[95] More serious was the wound of Pierre Soult, member of the 22nd Chasseurs, who obtained a heavy saber wound from a Mameluke in his occipital bone (back bottom of the skull). This cut divided the extensor muscles of his head as far as the sixth vertebra at which point the spinous process was cut. An enormous piece of skin was hanging on his shoulders and his chin fell on his chest. Though this wound looked horrible, Larrey sutured the infection and bandaged it. The patient was fully recovered after a short amount of time, though Larrey adds in a footnote that the soldier could not produce any children anymore after suffering from this wound.[96]

This Mameluke cut was clearly meant to cut off the head of the French soldier, but soldiers might not only lose their head in battle. Larrey gives several examples of operations in which the faces of soldiers were afflicted by saber wounds but nevertheless could be treated succesfully by suturing: Gardel (nose, cheek and part of his jaw bone),

---

[95] Larrey, *Mémoires de chirurgie militaire et campagnes,* I p. 212.

[96] Ibid., I, p. 280.

Thévenin (eyebrow, eyelid, cheekbone and cheek), Pierre Leclerc (nose and cheek), Jerdet and Lejuste (nose) and Rivière Brocard (left part of head near the ear).[97] General Dommanget received serveral saber blows in the battle of Moscow (1812), several cuts on his scalp, one on his lip and even a cut which damaged several teeth and made him look horrible and unrecognisable. Larrey removed several broken teeth, sutured the lip and the general could return to France. Later only a small scar was seen on his lip, but no other deformity.[98] Larrey was also successful in operating on the nose of a Russian colonel without leaving any deformity afterwards.[99] It is interesting to note that Larrey likes to add that he performed an operation which left the patient afterwards without any scar or only a small scar. Surprisingly not many images can be found of soldiers and officers with scars on their heads, as a result of saber wounds.

To my knowledge, only three clear images exist, which I present here:

Figure 25: Adam Adalbert von Neipperg (1775-1829) was heavily wounded in 1794: bayonet thrust in the right arm and saber cut on his right eye.
(Allgemeine Deutsche Biographie, 1886, 23, c. 408)
Source:
http://en.wikipedia.org/wiki/Adam_Albert_von_Neipperg#/media/File:Neipperg.jpg
(accessed 6 May 2015).

---

[97] Ibid., I, pp. 590-592.

[98] Ibid., II, p. 1148.

[99] Ibid., II, pp. 734-735.

Figure 26: During the Battle of Waterloo, Pierre-François Durutte (1767-1827), commander of the 4th devidion received two heavy saber blows: one in the face and one on the right hand, which had to be amputated the day after.
Source: http://fr.wikipedia.org/wiki/Pierre_François_Joseph_Durutte (accessed 6 May 2015).

Figure 27: Joachim Hyppolite Lepic (1768-1835), brother of the famous general Lepic, received several saber cuts in his entire career.
On this image one can clearly see the scar on his face, made by a saber in June 1807.
Source: http://fr.wikipedia.org/wiki/Joachim_Hippolyte_Lepic (accessed 6 May 2015).

But not only the upper part of the body was a target. François Bernard was wounded by a saber in his lower abdomen. Some of the intestines had already come out, but Larrey put them back and the patient survived after six weeks.[100] During the Russian campaign (1812) Larrey had to operate on a certain Arbette, who received a saber thrust in his lower abdomen. Though the patient suffered terribly from inflammation, he did recover after about one month.[101] Larrey also mentions the case of officer Netherwood who received a very deep cut from a Mameluke during the Egyptian campaign. A Mameluke saber cut him very deep in the right thigh but Larrey sutured Netherwood with about ten stitches, after which the patient walked as before.[102]

In certain cases, certainly when surgeons feared the risk of gangrene,[103] an amputation of the wounded member was necessary, as the case of colonel Sourd illustrates. Sourd was colonel of the 20th regiment of the Chasseurs à cheval and was wounded several times by saber cuts on the right arm. Two wounds were situated on the joints of the wrist and the elbow but a third cut had gone through the muscles in the arm until it reached the bone. Larrey and his assistants judged that an amputation was necessary and performed the operation, during which Sourd did not show any signs of pain and even dictated a letter to the Emperor asking that he be able to keep command of his regiment. The bandage was only just attached when Sourd mounted and went back to the battle and survived.[104] Sometimes amputation wasn't a success and the patient died immediately after, as the case of Joseph Grandi illustrated when he received a saber cut in the joint of his right knee.[105] The patient could also die after a few days: Jean Lapaix also suffered from a saber cut in his right knee. Lapaix asked for the amputation after five days, and in the beginning he seemed to heal but after fifteen days he died anyway. Larrey adds that he had seen many similar cases of people dying because the doctors were afraid to amputate.[106]

---

[100] Ibid., I, p. 592.

[101] Ibid., II, p. 865.

[102] Ibid., II, p. 1172.

[103] Ibid., I, pp. 455 and 642-643.

[104] Ibid., II, pp. 973 and 1182.

[105] Ibid., I, p. 443.

[106] Ibid., I, pp. 443-444.

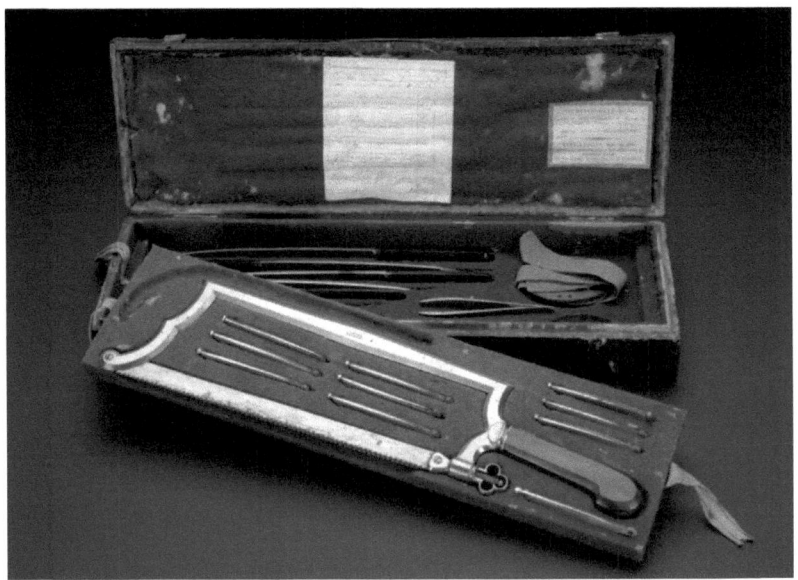

Figure 28: Amputation instrument set, Strasbourg, France, 1780-1820
Source: Science Museum London
≤http://www.sciencemuseum.org.uk/broughttolife/objects/display.aspx?id=5476> (accessed 6 May 2015)

The example of Sourd illustrates that the wrist and arm were a possible target and these are also the body parts where Pierre Larrey was wounded in 1810. Because Larrey saw inflammation of the wound, he executed the amputation in less than one minute and his patient survived.[107]

The most bizzare wound treated by Larrey happened during the second battle of Aboukir (1799). When general Dermoncourt was leading his troops, his saber was broken by a large musket ball. The broken saber blade flew through the air and struck a soldier behind Dermoncourt in his thigh penetrating about 4 to 5 cm deep. When other soldiers saw this wound, they were very angry at the enemy because they thought they charged their cannons with broken saber blades. Larrey added to this story that he explained to the soldiers what really had happened and that this wound was not so special for him because he had seen many similar cases during his entire campaign. Larrey also added that the healing of the soldier occured without any problem.[108]

---

[107] Ibid., I, p. 280.

[108] Ibid., II, p. 1142.

VI.3. Protection against saberblows to the head

Because many saber cuts were aimed at the head, soldiers wore shakos or sometimes even leather helmets, reinforced with a brass band.[109] The anecdote of Marbot in Spain illustrates how even simple shakos, without brass or iron bands, could provide a certain way of protection against blows to the head. Cuirassiers and carabiniers had beautifully decorated steel helmets which provided better protection.

Of course head protection could be lost, so a very popular method of giving extra protection to the head were the so called *cadenettes*: braids on both side of the head, sometimes around a wooden core. These cadenettes partially protected the side of the face against saber cuts.[110]

VII. OTHER WAYS OF USING THE SABER: PUNISHMENT AND PRIZE

Sometimes the flat of the blade was used to punish prisoners, or as in the case of Marie-Thérèse Figueur, the flat was used to encourage her not to slow down when she was taken away as prisoner.[111]

Sergeant Bourgogne tells the story about a Russian officer who uses the flat of his saber on his own soldiers who where trying to flee from the battlefield.[112]

When he was still general, Napoleon had the custom of giving honorary swords and pistols to brave and valliant soldiers. There was some discussion as to whether he really had the authority to do so, but nevertheless, he gave valuable, beautifully decorated and inscribed weapons to his soldiers as early as 1797 (In the Italian campaing he had given about one hundred sabers to his heroes) and in 1798.[113] In this practice, Napoleon was not an innovator because, already in 1796, the Directory government had started to give ornate weapons to brave soldiers or units.[114]

VIII. AND NAPOLEON HIMSELF?

Unfortunately not much can be found about Napoleon's own martial skills. As a young boy of ten years old, he went to the Ecole Militaire royale in Brienne-le-Château, near Troyes in the Champagne region. Every day the young students had eight hours of course: mathematics, Latin, history, German, geography, natural sciences, science of fortifications

---

[109] Crowdy, *Napoleon's infantry handbook,* p. 72.

[110] Ibid., p. 78.

[111] Figueur, *Les campagnes de mademoiselle Thérèse Figueur,* p. 107.

[112] Bourgogne, *Mémoires du sergent Bourgogne,* p. 112.

[113] Crowdy, *Napoleon's infantry handbook,* pp. 135-136 and Gallaher, *Napoleon's enfant terrible,* p. 112

[114] Crowdy, *Napoleon's infantry handbook,* p. 136.

and of weapons, dancing, music and also fencing. In 1784 Napoleon graduated at Brienne and was admitted to the very prestigiuos Ecole Royale Militaire near the Seine in Paris. Here he had the same courses as in Brienne, but without history of strategy and battle. New courses were musket shooting, military marching and horse riding.[115] In Brienne his achievements in fencing and dancing had been marked as 'very poor', but in Paris he became better and was known for the amount of blades he had broken.[116]

After the graduation of Napoleon at the Ecole Royale, there is not one reference to Napoleon's personnal achievements with the saber, though he had a huge collection of decorated sabers – even one in his coffin.[117] - and is almost always depicted with a saber or smallsword.

Figure 29: The fencing lesson: Little (though he was 1m68, which was an average height in his time) Napoleon is fencing against von Blücher while a British sailor is juding the match. Blücher is supported by German peasants and even a Russian cossack.
Ink and watercolour caricature made by the Prussian artist Johann Gottfried Shadow
Source: World digital Library (≤http://www.wdl.org/en/item/2944/>, accessed 6 May 2015)

One notable exception can be found at the end of Napoleon's military career. In the Battle of Arcis-sur-Aube (20 March 1814), the emperor himself was at the head of his

---

[115] Roberts, *Napoleon de Grote*, pp. 32 and 38.

[116] Cohen, *By the sword*, p. 96.

[117] Op de Beeck, *Napoleon, deel II*, p. 728.

own troops and fought, saber in hand. It is very well possible that he was searching for his death on the battlefield, but could not find it.[118]

In contrast to many of his officers (Ney, Marbot, Augereau, baron de Lasalle,...) there are no stories about Napoleon involved in duelling. When people challenged him to a duel, he simply declined, as was the case when the king of Sweden challenged him to duel with him.[119] According to Mike Loades, Napoleon would have said: "It's too bad that death often results from duelling, for duels otherwise help keep up politeness in society."[120] Though this quote seems to say that Napoleon didn't have any problems with duelling, in reality he saw this as a waste of manpower. According to Elting "he especially disliked the professional duellist, whom he compared to a cannibal."[121] Cohen also confirms this negative view of Napoleon against duelling: a good duellist made a bad soldier and besides this, many soldiers in his army had died or were seriously injured because of a matter of honour.[122] Parquin tells an interesting story about Napoleon's opposition against duelling. When the emperor saw the huge scar on the face of Captain Lion, which was caused by duelling, he asked him where the scar came from. Lion replied that it happened in Ulm. On hearing this, the emperor rewarded him because he thought it happened during the Battle of Ulm (16-19 October 1805). Lion didn't lie, because he received the wound in Ulm, not on the battlefield but in a duel... If the emperor had known this, he would never have rewarded Lion.[123]

IX. CONCLUSION

Without any doubt, the saber was not the most deadly, but certainly the most honourable weapon during Napoleonic warfare. Even today, it is still an iconic weapon, symbolizing the personal contact between two warriors, in which bravery and martial prowess played an important role. A scar obtained from a saber was not something to wear with shame, but was a proud mark of bravery on the battlefield or in a personal duel.

Though it was not the most deadly weapon, it still played an important role in the hands of an experienced cavalry soldier. Here, in combination with the speed and weight of a horse, and wielded by a large group of cavalrists it was the *conditio sine qua non* for a successful cavalry charge. These charges, as proven in the Battle of Eylau, could change the course of a battle from defeat into victory.

---

[118] Ibid. p. 530.

[119] Cohen, *By the sword*, p. 97.

[120] Loades, *Swords and swordsmen*, p. 459.

[121] Elting, *Swords around a throne*, p. 97.

[122] Cohen, *By the sword*, p. 97.

[123] Parquin, *Récits de guerre*, p. 43.

In this article, I have selected only a few stories of martial prowess, in which individual soldiers survived or became famous because of their talent in wielding the saber. Still, many more individual stories are waiting for scholars to be discovered. [124]

Are there conclusions to be made for people practising military saber in the world of Historical European Martial Arts? This research has certainly proven that in combat the afterblow was very frequent: hitting someone on the head certainly didin't cause his death – as in the case of Louis-Ferdinand - and it was very important to riposte the attack of a wounded opponent. It was also very difficult to leave a saber duel unharmed, wounds occurred frequently, but good surgeons could easily treat these. The fact of bein being wounded in a battle, even on the head, and continuing to fight, is something which can never be imitated in HEMA, where the use of sharp weapons is not possible and where no napoleonic uniforms are worn. Some questions will certainly be unanswerd: How sharp were individual blades of individual soldiers? How resistant was their body (covered in leather or other clothing) to a deep cut? When did soldiers feel pain enough to leave the battlefield? Personally, I strongly believe there is an uncrossable gap between our present day HEMA and the world of napoleonic soldiers who fought under harsh conditions, whose survival was dependent from their use of the sword, who wanted to achieve glory on the battlefield and shine in the eyes of their commanders or give the example in front of their men. Those are things from the past and can never return or simulated in a present day saber bout.

On the other side, it is possible today to set up rules concerning the target zone (head only or also other parts of the body?), the kind of hit (with a thrust or with a cut?), the amount of protection (fencing jacket, gloves or only fencing mask?) and concerning the afterblow (one, two or three afterblows?).

I also think it can be very valuable and interesting to experiment with different kind of sabers, because the French soldiers had to fence against Mamelukes with very curved sabers or cuirassiers with straight swords. Maybe this could be a challenge for the future of the military saber in HEMA?

X. BIBLIOGRAPHY

X.1. Primary Literature

Adrien Bourgogne, *Mémoires du sergent Bourgogne (1812-1813), publiés d'après le manuscrit original,* ed. by Paul Cottin and Maurice Hénault (Paris: Librarie Hachette et Compagnie, 1853, repr. 1910).

---

[124] An enormous amont of primary sources (more than 5000) is presented by the Fondation Napoleon, see: <http://www.napoleon.org/en/home.asp>.

Alexandre Muller, *La baïonette et son maniement: L'escrime militaire au début du XIXe siècle. Alexandre Muller (Manuel d'Instruction: vol. 1)*, ed. by Philippe Charlet and Jean-Jacques Pattyn (Gilly: Historic 'One, 2013).

Alexandre Muller, *Le sabre et l'escrime du cavalier: L'escrime militaire au début du XIXe siècle. Alexandre Muller (Manuel d'Instruction: vol. 2)*, ed. by Philippe Charlet and Jean-Jacques Pattyn (Gilly: Historic 'One, 2013).

Antoine Charles Etienne de la Roche-Aymon, *Troupes Légères, ou réflexions sur l'organisation, l'instruction et la tactique de l'infanterie et de la cavalerie légères* (Paris : Magimel, Anselin et Pochard, 1817)

Antoine Fortuné de Brack, *Light cavalry out-posts: Recollections by F. De Brack, translated from the fifth edition for F.M. The marquis of Tweeddale*, ed. by Lonsdale A. Hale and F.T. Hobson (London: W. Mitchell & Co. Military Publishers, 1876).

Denis Charles Parquin, *Récits de guerre: Souvenirs du capitaine Parquin 1803-1814* (Paris: Boussod, Valadon et Compagnie, 1842, repr. 1892).

Dominique Larrey, *Mémoires de chirurgie militaire et campagnes, I (1787-1811: Campagnes de l'Amérique Septentrionale, du Rhin, de Corse, des Alpes-Maritimes, de Catalogne, d'Italie, d'Egypte et de Syrie, de Boulogne, d'Ulm et d'Austerlitz, de Saxe, de Prusse, de Pologne, d'Espagne et d'Autriche avec planches* (Paris, Tallendier Editions, 2004).

Dominique Larrey, *Mémoires de chirurgie militaire et campagnes, II (Campagnes de Russie, de Saxe, et de France, relation Médicale de campagnes et voyages, annexes avec planches* (Paris, Tallendier Editions, 2004).

Friedrich Christian Christmann and G. Pfeffinger: *Theoretisch-Praktische Anleitung des Hau und Stossfechtens und des Schwadronhauens nach einer ganz neuen Methode bearbeitet* (Offenbach am Main: Pfeffinger (?), 1838).

Jean Baptiste Antoine Marcellin de Marbot, *The memoirs of Baron de Late*, ed. by Arthur John Butler (London: Forgotten Books, 2013).

Jean-Roch Coignet, *Les cahiers du capitaine Coignet (1799-1815) publiés par Lorédan Larchey, d'après le manuscrit original avec gravures et autographe fac-similé*, ed. by Lorédan Larchey (Paris : Librairie Hachette et Compagnie, 1883).

Joseph Abbeel, *Met Napoleon naar Moskou: De ongelooflijke overlevingstocht van Joseph Abbeel*, ed. By Joost Welten and Johan De Wilde (Leuven: Davidsfonds, 2011).

Louis Rilliet, *Journal d'un sous-lieutenant de cuirassiers 1810-1814, présenté et annoté par Olivier Lapray (Editions du Grenadier)*, ed. by Olivier Lapray (Paris : Bernard Giovanangeli Editeur, 2013).

M.J. de Saint Martin, *L'art de faire des armes réduit à ses vrais principes* (Vienna: Imprimerie de Janne Schrämble, 1804).

Nicolas Davout, *Le Maréchal Davout, Prince d'Eckmühl. Correspondance Inédite, 1790-1815 Pologne- Russie- Hambourg*, ed. by Adélaïde Louise d' Eckmühl de Blocqueville (London: Forgotten Books, 2013).

Pierre Jacques François Girard, *Nouveau traité de la perfection sur le fait des armes, dédie au roy, par le Sr. P.J.F. Girard, ancien officier de marine, enseignant la manière de combattre de l'épee de pointe seule, toutes les gardes étrangeres, l'espadon, les piques, hallebardes, baïonettes au bout du fusil, fléaux brisés et batons à deux bouts; ensemble à faire bonne grâce les saluts de l'esponton, l'exercice du fusil, et celui de la grenadière, tels qu'ils se pratiquent aujour'hui dans l'art militaire de la France* (Paris: Moette, 1736).

Pierre Jean Baptiste Nougaret, *Anecdotes militaires, anciennes et modernes, des Français; contenant les actions sublimes et courageurses des généraux, des grands capitaines, des officiers et des soldats, les traits de dévouement extraordinaire de plusieurs villes assiégées, des particularités sur plusieurs batailles mémorables, soit de terre, soit de mer, et sur les stratagèmes de guerre curieux et remarquables* (Paris, F. Louis, 1808).

Thérèse Figueur, *Les campagnes de mademoiselle Thérèse Figueur, aujourd'hui Madame Veuve Sutter, ex-dragon aux 15e et 9e régimens, de 1793 a 1815, écrites sous sa dictée par St.-Germain Leduc* (Paris: Dauvin et Fontaine, 1842).

X.2. Secondary sources

Amberger, Christopher, *The secret history of the sword: Adventures in ancient martial arts* (Burbank: Multi-Media Books, 1999).

Amberger, Christopher, *Saber fencing: Germany, 1838* (2008), available from Fencingclassics <https://fencingclassics.wordpress.com/2008/12/05/saber-fencing-germany-1838/≥ (accessed 4 April 2015).

Amberger, Christopher *The French connection: Christmann's practical self-defence* (2011), available from Fencingclassics <https://fencingclassics.wordpress.com/2011/12/06/the-french-connection-christmanns-practical-self-defence/> (accessed 4 April 2015).

Barbero, Alessandro, *Waterloo. Het verhaal van de veldslag* (Amsterdam: Mets & Schilt Uitgevers, 2010).

Briost, Pascal., Hervé Drévillon and Pierre Serna,*Croiser le fer. Violence et culture de l'épée dans la France moderne (XVIe-XVIIIe siècle) (Les Classiques de Champ Vallon)* (Seyssel: Champ Vallon, 2002).

Cardoza, Thomas, *Intrepid women. Cantinières and vivandières of the French army* (Indiana: Indiana University Press, 2010).

Cohen, Richard, *By the sword: gladiators, musketeers, samurai, swashbucklers, and Olympic champions* (London: Simon and Schuster UK Ltd, 2010).

Crowdy, Terry E., *Napoleon's infantry handbook* (Yorkshire: Pen and Sword Military, 2015).

Elting, John.R., *Swords around a throne: Napoleon's Grande Armée* (New York: Da Capo Press, 1988, repr. 1997).

Fermont Barnes, Gregory (ed.), *Encyclopedia of the French Revolutionary and Napoleonic Wars. A political, social and military history* (Santa Barbara, Denver and Oxford: ABC Clio, 2006).

Gallaher, John G., *Napoleon's enfant terrible: General Dominique Vandamme (Campaigns and commanders 15)* (Oklahoma: University of Oklahoma Press, 2008).

Haythornthwaite, Philip (text) and Patrice Courcelle (Illustrations), *Napoleon's commanders (1) c. 1809-15 (Osprey Elite 72)* (Oxford: Osprey Publishing, 2001).

Haythornthwaite, Philip (text) and Patrice Courcelle (Illustrations), *Napoleon's commanders (2) c. 1809-15 (Osprey Elite 83)* (Oxford: Osprey Publishing, 2002).

Haythornthwaite, Philip, *Napoleonic cavalry (Napoleonic weapons and warfare)* (London: Cassell, 2002).

Histoire de la guerre d'Espagne contre Napoléon Buonaparte, par une commission d'officiers de toutes armes établie à Madrid auprès de S. Ex. Le ministre de la guere, tome I. (Paris: Le Normant, 1818).

Hughes, Basil P., *Firepower: weapons effectiveness on the battlefield 1630-1850* (New York: Sarpedon, New York, 1997).

Loades, Mike, *Swords and swordsmen* (Yorkshire: Pen and Sword Military, 2010).

Massoni, Gérard-Antoine, *Histoire d'un régiment de cavalerie légère : le 5e hussards 1783-1815* (Paris: Archives & Culture, 2008).

Napoleon, his army and enemies: armies – battles- tactics- commanders, *Napoleon's guard cavalry*, available from Napoleonistyka <http://napoleonistyka.atspace.com/IMPERIAL_GUARD_cavalry_1.html> (accessed 15 April 2015).

Napoleon, his army and enemies: armies – battles- tactics- commanders, *Infantry tactics and combat during the Napoleonic wars, part 1*, available from Napoleonyska <http://www.napolun.com/mirror/napoleonistyka.atspace.com/infantry_tactics_2.htm> (accessed 15 April 2015).

(1886) 'Neipperg, Adam Adalbert Graf von', *Allgemeine Deutsche Biographie* (Leipzig: Duncker und Humbolt, 1886), vol. 23, c. 408-412.

Nosworthy, Brent, *With musket, cannon and sword: battle tactics of Napoleon and his ennemies* (London: Da Capo Press, 1996).

Op de Beeck, Johan, *Napoleons nachtmerrie. 1812: hoe de Keizer en zijn soldaten ten onder gingen in Rusland* (Berchem: Epo, 2012).

Op de Beeck, Johan, *Napoleon, deel I: Van strateeg tot keizer* (Amsterdam: Manteau, 2014).

Op de Beeck, Johan, *Napoleon, deel II: Van Keizer tot mythe* (Amsterdam: Manteau, 2014).

Pawly, Ronald (text) and Patrice Courcelle (illustrations), *Napoleon's carabiniers (Men-at-Arms 405)*. (Oxford: Osprey Publishing, 2005).

Pawly, Ronald (text) and Patrice Courcelle (illustrations), *Napoleon's mamelukes (Men-at-Arms 429)*. (Oxford: Osprey Publishing, 2006).

Roberts, Andrew, *Napoleon de Grote* (Amsterdam: Prometheus, 2015).

Reinhard, Hank, *The book of swords* (New York: Baen Books, 2009).

Roucaud, Michel., 'Etude des Avant-postes de cavalerie légère par le général de Brack', *Revue Historique des Armées* 249 (2007) pp. 110-113.

SabresEmpires, *Napoleonic swords and sabers collection*, available from Swordscollection <http://swordscollection.blogspot.co.uk/2012/02/my-napoleonic-sword-collection.html> (accessed 15 April 2015).

Westwood, David, 'French Army' in Gregory Fermont Barnes (ed.), *Encyclopedia of the French Revolutionary and Napoleonic Wars. A political, social and military history* (Santa Barbara, Denver and Oxford: ABC Clio, 2006) pp. 373-378.

Westwood, David, 'musket' in Gregory Fermont Barnes (ed.), *Encyclopedia of the French Revolutionary and Napoleonic Wars. A political, social and military history* (Santa Barbara, Denver and Oxford: ABC Clio, 2006) pp. 668-669.

Westwood, David, 'rifle' in Gregory Fermont Barnes (ed.), *Encyclopedia of the French Revolutionary and Napoleonic Wars. A political, social and military history* (Santa Barbara, Denver and Oxford: ABC Clio, 2006) pp. 373-378.

Westwood, David, 'Musket' in Gregory Fermont Barnes (ed.), *Encyclopedia of the French Revolutionary and Napoleonic Wars. A political, social and military history* (Santa Barbara, Denver and Oxford: ABC Clio, 2006) pp. 818-819.

Wikipedia, *Joachim Hyppolite Lepic*, available from Wikipedia <http://fr.wikipedia.org/wiki/Joachim_Hippolyte_Lepic> (accessed 6 May 2015).

Wikipedia, *The Duellists*, available from Wikipedia <http://en.wikipedia.org/wiki/The_Duellists> (accessed 6 May 2015).

Wikipedia, *Pierre François Durutte*, available from Wikipedia <http://fr.wikipedia.org/wiki/Pierre_François_Joseph_Durutte> (accessed 6 May 2015).

DOI 10.1515/apd-2016-0005

Income and working time of a Fencing Master in Bologna in the 15th and early 16th century

Alessandro Battistini and Niki Corradetti
translated by Luca Dazi,
Sala d'Arme Achille Marozzo (www.achillemarozzo.it)
alessandro.battistini@achillemarozzo.it, niki.corradetti@achillemarozzo.it

Abstract – Since ancient times, the master-at-arms profession has always been considered essential for the education of the nobility and the common citizenship, especially in the Middle Ages. Yet, we know nothing about the real standard of living of these characters. The recent discovery of documents, which report the sums earned by fencing masters to teach combat disciplines, has brought us the possibility to estimate how highly this profession was regarded, and what its actual economic value was in the Italian late Middle Ages. They also give us also a material view into the modes of operation of a *sala d'arme* in those times.
Using different comparative methods based on the quoted currencies, primary goods and the cost of living, it was possible to analyze prices and duration of various military teachings offered by the fencing Masters in the late Middle Ages and equivalent viable activities of the time. We use three ways to calculate equivalent income levels in euros: from the silver content of the coins (bolognini, equivalent to the soldo); from purchasing power in relation to bread prices; and from equivalent wages. As a result we were able to define more accurately both the accessibility of these services for citizens and the relative value to other professions.
This cursory research study also aims to estimate approximately the current equivalent wages of a fencing master operating in the Italian peninsula in the 15th and early 16th century, confirming that this job was comparable to a modern, highly specialized, profession.

Keywords – Fencing Masters, Medieval Economy, History of Fencing, Medieval Bologna, Ancient Coins

Acknowledgements

We thank Prof. Trevor Dean for making his studies available to us.

I. INTRODUCTION

The main source for this research is a bundle of documents kept at the Archivio di Stato of Bologna[1] and dated 1443, based on the date of the latest annotation (December 1443). These documents contain a series of letters, presumably written during a span of several years, between Filippo Dardi and the government of the city of Bologna[2].

Filippo (or Lippo) di Bartolomeo Dardi was an astrologist and mathematician from Bologna, where he lived and held a *sala d'armi* starting from 1413 to his death, in 1464[3]. The *sala d'armi* was located on Pietralata Road where Dardi resided. From the archives of the University of Bologna we know also that he was Reader in Arithmetic and Geometry from 1443 to 1463. In 1444 he was also Reader in Astronomy[4].

The second document to be taken into account is the treatise from the famous Master Achille Marozzo, also from Bologna, where some other price information is obtainable.

Achille Marozzo was born in 1484 and had a fencing school in Bologna at the beginning of the sixteenth century. His *sala d'armi* was located on Riva di Reno Road where he lived. He certainly studied fencing in the school of the great Bolognese master Guido Antonio di Luca[5]. His book is one of the most famous fencing treatises and was reprinted several times over the centuries[6].

Due the quality of his treatise, Marozzo, who declares himself "General Master of the Arts of Weapons", is considered the fundamental master of renaissance fencing in Italy. But also Dardi is a very important figure in the Historical European Martial Arts, because he is considered the founder of the Ancient Bolognese Swordsmanship, to the point that this school is sometimes known also as "Dardi tradition" or "Dardi school".

This modern ascription probably derive from the supposed lineage between the Bolognese masters Dardi, De Luca and Marozzo[7]. Without detracting importance to Dardi, authors do not agree with this thesis. While the lineage between De Luca and

---

[1] Dardi, *Letters* (see bibliography). These documents were recently discovered and transcribed by Prof. Trevor Dean. The first complete transcription of the manuscript document is on Medieval Crime History blog (<https://medievalcrimehistory.wordpress.com/2015/06/>, Transcription by Trevor Dean, dated May 2015, last accessed 27 January 2016). Full transcription of the document in Appendix (reproduced with permission of the author).

[2] Government inference to regulate prices of goods and services in medieval cities was a common practice in Italy due the difficulty of the society to regulate itself (Welch, *Making money*, pp. 73,74, 76).

[3] Gelli, *Scherma Italiana*, p. 6, and Orioli, *La scherma a Bologna*, p. 2.

[4] Mazzetti, *Repertorio di tutti i professori*, p. 110.

[5] Marozzo, *Opera Nova*, proem, where Marozzo cites de Luca as the one who showed him the art.

[6] Pantanelli, *Scherma e maestri di scherma bolognesi*, p. 47.

[7] First hypothesized by Orioli, *La scherma a Bologna*, p. 2, and then re-proposed by Pantanelli, *Scherma e maestri di scherma bolognesi*, p. 47.

Marozzo can be supported directly by Marozzo's words, the lineage between Dardi and De Luca actually is purely hypothetical and no fencing writings of these masters are known. Other treatises of the Bolognese masters of the same period are now known without any proved relation with the other cited masters[8]. Some masters, like one named Nerio, are known to operate in Bologna before Dardi[9]. Authors are of the opinion that the ancient Bolognese school of fencing was spread in Bologna and near territories by a plurality of masters, derived directly from a fencing medieval matrix through mutual interrelationships, but without a common well defined single founder or influencer like Liechtenauer in German fencing tradition.

However, no research on either of these masters has been published yet. There is some information from independent researchers available[10], but it deserves further academic research outside of the scope of this article.

Despite this, documents found are very important because, for the first time, they tell us important information about a medieval fencing classroom, like payment required for every lesson, possible number of students and pace of training. Besides confirm some information already known about Dardi himself. Almost certainly these documents are the same used by fencing bibliographers that have wrote about Dardi[11], but they are interested and have reported only bibliographic information, while the documents contain much more.

II. PRICES IN SOURCES

The first part of previously mentioned letters shows how the work of Filippo Dardi was well regarded by the city government, to the point that he was granted annual wages of 200 *lire* of *bolognini* to practice astrology: 'they will give you the stated 200 *lire* of *bolognini* each year, and they do this so that you have reason to practice astrology more willingly for our community." (App., l. 14-16).

The city council also stated the maximum price he could ask when teaching martial arts in exchange for these annual wages. In practice the prices requested by the Bolognese Master for his fencing lessons were more than halved in return for a fixed annual payment provided by the city itself. This public investment was justified by the benefits of teaching fencing to the youths of Bologna, something that was highly valued by the city government.

---

[8] Manciolino, *Opera Nova*, and Anonymous, *Arte di Scherma*.

[9] Gelli, *Scherma Italiana*, p. 5.

[10] To learn more biographical details and read quotes on Filippo Dardi and Achille Marozzo refer to Scrimipedia (<http://www.scrimipedia.it>), only Italian, or Wiktenauer (<http://www.wiktenauer.com>) and related links on the relevant entries.

[11] Gelli, *Scherma Italiana*, p. 6, and Orioli, *La scherma a Bologna*, pp. 1-2.

[…] where you ask for the play of two-handed sword 23 *Lire* of bolognini, I want you to take up to 8 *Lire* of *bolognini*, and where you want 7 *Lire* for the play of sword and buckler I want you to take only 3 (*Lire*) of *bolognini*, and where you take 12 *lire* for the play of the dagger you'll take 5 *Lire* of *bolognini*, and where you want 7 *Lire* for the stick play you will take 3 L of *bolognini*, and where you take 10 L for the wrestling you will take 3 *Lire* of *bolognini*, and where you take 8 *Lire* for the play of rotella or targone you will take 3 *Lire* of *bolognini* (App., l. 22-27).

This obligation by the city council is probably dated back to the opening of the *sala d'arme*, and is summarized in Table 1.

Discipline	Requested by Dardi	Set by the Council
Two handed sword	23 lire of bolognini	8 lire of bolognini
Sword and buckler	7 lire of bolognini	3 lire of bolognini
Dagger	12 lire of bolognini	5 lire of bolognini
Stick	7 lire of bolognini	3 lire of bolognini
Wrestling	10 lire of bolognini	4 lire of bolognini
Sword and rotella or targone	8 lire of bolognini	3 lire of bolognini

Table 1: Dardi - earnings before 1443

Following this excerpt there is a letter in which Dardi express his concerns, after some years, that the low prices for his teaching could attract more students than he could handle and than would actually fit into the *sala d'armi*, which he sets at a maximum of 20 students at a time. He also writes about the optimal educational path for a fencer attending his lessons: two hours a day. He then declares he is not bound to teach a student for more than one year:

[…]he will learn the theory of the two-handed sword in two and a half months, and the practice in as many days, and the theory of the bucklers in one month and a half and in as much time the practice, and for each other play they learn the theory in one month each, and the practice in as much time (App., l. 40-43).

Table 2 shows the average learning times for each discipline, based on the documents.

Discipline	Theoretical Part	Practical Part	Total
Two handed sword	2.5 months	2.5 months	5 months
Sword and buckler	1.5 months	1.5 months	3 months
Dagger	1 month	1 month	2 months
Stick	1 month	1 month	2 months
Wrestling	1 month	1 month	2 months
Sword and rotella or targone	1 month	1 month	2 months

Table 2: Dardi – learning times for each discipline

In the end Dardi suggests to the city council that they transfer him into an academic tenure for teaching geometry, possibly with the same compensation. Since both astrology and fencing are subjects strictly related to geometry he was able to demonstrate his qualification. In this regard it has to be noted how the title of Reader was related to a tenure in the University; belonging to this corporation would guarantee, in the medieval Bologna, and elsewhere, a certain standing and some privileges[12].

Following this request Lodovico Caccialupi and Simone Manfredi, both belonging to a corporation designated by the city council to collect taxes (created in 1440[13]), suggest that the council accept the proposal, but also reduce the annual wages from 200 to 150 *lire* of *bolognini*:

> [...]in his practice and works of astrology and geometry and fencing he can continue and move on, and it will be that despite his higher demand, each year he will be payed only one hundred fifty *lire*, that is 150 L of *bolognini* (App., l. 79-82).

In compensation for this decreased wages, Dardi was granted an increase of his teaching prices, as reported in Table 3. "For the play of two-handed sword 10 L of *bolognini*, for the play of sword and buckler 4 L, and for the play of dagger 6 L, and for the play of stick 4 L, and for the play of wrestling 5 L, and for the play of rotella or targone 4 L of *bolognini*" (App., l. 84-87).

Discipline	Set by the Council
Two handed sword	10 lire of bolognini
Sword and buckler	4 lire of bolognini
Dagger	6 lire of bolognini
Stick	4 lire of bolognini
Wrestling	5 lire of bolognini
Sword and rotella or targone	4 lire of bolognini

Table 3: Dardi - earnings after 1443

An approximate calculation show a raise of 1 *Lira* for each discipline (except the two-handed sword, which was raised by 2). This related to a full capacity of 20 students with an average duration of 2.5 months for each course. This granted Dardi an average added revenue of 100 *lire* of *bolognini* per year, which well compensates the 50 *lire* annual decrease in wages. This was provided the school filled his classes, which seems evident given the previous proposal by Dardi. This deal favored both the Master and the city treasurers.

---

[12] Haskins, *The Rise of Universities*, p. 17.

[13] Muzzi, *Annali della citta di Bologna*, Vol. IV, p. 269, where it also possible see that the '40s of the fifteenth century was a period of financial strain for the treasury of Bologna.

After this, it's possible to find a bit of other similar information analyzing Marozzo treatise. In effect, Achille Marozzo doesn't give hints on his prices in his treatise on the teaching of fencing, except for a sentence in the third book:

> [...] because you know that for the wide play of sword versus sword, two-handed, I take seven *lire* of *bolognini*, and for the close play, also sword versus sword, and versus pole weapons, I take as much, which in total are fourteen *lire* of *bolognini*;[14]

From this excerpt we have a confirmation of the prices for two disciplines.

Discipline	Requested by Marozzo
Two handed sword – wide play	7 lire of bolognini
Two handed sword – close play and against pole weapons	7 lire of bolognini

Table 4: Marozzo – earnings mentioned in 1536

Even if limited to just one discipline, we can see how after little more than a century the price for the teaching of two-handed weapons has almost remained the same.

III. *LIRE* AND *BOLOGNINI*

In the Middle Ages the official currency in Italy was the *Lira*. The name *Lira* comes from the Latin *libra* (scale / pound). It represents a unit of weight, which varies considerably according to zones and time frames, whose equivalent in silver formed the currency unit. The measure, in weight, of one pound was, on average, from 300g to 350g (0.66lb to 0.77lb), with considerable variations. In Bologna it was reported to be 361.85g (0.79lb)[15]. Factually, the *Lira* didn't exist as a currency, and it merely represented the base of the monetary system, which was based on sub-multiples. This was the case until 1472, when the so-called *Lira Tron* was first forged in Venice (named after the Venetian Doge Nicolò Tron). From then on, the *Lira* started to be forged also in other cities, including Bologna in 1529[16]. The *Lira* was divided into 20 *soldi* (singular *soldo*), and each *soldo* was in its turn divided into 12 *denari*[17] (singular *denaro*).

---

[14] *perché sapendo tu che di gioco largo a spada contra spada da due mane io li toglio lire sette di bolognini & de giocho stretto, pure a spada contra spada e contra armi inastate, io toglio altre tante, che sono in tutto lire quatordici de bolognini*; Marozzo, *Opera Nova*, book III, p. 58.

[15] Dornbusch, *Gewichts-Reductions-Tabellen*, p. 4.

[16] This *Lira* was dubbed *della carestia* (of the Famine), due to the terrible famine of that year, and by the fact it was forged using founds from the Domenican fathers (Salvioni, *Il valore della lira bolognese*, p. 233).

[17] This monetary partition, commonly present in the whole of Europe, was derived from the Carolingian currency, the monetary form which replaced the old Roman currency, and ruled the monetary regulations until the French Revolution. Indeed the system was much

The *Bolognino* (plural *bolognini*), or *soldo bolognese*, was the coin forged and commonly used in Bologna. Starting from 1236, two variations of the *bolognino* began to circulate in the city: the small alloy *bolognino*, already forged from 1192, and the big silver *bolognino*[18]. A small *bolognino* was the equivalent of one denaro, while the big silver *bolognino* was the equivalent of the soldo, maintaining in this way a formal canonical match with the reference *Lira*[19]: 1 *Lira* = 20 big silver *bolognini*, 1 silver *bolognino* = 12 small *bolognini*.

Although *bolognino* in the 13th cent. commonly referred to the small alloy one, in the 15th cent. the official *bolognino* became the big silver one[20]. Later on, after 1380, Bologna also forged the gold *bolognino*, having the same weight and title of the *Ducato*. The initial exchange rate was established to be 1 gold *bolognino* to = 40 silver *bolognini*[21], and after that the gold *bolognino* was used to commonly identify all the *Ducati* forged in Bologna.

It is worth noting that, although the silver content in the *bolognino* was held constant its quality was probably worse than the many equivalents of the *soldo*, forged by many foreign courts, which were commonly found in Bologna. The lower silver content could justify the higher diffusion among the population of Bologna, based on Gresham's law[22]. Starting from Bologna, in fact, the *bolognino* spread to all the Pontificial domains, sometimes even forcedly[23], becoming the synonym and replacement of the *soldo*. This fact is confirmed by the references to the many currencies coined in several Italian cities from the 14th to 18th cent., which took their names from the exchange rate with the *bolognino*[24]. The nominal rate of 20 between *bolognino* and *Lira* was constant, and the term *bolognino* was so widespread in the Papal States to the extent that many currencies with the same name and nominal value were forged in several other cities, like for example the *bolognino*

more complex. There were a wide variety of different coins circulating in a large medieval city, and it was difficult to find a fixed exchange rate between them (Welch, *Making money*, pp. 71, 72, 80).

[18] Guidicini, *Cose notabili della Città di Bologna*, Vol. I, p. 32.

[19] Fanti, *Confraternite e città a Bologna nel Medioevo e nell'Età moderna*, p. 215

[20] The latest reference to the small *bolognino* is documented in 1377. After this date there are only references to the *denaro*.

[21] Guidicini, *Cose notabili della Città di Bologna*, Vol. V, p. 203. In Chimienti, *Monete bolognesi*, the author reports an exchange rate between Ducato and silver *bolognino* ranging from 34 in 1381 to 74 in 1520.

[22] Economic law stated by Thomas Gresham (1519-79), financial agent for Queen Elisabeth I, for which "When a government overvalues one type of money and undervalues another, the undervalued money will leave the country or disappear from circulation into hoards, while the overvalued money will flood into circulation." It's in fact worthy melting the higher silver content coins in order to obtain more coins of lower quality, but the same nominal value.

[23] Frati, *Statuti di Bologna dall'anno 1245 all'anno 1267*, Vol. III, p. 319, references to the obligation on using the *bolognino* as currency in Cesena and Ravenna.

[24] Entry about *Bolognino* in LaMoneta.it Network di Numismatica e Storia (<http://numismatica-italiana.lamoneta.it/nominale/Bolognino>, accessed 15 July 2015).

of Ravenna[25]. Even when Rome started imposing its own currency, the *bolognino* continued being forged in Bologna; together with the official ones imposed by the Church State[26]. Even when it stopped being forged, the old *bolognino* with its ratio of 20 to 1 with the Lira, continued to be used as the reference value for any other currency, and standard in commercial document of the northern Pontifical delegations, to the extent that in the 17th cent. the Papal States had to publish several bans to avoid the drafting of commercial documents using bolognini[27].

It is, however, extremely difficult to have a complete picture of monetization in Italy, or in Bologna, due to the large amount of economical and territorial factors at play in such a large span of time. The present study is limited to a functional approach in order to obtain easily computable and deducible results, without any claim for completeness[28].

IV. PURCHASING POWER

Establishing the current value of a currency is maybe even harder than retracing its history. The currency named bolognino could have different values from place to place[29]. Fortunately, the bolognino of Bologna was taken as a reference in the majority of the Papal States, as we have seen before.

We decided to show three different approaches to find the most realistic and consistent result. First, we defined the value based on the amount of metal. Second, we assessed its purchasing power to the price of primary goods. Third we compared modern wages with those of late Medieval Bologna using similar professions between then and now. We recognize that each of these approaches involves large simplifications and could thus be subject to obvious methodological critiques. Except for some data, here reported for completeness, we tried to apply a temporal frame ranging from 1380 to 1525. Those years

---

[25] Battaglini, *Memorie istoriche di Rimino e de'suoi signori*, p. 63 and following.

[26] Entry about the mint of Bologna from 1506 to 1600 in Monete e dintorni site (<https://sites.google.com/site/moneteedintorni/la-zecca-di-bologna/la-zecca-di-bologna-dal-1506-al-1600>, accessed 15 July 2015).

[27] Decree by Pope Alexander VII, which states: ...*Prohibisce le Lire, e Bolognini nelle Province di Bologna, Ferrara, Romagna e Ravenna, volendo che vi si introduchino li giuli, e bajocchi. Edita A.D. 1660*. There we can also find the exchange rate applied to the official currencies, which is 2 giuli = 1 *Lira* and 1 giulio = 10/11 bolognini. This once again confirms the official rate of 20 to 1 of the *bolognino* to the *Lira*.

[28] For an insight on the interesting story of the *Lira* as a currency refer to Cipolla, *The adventures of the Lira*. For the complete evolution of the monetization in Bologna throughout the centuries, refer to the relevant item in Chimienti, *Monete bolognesi*.

[29] Argelati, *De monetis Italiae*, Vol. IV, p. 323 and following.

roughly include our case study and stand out due to a high amount of silver content in the bolognino[30] and strong stability in prices[31].

IV.1. Value based on metal

The most common approach to assessing value is to convert the quantity of precious metal contained in the coin to its current value in the modern market. If we want to proceed in this way, we find that it's not really easy to find the exact weight and silver content in thousandths of the *bolognini* in Bologna between the 15th and 16th cent. On one side, there is the extreme heterogeneity of the coin in various cities of the peninsula, on the other, there are several famines and general crisis periods which can influence the quantity of precious metal added to the coins, which would, in spite of this, maintain the same nominal value.

We know that the silver *bolognino*, since its very origins, maintained a rather constant silver content throughout the years. The *bolognino* of 1236 had an official weight of 1.57g (24gr), with 883/1000 silver content[32]. However, the weight of the coin slowly decreased during the centuries. Even though we observe a match of 1.5g (23gr) in the 14th cent., this weight drifts down to 1.3g/1.2g (19gr) in the early 15th cent., oscillating down to 1g (15gr) in the following centuries[33]. Although the coins in Bologna in our reference period seem to have a constant weight, and never drop under 1.2g (18.5gr), in our calculations we have taken note of the natural deterioration of the existing, original, samples.

---

[30] Other than the aforementioned introduction of the silver *Lira* in 1529, in 1526 the Mint of Bologna issued for the first time an mixed *bolognino*. This new coin became known as the muraiola, so called due to its color (*muro* means wall in Italian), whose value was 2 bolognini. Even the gold *bolognino*, issued in 1380, was replaced in 1553 by the golden scudo "of the sun", of French origins (Chimienti, *Monete bolognesi*).

[31] English economists divide the economy from the XII to XX cent. into 6 macro-periods: there are two phases of strong stability (1380-1510 and 1630-1760) and two phases where there is a general rise in prices (1270-1380 and 1815-1914). Between 1510 and 1630 there was a fall in prices, whose low point was reached in 1597 (Phelps-Brown and Hopkins, *Seven Centuries of the Prices of Consumables*). The time frame from 1380 to 1510 almost overlaps with our case study, with the closed link being at the end of the period. The inflation observed in this model doesn't only apply to the Anglo-Saxon world, but seems to be widespread in the whole of Europe with almost the same time scales. Similar statistics research performed on Tuscany, Lombardy and, in general, on the Central-Northern Italy, highlight very similar tendencies for prices. In particular, the first stability period tends to expand from 1381 to 1524 (Malanima, *Statistical Appendix*).

[32] Ditaranto et Al., *Caratterizzazione spettroscopica e morfologica di monete (bolognini) medievali*.

[33] As ascertained by consulting various Italian numismatic and auctions catalogs, especially for silver bolognini not forged in Bologna.

As an example, we report in Table 5 the values of the silver *bolognini* (the big ones) or equivalent ones forged in the Mint of Bologna and classified in the numismatics bulletin[34]:

Coin	Ruler	Years	Maximum weight
Bolognino Grosso	Republic (Emperor Enry VI)	1236-1337	1.49 grams 23 grains
Grosso or Bolognino	Giacomo and Giovanni Pepoli	1337-1350	1.34 grams 21 grains
Bolognino	Giovanni Visconti Lord of Milan	1350-1360	1.34 grams 21 grains
Bolognino	Urbano V Pope	1362-1370	1.31 grams 20 grains
Bolognino	Republic (Autonomous)	1376-1401	1.24 grams 19 grains
Bolognino	Martino V Pope	1421-1428	1.17 grams 18 grains
Bolognino	Pontificial Anonymous	2nd half XVI cent. 1st half XV cent.	1.15 grams 18 grains
Bolognino	Filippo Maria Visconti Duke of Milan	1428-1443	1.16 grams 18 grains

Table 5: Summary statistics of rediscovered Bolognini

As of today silver has a value of 430.15€ per kilogram ($472.18 /Kg, $14.69 /oz). Supposing a silver content of 883/1000 and an average weight of the *bolognino*, in the early 15th cent., of 1.2g (19gr), we can estimate an up to date value of the silver *bolognino* of 1.2 x 0.001 x 0.883 x 430.15 = 0.43€ ($0.47).

For the sake of completeness we will also report the calculation for the gold *bolognino* of 1380, even if, as mentioned before in contractual references like our case study, the referred exchange rate was for the silver *bolognino*. If we assume the gold *bolognino* had a gold content of 995/1000 and weighed 3.45g (53gr)[35], considering a current exchange of 32,192.48€ /Kg ($35,338 /Kg, $1,099.13 /oz)[36], we get a current value in gold of the *ducato*/gold *bolognino* of 0.995 x 32,192.48 = 110.51€ ($121.28).

If we move ahead 80 years, we can refer to the city council decree on the exact composition of the coin in 1464[37]. There we can find that the silver *bolognini* is made from

---

[34] State Numismatic Bulletin, IUNO MONETA database (<http://www.numismaticadellostato.it>, accessed 11 September 2015), research on currency coined by the Mint of Bologna.

[35] The *Bolognino* forged by the Mint of Bologna for the Republic of Bologna (1376-1401), <http://www.gloriainarte.it/BOLOGNINO.pdf>, accessed 26 December 2015 .

[36] There are several online sites that provide this financial information, for this article we used BullionVault (<https://oro.bullionvault.it/Prezzo-Argento.do>, accessed 25 July 2015).

[37] Argelati, *De monetis Italiae*, Vol. IV, p. 311 and following.

an alloy of 9 ounces and 5/6 of silver for every pound (=12 ounces), resulting in a silver content of 819/1000. We can also find that a pound should make 396 coins, and an ounce 33 coins (12 ounces = 1 pound). With both these relations we can obtain a weight of 0.91g (14gr) per *bolognino*. This leads to a current value in silver equivalent to 0.91 x 0.001 x 0. 819 x 430.15 = 0.32€ ($0.35) per bolognino. A pound should be equivalent to 103 gold *bolognini*, which gives us a weight of 3.51g (54gr) per coin, forged at 18+76/103 = 18.74 carats, equivalent to 781/1000 of gold. We can so obtain a current value of the gold *bolognino* equivalent to 3.51 x 0.001 x 0. 781 x 32,192.48 = 88.25€ ($96.84).

In reviewing these actualized values for both silver and gold coins, we can obtain a relation of 1 to 250 in both cases, well away from the nominal relation of 1 to 40 in the 15th cent. This discrepancy can be linked to historical realities that separate modern life from the medieval one, especially the discovery of the New World, with the subsequent inflow of rare and precious metals, which caused a relative devaluation of silver. From 1344 up to 1830 there had always been an almost fixed ratio of 1 to 16 between gold and silver. In the late 19th cent., when silver was no longer used for monetization, this ratio began rising until reaching a record of 1 to 153 in 1939, then lowering to 1 to 28 in 1971, and raising back to 1 to 110 in 1992[38].

Even today, the values of these precious metals are unstable and not proportional to each other, especially in the past few years, so are unreliable as an absolute reference. Note that after a stable period of almost 20 years, the value of gold oscillated from almost 10,000€ /Kg ($10,974) in 2004 to over 42,000€ /Kg ($46,092) in 2012, while the value of silver rose to the equivalent of 124€ /Kg ($136) in 1996 to over 1,000€ /Kg ($1,097) in 2011.

It is also worth noting that a coin, although of good real value, always remains associated to a fiducial value, whose intrinsic worth is lower than its nominal worth, or rather its purchasing power as recognized in the community. As a matter of fact, this line of reasoning can give us an insight on the current "minimum" market value of the currency, equivalent to the mere value of the precious metal contained in the coin, extrapolating it from the social context in which it gets used. If we in fact analyze the exchange ratio between small (alloy) and big (silver) bolognino in 1236, conventionally stated as 12 to 1, it results in a higher ratio than that of the silver content, roughly equivalent to 8 to 1, contained in the coins[39].

IV.2. Purchasing power based on prime goods

A different approach, although not devoid of errors and approximations, is based on analyzing the acquisition price for several, commonly used, prime goods. One of the most used goods for these kinds of comparisons is bread, which we can find quoted in many

---

[38] McKinley-Degregori, *Le Opzioni*, p. 67, where there are also references to its highest value in 1477.

[39] Milani, *Monete, cambiatori e popolo*, pp. 133-134.

accounts and chronicles, even if its value is also greatly influenced by periods of famine and crisis in the place where it was produced. Fortunately though, precisely for its importance, a fixed price is often imposed in these periods[40]. Whether these prices were then respected or not is out of the scope of this analysis.

By consulting several chronicles of the 15th and 16th centuries, we can find how with one bolognino (we suppose a silver one) one could buy a widely variable quantity of bread, changing based on the year, the city, and obviously, whether there was famine or not. If we take, for example, the period of the Italian Wars (1494-1559) it is quite obvious how the value of bread rises up due to the famine generated by the war. In Table 6 we show some prices of bread in *bolognini*, for times when it was possible to retrieve it[41]:

Year	Place	Distance from Bologna	Price of bread	Note
1310	Forlì	65 km 40 mi	12 denari = 1 bol. = 12 or 18 oz of bread	Period of war
1430	Bologna	Countryside included	1 bol. = 36 oz of bread = 3 lb	Period of crisis, but abundance of goods
1464	Cervia	85 km 53 mi	33 bol. = 115 lb of bread from which 1 bol. = 3.48 lb of bread	Expences for the transit of Federico da Montefeltro
1477	Viterbo	240 km 149 mi	1 bol. = 8 or 6 oz of bread	Famine
1500	Forlì	65 km 40 mi	1 bol. 35 lb of bread	Imposed by Cesare Borgia
1505	Imola	30 km 19 mi	1 bol. = 8 to 4 lb of bread or less	Prices to be applied in function of the price of wheat
1505	Bologna		1 bol. = 4 oz of black bread	Famine

---

[40] Actually, calculations of this kind should be done through statistics based on the average prices of a full set of primary goods and services, carefully chosen among material for which there is historic data available during the years. A good example of a well chosen set of primary goods could be the sum of wheat, other minor cereals, meat, wine, olive oil, firewood, cloth and accommodation expenses (Malanima, *Measuring the Italian Economy 1300-1861*), but the current dissertation has a pure illustrative purpose, and we refer you to other publications on statistics on the medieval economy reported in the bibliography, for further details.

[41] Information obtained from: Muratori, *Rerum Italicarum*, vol. 14, p. 57; Muzzi, *Annali della città di Bologna*, Vol. IV, p. 204; Cognasso, *L'Italia nel Rinascimento*, Vol. 1, p. 248; Ciampi, *Cronache e statuti della città di Viterbo*, p. 414; Pasolini, *Caterina Sforza*, p. 352; Alberghetti, *Compendio della storia civile ecclesiastica e letteraria della città d'Imola*, Vol. I, p. 284 (in the same document it is stated how the price of wheat reached its maximum in 1505, but the relative price of bread is not indicated); Muzzi, *ibid.*, Vol. V, p. 468; Iacopi, *Pane e panettieri in assisi del medioevo*; Gionta, *Il fioretto delle croniche di Mantova*, p. 80; Muzi, *Memorie ecclesiastiche e civili di Città di Castello*, Vol. II, p. 111.

Year	Place	Distance from Bologna	Price of bread	Note
1514	Assisi	190 km 118 mi	1 bol. = 4 lb of bread	Decree of podestà
1526	Mantova	85 km 53 mi	1 bol. = 3 oz of bread	Famine
1539	Città di Castello and rest of Italy	135 km 84 mi	1 bol. = 1 lb of bread = 12 oz	Famine

Table 6: Prices of bread around 15th century

The weight of an ounce in grams is now fixed to 28.35 grams, while in the Middle Ages it strongly depended on the place and the year, ranging from 25 grams to 39 grams. The value of the ounce in Bologna, pre-unity, was 30.15 grams[42], equivalent to 1/12 of the bolognese pound (361.85g). To ease calculation, we can assume a standard ratio of 30 grams throughout the peninsula.

We can also isolate the prices from relatively quiet times, or from those when prices were imposed (2, 3, 5, 6 and 8). Fortunately these are quite coherent and refer to places moderately near to Bologna, if not to Bologna itself, and are issued in the time frame of reference for our case study: the mid 15th cent. and early 16th cent. In all five cases, we see how a quantity of bread of 3 to 4 pounds was valued at 1 bolognino, approximately 1 to 1.5 kg (2.2 to 3.3 lb). The price seems to keep itself almost stable during those years, until the great changes of the 16th cent. (Italian Wars and discovery of America). Basically it seems the devaluation only affected the quality of the coin, as we have already seen, and not its real purchasing power. In periods of crisis, obviously, the quantity of available bread drops a lot, but we can assume that the documents we are analyzing were not taking these aspects into consideration, and were referring to "normal" periods.

Based on this reasoning, we can estimate the purchasing power of a *bolognino* based on the current value of a primary good, such as bread. As of June 2015, the price of bread in Bologna ranges from 1.29€ /kg ($0.66 /lb) to 5.6€ /kg ($2.87 /lb), with an average value of 4€ /kg ($2.04 /lb)[43]. Using this average value, we obtain a cost of 0.004€ per gram of bread. We can then estimate the actual purchasing power of a silver *bolognino* to be from 0.004 x 361.85 x 3 = 4.34€ ($4.90) to 0.004 x 361.85 x 4 = 5.79€ ($6.54). Or more easily, we can propose 1 *bolognino* = 4-6 current euros.

As we can see, this second approach leads us to an estimated value over ten times higher than the value calculated on the base of the precious metal content of the coin. This result

---

[42] Savigny, *Storia del diritto romano nel Medioevo*, Vol. III, p. 209.

[43] Prices and Fares Observatory, Ministry for the Economic Development, Goods and services of wide usage, observed prices – June 2015 (<http://osservaprezzi.sviluppoeconomico.gov.it>, accessed 26 June 2015). It is impossible to have a valuable average for the whole of Italy, so we focused our research on the city of Bologna.

is certainly more realistic, but probably a bit low, based on the abundance of edible goods in today's everyday life.

IV.3. Purchasing power based on equivalent wages

The last approach analyzes the wages of jobs in medieval Bologna to those commonly found in current times. Through the analysis of some chronicles of the city of Bologna[44] we were able to find examples for wages, assigned by the city council, on which we can base our study. When looking at this data, we need to take into account that different workers, with the same job title, conducted different tasks and there were no national contractual agreements to which we can refer. For these reasons each individual was a case on his own and earned based on his abilities. In this scenario it's really difficult to establish an average for any category.

Year	Profession	Salario
1390	Chief bricklayer	10 *bolognini* for every work day
1392	Architect or Engineer	30 *lire* al month
1393	Preacher Bishop	60 *lire* per year
1393	Notary	5 *lire* per month
1393	Keeper of the Asinelli Tower	5 *lire* per month
1429	Treasurer	12 *lire* per month
1429	Overseer	12 *lire* per month
1431	Member of the Elders' College	5 *lire* per month
1431	Chaplain	10 *lire* per month
1464	Architect	15 *lire* per month
1490	Organist	12 *lire* per month

Table 7: Wages in Bologna around the 15th century

In Table 7 we did not report borderline professionals, like the legate, who in 1447 earned more than 500 *Lire* per month[45], or complex social figures like readers, auctioneers and law doctors, whose prestige affected their pay in Middle Age Bologna[46]. Among these it's interesting to report the wage of a Judge in the Merchants' Forum, who in 1490 received a 500 *Lire*/month salary, and of the relative wage of an Appeal Judge, who earned 100 *Lire*[47]. It was an important position, which was assigned once every six months only to

---

[44] Information obtained from: Guidicini, *Cose notabili della Città di Bologna*, Vol. III, pp. 361, 363, 364, 367, 371; Ghirardacci, *Della historia di Bologna*, p. 485; Muzzi, *Annali della città di Bologna*, Vol. IV, p. 214;

[45] Muzzi, *Annali della città di Bologna*, Vol. IV, p. 379.

[46] Wages of these individuals varied broadly and were more truly linked to the person and his actual political history in the city. We can find salaries of 300 *Lire* per year in 1384, 550 *Lire* per year in 1439, 400 *Lire* per year in 1444, and as high as 1200 *Lire* per year in 1460 and 1000 *Lire* per year in 1498 (Muzzi, *Annali della città di Bologna*, Vol. V, pp. 327, 324, 299, 367, 315).

[47] Muzzi, *Annali della città di Bologna*, Vol. V, p. 161.

the doctors of law who had shown themselves most worthy of consideration, and it was a source of pride for the whole profession. We would not be too wrong if we were to compare this position with the highest positions in today's State organizations.

On the base of these wages and on a pure empiric reasoning, we are confident in speculating the actual value of a *Lira* from 150€ to 200€ ($170 to $225), which equates the current value of one *bolognino* to be 7.5€ to 10€ ($8.40 to $11.30). This value is slightly higher than the one proposed using the price of bread, but certainly comparable. It should also be highlighted how the reported salaries are not those of popular jobs[48], even so, we don't think this invalidates our analysis.

V. CONCLUSIONS

Due the difference between fiducial and intrinsic value of a coin previously explained, we can discard the first approach. Leaving our analysis with the other two, we can postulate a hypothetical *bolognino*/EUR exchange rate of 1 to 7.5, with a possible variability range of 30%. We should always take note that the simplifying approximations we introduced make the following estimations a rough indicative value, which should be taken into consideration only to give an order of magnitude for comparison, and nothing more. Based on the previous analysis, we can make some assumptions and correlations between modern life and what we see in the documents. Supposing an exchange *bolognino*/EUR of 7.5 (±2.5), we find that, up to 1443, Filippo Dardi, through his city of Bologna wages, earned 200 *Lire* = 4000 *bolognini* = 30,000€ per year (±30%), in order to work, we suppose for free, the job of astrologist/astronomer for the city. Wages that in 1443, in years of monetary crisis of the city, were lowered to 150 *Lire* = 3000 *bolognini* = 22,500€ (±30%), granting the role of reader in Geometry, in exchange.

In the same way we can transpose in Table 8 his earnings as a fencing Master, as shown in Table 1 and Table 3. From now on, we consider all the actualized prices to have the 30% aforementioned margin:

Discipline	Requested by Dardi	Set by the Council before 1443	Set by the Council after 1443
Two handed sword	3450 euro	1200 euro	1500 euro
Sword and buckler	1050 euro	450 euro	600 euro
Dagger	1800 euro	750 euro	900 euro
Stick	1050 euro	450 euro	600 euro
Wrestling	1500 euro	600 euro	750 euro
Sword and rotella or targone	1200 euro	450 euro	600 euro

Table 8: Dardi - actualized earnings

---

[48] On the wages of the less wealthy classes, we can report the current daily wages that were found in the building sector, in Tuscany, in late XVI cent.: women 4-5 soldi; manual workers 8-12 soldi; chiefs 15-20 soldi (Pinto, *Il lavoro, la povertà, l'assistenza*, p.39); while in 1474 and 1475 the workers hired for the excavation of an irrigation ditch near Pavia were payed 3 soldi per day (Zanoboni, *Donne al lavoro nell'edilizia medievale*, p. 109-132).

We can actualize the earnings of Master Marozzo in the same way from Table 4:

Discipline	Requested by Marozzo
Two handed sword – wide play	1050 euro
Two handed sword – close play and against pole weapons	1050 euro

Tabella 9: Marozzo - actualized earnings

Other than that, we can estimate a monthly or even hourly cost based on the durations of the courses, as noted by Dardi in Table 2. We suppose that the 2 hours per day dedicated to each student were held 6 days per week, excluding Sundays. This places the total for each month, composed by an average of 26 days of study, at 52 hours. The result of the calculation is noted in Table 10.

Discipline	Duration	Monthly/hourly cost before 1443	Monthly/hourly cost after 1443
Two handed sword	5 months = 260 hours	240 euro / 4.61 euro	300 euro / 5.76 euro
Sword and buckler	3 months = 156 hours	150 euro / 2.88 euro	200 euro / 3.84 euro
Dagger	2 months = 104 hours	375 euro / 7.21 euro	450 euro / 8.65 euro
Stick	2 months = 104 hours	225 euro / 4.32 euro	300 euro / 5.76 euro
Wrestling	2 months = 104 hours	300 euro / 5.76 euro	375 euro / 7.21 euro
Sword and rotella or targone	2 months = 104 hours	225 euro / 4.32 euro	300 euro / 5.76 euro

Table 10: Dardi – actualized prices per discipline

The first thing to note is how the most economic discipline to learn was sword and buckler, probably the most commonly diffused discipline in Bologna at the time[49]. The most expensive one is instead the dagger, which is quite obvious if you consider that it was the base for self-defense in a turbulent city like Bologna in the 15th century[50].

These prices are more or less consistent with the prices of a modern martial arts gym. In an hypothesis of a two-day workout session per week, of 2 hours, approximately 17 hours per month, and basing on a monthly fee of 100€ ($113), we have an hourly cost of about 6€ ($6.8), which can often be lowered with multi-month or annual subscriptions. To this comparison it should be underlined how today offers for sports courses are much more

---

[49] The main known fencing treatises of early 16th century in Bologna are written by Marozzo Achille and Manciolino Antonio (see bibliography), the base discipline of the teachings of both Bolognese Masters is sword and buckler.

[50] Further information the law and the duels in XV century Bologna can be found in: Cavina, *Il sangue dell'onore*, and Dean, *Criminal justice in mid-fifteenth-century Bologna*.

diversified and widespread, while in the 15th cent. fencing was an exclusive teaching, and Dardi can be considered as a sort of luminary in the matter, to the extent he had to be limited by the city council so to diffuse his teachings as much as possible. It should be noted how in the start Dardi was requesting more than three times the wages the city council established.

Presuming the teaching was equally distributed in all the disciplines during the lessons, we have an average of 4.86€ per hour ($5.50) before 1443, and 6.17€ per hour ($7) after 1443. Supposing a working schedule of 6 days per week (approximately 310 days per year, removing Sundays and some holidays), limiting the teaching of fencing to 4 hours per day, so to leave the remaining hours for the job of astrologist, we can push the estimations of an hypothetical total annual earning for Filippo Dardi to around 120,000€ (c. $138,000) per year before 1443, and 150,000€ (c. $170,000) per year after 1443, for the teaching of fencing only. We also have to add wages of 30,000€/$22,500 (c. 35,000€/$26,000) per year for the job as an astrologist/astronomer. It should be noted that these estimates refer to years with a full schedule of 20 students in the classes, with courses of 2 hours, 2 times per day. It is highly probable that this estimate is quite optimistic 0and doesn't reflect the real rhythms of the sala d'arme. It's way more probable that the teachings were limited to only the 2 hours per day stated in the document. In this case the earnings would have to be halved to almost 60,000€ (c. $70,000) per year before 1443 and almost 75,000€ (c. $85,000) per year after 1443, always on the hypothesis of a full schedule. In any case, these estimates put Dardi's earnings to the level of a modern highly specialized professional, if not more[51].

Moving the focus to Achille Marozzo, we don't have indications on the duration of his course on two-handed sword, but using the base of information from Dardi, we can presume about 3 months for the theory and practice of the wide play of two-handed sword, and the same for the close play. The additional month, not included by Dardi in his teaching of the two-handed sword, comes from the defense against pole weapons material, included by Marozzo. Pole weapons were slowly becoming the rulers of the battlefield. Results are in Table 11.

Discipline	Duration	Monthly/hourly cost
Two handed sword – wide play	3 months = 156 hours	350 euro / 6.73 euro
Two handed sword – close play and against pole weapons	3 months = 156 hours	350 euro / 6.73 euro

Table 11: Marozzo – actualized prices per discipline

These prices are aligned with the ones imposed on Dardi by the City Council. Although it seems the wages of Marozzo are higher than those of Dardi, the period of activity of

---

[51] Federica Micardi, on "Sole 24 Ore" of December 11th, 2014, states the average annual earnings of the wealthier professions of 2014, basing on the relative welfare treasury: Notaries 101130 euro, Medics 75308 euro, Journalists 61180 euro, Accountants 60288 euro, Bookkeepers 57033, Lawyers 43815 euro.

Marozzo is far nearer to the time frame of relative price stability we noted before. The year 1536, publishing year of his treatise, is already fully inside the Italian Wars, and several famines have already hit Italy, starting in the first two decades of the 16th century. It is possible that for this reason his wages, although being formally higher than Dardi's, are affected by a far lower purchasing power of the currency. It is also totally possible that the prices stated by Marozzo were written well before the publishing date of the treatise. We don't have (yet) other information on the courses held by Marozzo, so we cannot make other assumptions. That being said, the principles of the analysis done on the earnings of Dardi can be applied also to Master Marozzo, almost a century later.

VI. BIBLIOGRAPHY

VI.1. Primary sources

Anonimo Bolognese (Ravenna, Classense Library, MS 345 and MS 346). Edited by Marco Rubboli and Luca Cesari, *L'Arte della Spada. - Trattato di scherma dell'inizio del XVI secolo* (Rimini: Il Cerchio, 2005), 382p.

Filippo Dardi, *Letters between Lippo di Bartolomeo Dardi and the government of Bologna* (Archivio di Stato, Bologna, Comune, Governo, envelope N°318, "Riformagioni e provvigioni", Miscellaneous series, envelope N°5), first transcription by Trevor Dean on Medieval Crime History blog (https://medievalcrimehistory.wordpress.com), May 2015.

Antonio Manciolino, *Opera Nova per Imparare a Combattere, & Schermire d'ogni forte Armi*, Venezia, N. d'Aristotile detto Zoppino, 1531. Reprinted with technical comments by Alessandro Battistini and Marco Rubboli (Rimini: Il Cerchio, 2008), 240p.

Achille Marozzo, *Opera Nova de Achille Marozzo, Mastro Generali de l'Arte de l'Armi* Modena, D. Antonio Bergolae, 1536.

VI.2. Secondary sources

Alberghetti, Giuseppe, *Compendio della storia civile ecclesiastica e letteraria della città d'Imola* (Imola: tipi comunali per G. Benedetto Filippini, 1810), 2 vol.

Argelati, Filippo, *De monetis Italiae variorum illustrium virorum dissertationes* (Milano: Stamperia della Società Palatina, 1750-59), 6 vol.

Battaglini, Francesco Gaetano, *Memorie istoriche di Rimino e de'suoi signori artatamente scritte ad illustrare la zecca e la moneta riminese di F. G. B., pubblicate e corredate di note da Guid'Antonio Zanetti* (Bologna: Stamperia di Lelio della Volpe, 1789), 314p.

Cavina Marco, *Il sangue dell'onore. Storia del duello* (Bologna: Laterza, 2005), 327p.

Chimienti, Michele, "Monete bolognesi e circolazione monetaria a Bologna", *Strenna Storica Bolognese*, 58 (2008), pp. 93-131.

Ciampi, Ignazio, *Cronache e Statuti della città di Viterbo* (Firenze: Tipi di M. Cellini e c., 1872), 653p.

Cipolla, Carlo M., *Le avventure della lira* (Bologna: Il Mulino, 2012), 162pp.

Cognasso, Francesco, *L'Italia nel Rinascimento* (Torino: Unione Tipografico-Editrice Torinese, 1965), 2 vol.

Dean, Trevor, *Criminal justice in mid-fifteenth-century Bologna, Crime, Society and the Law in Renaissance Italy* (Cambridge: Cambridge University Press, 1994).

Dean, Trevor, and Lowe, Kate, *Crime, Society and the Law in Renaissance Italy* (Cambridge: CUP, 1994), 281p.

Ditaranto, Nicoletta, Colucci, Silvia, van der Werf, Inez, Sabbatini, Luigia, *Caratterizzazione spettroscopica e morfologica di monete (bolognini) medievali* (XX Congresso Nazionale di Chimica Analitica, Viterbo, 16-20 Settembre 2007).

Dornbusch, F.W. (pseudonym of Fritzsche, Friedrich Wilhelm), *Gewichts-Reductions-Tabellen zur Verwandlung des bisherigen Preussischen Handelsgewichts sowie des Wiener, des Hamburger, des Englischen und des Russischer Handelsgewichts in neues Preussisches oder Zollgewicht und umgekehrt* (Berlin: Franz Duncker, 1858), 21p.

Fanti, Mario, *Confraternite e città a Bologna nel Medioevo e nell'Età moderna* (Roma: Herder Editrice e Libreria, 2001), 645pp.

Frati, Luigi, *Statuti di Bologna dall'anno 1245 all'anno 1267* (Bologna: Regia Tipografia, 1869-1877), 3 vol.

Gelli, Jacopo, *Scherma Italiana, sui principii ideati da Ferdinando Masiello del Cav. Jacopo Gelli*. (Milano: Hoepli, 1891), fifth edition, *Scherma Italiana, con accenni agli schermitori di jeri e d'oggi* (Milano: Hoepli, 1932), 273p.

Goldthwaite, Richard A., *The Economy of Renaissance Florence: An Economic and Social History* (Baltimore: The Johns Hopkins University press, 1980). Translated in Italian in *La costruzione della Firenze rinascimentale: una storia economica e sociale* (Bologna: Il Mulino, 1984), 630p.

Gionta, Stefano, *Il fioretto delle croniche di Mantova raccolte da Stefano Gionta* (Verona: per Bastian dalle Donne & Giouanni fratelli, 1570) edited by Amadei, F. (Mantova: Giuseppe Ferrari, 1741), 241pp.

Ghirardacci, Cherubino, *Della historia di Bologna, fino all'anno 1425* (Bologna: Giovanni Rossi, 1596), 2 vol.

Guidicini, Giovan Battista, *Cose notabili della Città di Bologna ossia Storia cronologica de'suoi stabili sacri, pubblici e privati* (Bologna, Tip. delle scienze di G. Vitali, 1868-73, reprinted in Sala Bolognese: A. Forni, 1972), 5 vol.

Haskins, Charles Homer, *The Rise of Universities* (New York : Henry Holt and Company, 1923), reprinted with new introduction by Lionel S. Lewis (Piscataway: Transaction Publishers, 2002), 134p.

Iacopi, Massimo, "Pane e panettieri in assisi del medioevo" (Published in quarterly newsletter "Il Subasio" in Assisi n. 3/17, December 2009, and in the weekly publication "Arte Bianca" by Federazione Italiana Panificatori in Padova, September 20, 2010).

Malanima, Paolo, "Measuring the Italian Economy 1300-1861", *Rivista di Storia Economica*, 19 (2003), pp. 265-295.

Malanima, Paolo, *Statistical Appendix, Consumer Price Indices and Wages in Central-Northern Italy and Southern England 1300-1850*. (Available on the website of the author http://www.paolomalanima.it/default_file/Italian Economy/StatisticalAppendix.pdf with data in EXCEL format, accessed 22 December 2015).

Mazzetti, Serafino, *Repertorio di tutti i professori antichi, e moderni, della famosa università, e del celere istituto delle scienze di Bologna, compilato da Serafino Mazzetti Bolognese, Archivista Vescovile* (Bologna: Tipografia San Tomaso d'Aquino, 1847), 378p.

McKinley, John, Degregori, Italo, & Partners, *Le Opzioni*, (Quaderni di finanza 13, Edizioni R.E.I., 2014), 228p.

Milani, Giuliano, "Monete, cambiatori e popolo. Un tentativo di riforma monetaria bolognese nel 1264", *Annali dell'Istituto Italiano di Numismatica*, 57 (2011), pp. 131-156.

Muratori, Ludovico Antonio, *Rerum Italicarum scriptores* (Milano, ex typographia Societatis Palatinae in Regia Curia, 1729-1751), 25 vol.

Muzi, Giovanni, *Memorie ecclesiastiche e civili di Città di Castello, raccolte da M. G. M. A. V. di C. di C.* (Città di Castello: Francesco Donati, 1842-44), 7 vol.

Muzzi, Salvatore, *Annali della città di Bologna dalla sua origine al 1796* (Bologna: tipi di S. Tommaso d'Aquino, 1840-46), 8 vol.

Orioli, Emilio, "La scherma a Bologna" (published in "il Resto del Carlino" n. 140, May 20-21, 1901, 3p).

Pantanelli, Guido, "Scherma e maestri di scherma bolognesi", *Strenna storica bolognese*, 3 (1930), pp. 45-49.

Pasolini, Pier Desiderio, *Caterina Sforza* (Roma: E. Loescher, 1893), 3 vol.

Phelps-Brown, E. Henry, Hopkins, Sheila, "Seven Centuries of the Prices of Consumables, Compared with Builders' Wage Rates"', *Economica*, 23(1956), pp. 296-314.

Pinto, Giuliano, *Il lavoro, la povertà, l'assistenza. Ricerche sulla società medievale* (Roma: Viella, 2008), 240p.

Salvioni, Giovanni Battista, "Il valore della lira bolognese nella prima metà del secolo XVI", *Atti e memorie della R. Deputazione di Storia Patria per le Provincie di Romagna, Terza serie*, 23 (1905), pp. 233-245.

Savigny, Friedrich Carl, *Geschichte des römischen Rechts im Mittelalter* (1815-1831), 6 vol. Translated in Italian, *Storia del diritto romano nel Medioevo* (Torino: Gianini e Fiore, 1857), 6 vol.

Tiraboschi, Girolamo, *Storia della letteratura italiana del cavaliere abate Girolamo Tiraboschi* (II ed., Modena: Società Tipografica, 1787-1794), 16 vol.

Welch, Evelyn, "Making money: pricing and payments in Renaissance Italy", in: *The Material Renaissance*, ed. by id. and M. O'Malley (Manchester: Manchester University Press, 2007), pp. 71-84.

Zanoboni, Maria Paola, "Donne al lavoro nell'edilizia medievale", *Archivio Storico Italiano*, 132/1 (2014), pp. 109-132.

APPENDIX

Archivio di Stato, Bologna, Comune, Governo, envelope N°318, "Riformagioni e provvigioni", Miscellaneous series, envelope N°5.

Transcription by Trevor Dean, May 2015.

Dilecto nobis magistro Lippo quondam Dardi Bononie civi salutem. Exhibita nobis fuit tui parte petitio sive supplicatio tenoris et continentie subsequentis, vz

M.D.V. Magnifici e potenti Signuri, Io Lippo de Bartolamio de Dardo de Dardi vostro minimo servidore supplico ale V.M.S. [Vostri Magnifici Signori] che a vui piaza de essere cason de uno honoro e utilita a questa magnifica cita, zoe che le V.M.S. dignino inverso de mi de uno certo honore e bene, el quale za piu tempo fa mi fo proferto e promesso, non cerchando quello, da uno certo citadino al quale iparve de volerme meritare per questa via, per caxon de le opere per mi facte in estrologia a quello stato popularo, el quale quello non e anche finito, e cusi piaqua a Jesu Christo che ello duri imperpetuo in felice stato E pertanto notifico ale V.M.S. como li detti beni proferti forno questi, zoe

Sapiti Lippo como io o deliberato per honore di questa cita che tu habii uno mandato de livre doxento de bolognini per zaschaduno anno sopra uno dacio, elquale quando se vendesse o no se vendesse che per li officiari de quello illi te debiano dare omne anno le dicte livre doxento de bolognini, e questo fo perche tu habii caxon de adoperarte piu volentiera in extrologia sopra el stato nostro, e anche per meritarte per quello che tu za fatto a questo stato, ma sapi che questo non e chuno motivo perche a ti fazo questo, avisandote che el dicto motivo sie che io voglio per utilita deli zuveni de questa cita, e onore de questo stato, e a utilita de ti, io voglio che tu adopri el to mistieri per altro modo che tu non ai facto per lo passato, quanto e per li presii grandi li quali tu toi ali zuveni de questa cita, e dimperzo te voglio tassare a mio modo tutti li tuoi zuoghi, zoe dove tu voi del zuogo dela spada da doe mane livre xxiii de bolognini, io voglio che to non toglii senon livre otto de bolognini, et dove tu toi livre sette del zuogo dela spada del bochilieri voglio che tu noe toglii che iii de bolognini, e dove tu toi L xii del zuogo dela daga tu ne tora L v de bolognini, e dove tu toi L vii del zuogo del baston tu ne tora L iii de bolognini, e dove tu toi L x del zuogo dele braze tu ne tora L iiii de bolognini, e dove toi L otto del zuogo dela rodella o targon tu ne tora L iii de bolognini.

E io a questo rispuxi che io ero contento, cum queste conditione che se caso fosse che a uno tracto me vignisse troppo scolari per caxon del pocho prexio non consueto, io non voglio essere obligato a torre piu che vinte scolari per volta, azo che a quilli possa imeglio insegnarglie, e anche percaxon che la scola non e capace a piu scolari, e a questi voglio averglie insegnato la teoricha dela spada grande infra dui mesi e mezo vignando quilli / do hore del di ala scola, et imparato che quelli avano la detta theoricha ne possa vignire altre tanti, e cusi distinguando per lordine detto, ma in men tempo voglio insegnare la teorica e arte del bocholieri, e cusi de tutti li altri zuoghi glieva men tempo a insignare como e noto in la mia scola tale theoriche, avisando ali V.M.S, che la pratica illi se la convenno a fatichare in zugare cum li altri scolari. Ancora [...] che io non volea essere tenuto ne obligato a insignare a zaschaduno senon uno anno, seno quanto paresse a mi de mia nobilita, avisando ale V.M.S. che se uno fosse piu grosso chel da buda ello imparara la theoricha overo larte dela spada da doe mane in dui mixi e mezo, e la praticha in altri tanti di, e la theoricha del bocholieri in uno mexe e mezo e in altri tanti la praticha, e de zaschuno deli altri zuochi quanto e per theoricha impararano uno da persi da laltro in uno mese, e la praticha in altrotanto, siche zaschuno de quisti voleno li suoi dui misi, tra imparare larte e la pratica, siche zaschuno a sette misi piu a potere imparare, e de tali zuochi ano nove mixi, e tali x misi, siche se illi non impararano in li dicti tempi non impararano mai piu. Anchora che volea chel me fosse facto decrieti segondo li pacti novamente facti li quali fosseno de quella natura li quali e li decrieti che za trenta anni fa o ottenuti da tutti li stati de Bologna in suso li quali se contene che one zudexe competente dela cita de Bologna a mi debiano fare una raxon summaria, e che ale mie libri siano dati piena fede contra zaschuno menore de xxv anni e contra zaschuno che fosse in podesta del padre, e cusi contra zaschuno che fosse # [sic] segurta per caxon deli dicti zuochi segondo che se contene in su la tavola de mia scola, li quali zuveni dami havesseno principiadi o fenire o no fenire quilli, avisando ale V.M.S. como a tale arte non impara seno zuveni, e imperzo a mi e stato concesso tali decrieti. E pertanto supplico ale V.M.S. che siate casone de tale honore e utilita segondo lordine dato, azo che li zuveni de questa cita habiano casone de imparare tale virtu, perche considerato il pocho prexio non consueto multi vigniranno a imparare. Ma considerato che le V.M.S. non hanno per si soli a poterme fare tale domanda, io ve demostra uno modo che cum vostro honore le V.M.S. il porano fare, zoe sopra le tasse di docturi, considerando che de lanno passato e del presente il sia insuso il rotulo ala lectura de zeumetria, la quale e conforma al arte del scrimere perche in quella non e altro che mesura propria la quale posso per lectura demostrare, cum zo sia chosa che ... facto libero ordinato a potere ... a chi ipiacesse, avisando ale V.M.S. che quilli liquali forno cason de farme mettere a tale lectura el... de quella si fo per meritarme dele fatiche passate in astrologia, la quale / e di natura geumetrale. E imperzo priego ale V.M.S. che inanci che se tassi ve piaza de tassirme como o detto per lo passato, e anche per li anni che ano adevenire perche a mi ne fariti grande apiacere, e anche utilita ad altri.

Qua quidem supplicatione per nos visa et lecta, de contentis in ea certam noticiam non habentes, commissimus Lodovico de Cazalupis et Simoni de Manfredis ut de ipsis omnibus se informarent nobisque refferent, qui postmodum nobis relationem eorum in scriptis fecrunt in forma infrascripta, viz:

Refferisseno ale V.M.S. Lodovico di Cazalupi e Simone Manfredi che vezuda la soprascritta domanda de Maestro Lippo de Dardo di Dardi, e quella examinata e conferitone cum piu persone circha quello che in essa se contene, ex parte considerando quanto beneficio torna le virtu del detto Maestro Lippo a questa nostra cita, perche lui e solicito a larte dela strologia, e poi avendo consideracione quanto esso il so mestiero dela spada da doe mane, buchulieri, e altri zuochi sopra zio sono utile ali zuveni de Bologna per deffesa de lora e etiandio de la re publica, ce pareria che dale V.M.S. fosse provisto in modo che neli soi exercitii e mestieri de strologia e geumetria e dela spada si potesse mantenire e perseverare, el quale serene che ogni anno non obstante la soa domanda de mazore soma fosse tassato solamente livre contocinquanta, zoe liv. 150 de bolognini, lanno insuso le tasse deli docturi, comenzando lanno mccccxliii e del mccccxliiii che cusi e rotolato, e cusi seguendo ... anno in anno, cum questo che deli zuochi infrascritti avesse infrascritte tasse e prexii, zoe del zuocho dela spada da doe mani livre diece de bolognini, del zuocho dela spada e buchelieri livre quatro, e del zuogo dela daga livre sie, e del zuocho del baston livre quatro, e del zuocho dele braze L cinque, e del zuocho dela rotella o targon L quatro de bolognini. E anche ce pareria che fosse dato piena fede ali soi libri contra qualonqua scolaro vignira a imparare da lui e che ogni zudexe consueto dela cita de Bologna li debia fare raxon sumaria e sianoli observati suoi decreti segondo se contene in li pacti dela scola. E cusi refferimo ale V.M.S., nientedemeno quelle provegono como a loro pare.

Cuius relationis tenore postea per nos viso et mature considerato precibus tuis utpote iustis benigniter annuentes nostri magistratus auctoritate in omni alio modo iure et forma quibus melius fieri potest, presenti nostro decreto decernimus et committimus fieri et tibi observari per omnia volumus et mandamus omnia et singula in suprascripta relatione contenta, expresse iniungentes omnibus et singulis ad quos spectat spectareque poterit in futurum quatenus presens nostre concessionis decretum observetur illudque faciant inviolabiliter observari sub nostri indignationis incursia. Dat. Bon. die xxiiii decembris 1443.

DOI 10.1515/apd-2016-0006

Pole-weapons in the Sagas of Icelanders: a comparison of literary and archaeological sources

Jan H. Orkisz,
Chapitre des Armes (Paris),
orkisz.jan@gmail.com

Abstract – The Icelandic sagas are a major source of information on the Vikings and their fighting prowess. In these stories, several mysterious pole-weapons appear, which are often called "halberds", for lack of a better word. In order to better identify what these weapons could have been, and to provide a better understanding of how the sagas relate to the Viking-age events they describe, we confront textual and archaeological evidence for several of these weapons (the *höggspjót*, the *atgeirr*, the *kesja*, the *krókspjót*, the *bryntroll* and the *fleinn*), keeping in mind the contextualisation of their appearances in sagas. The description of the use of each weapon allows to pick several candidates likely to correspond to the studied word. Without a perfect knowledge of what context the authors of the sagas wanted to describe, it appears to be impossible to give a final answer. However, we show that some specific types of spears are good candidates for some of the studied weapons.

Keywords – Early Middle Ages; Viking Age; pole-weapons; archaeology.

I. INTRODUCTION

I.1. Context

Vikings, their weapons and fighting prowess have fascinated people and raised a great interest since the 19th century, with the rise of romantic nationalism. Among the major sources that stimulate the imagination about these Scandinavian warriors are the Icelandic sagas, which tell the tales of many Viking-age heroes.

Among the weapons used by these Norsemen to achieve glory and bloodshed, some are very common, like the sword, axe or spear. But some weapons are much rarer, appearing only a few times in the sagas, and have names of unclear meaning in Old Icelandic (Old Norse). For lack of a better word, their names are often rendered as "halberd" or "bill", in literary translations of the sagas. For pole-weapons of an unknown nature, it can be a good option to put them under such umbrella terms, which in later medieval times referred to weapons with a huge variety of shapes.

However, is there any ground to compare e.g. a *kesja* or an *atgeirr* to what later became known as a halberd (Fig. 1)?

It seems that the path of thought followed by most translators is the following: if a pole-weapon is not a spear, and is able to cut and thrust, it means that it has a complicated shape, which makes it akin to a halberd. Others are more conservative, and assume that the shape of that weapon cannot be as complex as a halberd, and settle for something simpler, like a bill (or glaive). At best, intertextual studies relate these weapons to one another[1] or to other European weapons[2]. However, in these translations and comparisons, there is no sign of research into the archaeological evidence and martial arts of the time, and there is a general agreement on the fact that we don't really know what Viking-age "halberds" were, maybe because they were so rare that not a single specimen survived to our day.

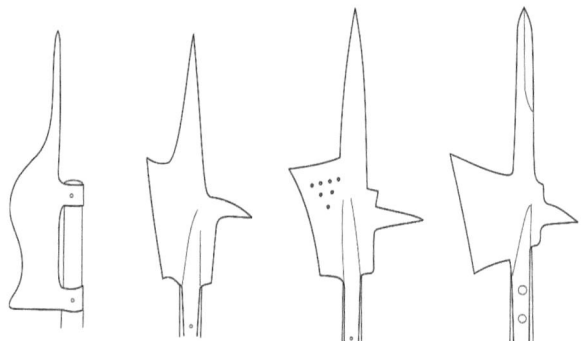

Figure 1: Examples of European halberds (to scale) from about 1400 to 1500, based on examples of the Metropolitan Museum (New York).

Our goal is to do this archaeological and martial research, to try and provide viable archaeological candidates for these unknown weapons, and a better understanding of the way they might have been wielded.

I.2. Methodology

The goal of our study is to compare the description that is made of these pole-weapons in the sagas with archaeological and pictorial evidences, in order to identify what kind of weapon was designated by a given word.

To do this comparison, there is a major caveat that has to be taken into account, namely the literary context of the sagas. The sagas describe events that happened in the Viking Age, between the 9th and the 11th century. However, the texts were not written down until the 13th century, some of the latest sagas being even dated to the early 14th century. Even if many sagas refer to historical characters and events, they are by no means history books, but rather literary works. Therefore, one does not expect them to give a realistic account of what happened – it is likely that instead, the authors distorted the facts to enhance the legendary or heroic nature of their protagonists. For example, elements of magic can be present in sagas which mention undoubtedly historical characters. It is also unlikely that

---

[1] Cleasby and Vigfusson, *An Icelandic-English Dictionary*, e.g. entry "atgeirr".

[2] Falk, *Altnordische Waffenkunden*, chapters 3 and 5.

the authors referred properly to 300-year old weapons: as it can be seen in paintings and manuscripts throughout all of the Middle-Ages (and, to some extent, in later periods as well), ancient characters are often wearing clothes, equipment and weapons that are either contemporary to the artist, or at most a few decades outdated □ which was deemed enough to give the impression of a time long past[3]. Besides, the authors of the sagas are not expected to be experts on military topics. They might therefore be misusing the names of the weapons, either involuntarily, by simple ignorance, or voluntarily, to embellish their text at the cost of technical accuracy.

When studying the descriptions of the weapons and their uses in the sagas, we must be careful with three things:

- the setting of the saga might be quite historically accurate for the Viking Age, or it can be contemporary to the author, and correspond to anywhere between the 10th and the 13th century.

- the related feats of arms can describe a realistic way of using the weapon, which the author can have heard (in the case of Viking-age weapons) or seen by himself (for 13th-century weapons), or it can be a literary overstatement that should be taken with a pinch of salt.

- the names of the weapons can sometimes by voluntarily or involuntarily misused by the authors. Since this last point is virtually impossible to verify, we will have to carefully check whether the various accounts on a given weapon are consistent with one another.

To carry out our study, we use an extensive list of references to weapons, armour and combat in the Sagas of Icelanders[4] to find the occurrences of the names of the studied weapons: the *höggspjót*, the *atgeirr*, the *kesja*, the *krókspjót*, the *bryntroll* and the *fleinn*. This database is constructed thanks to the full text of the Icelandic Sagas[5], and their full translation in English by Viðar Hreinsson and Katrina C. Attwood[6]. The search in the database is carried out according to the Icelandic text, since the English translation can be somewhat inconsistent, and the weapons that we study can be found under the names of "halberd", "thrusting spear", "spear", "bill", "double-bitted axe" or "pike". The identified sections of the sagas are cross-checked with their (Old) Icelandic and English versions, when available, in an online database[7].

---

[3] See, e.g., the depiction of Biblical times in the *Maciejowski Bible*, ca. 1245 (New York, Morgan Library, Ms. M. 638), or the depiction of Norse heroes in Renaissance manuscripts of the Icelandic Sagas.

[4] Short, *Arms and Armor in Sagas*.

[5] Anonymous, *Íslendinga sögur*, ed. Halldórsson et al.

[6] Anonymous, *The Complete Sagas of Icelanders*, ed. Hreinsson, transl. Attwood.

[7] Available at <http://sagadb.org/index_az> (accessed 01 December 2016).

For each weapon, we start by narrowing down our search for archaeological candidates by explaining the meaning of the name and its etymology. After that, we make an extensive list of the appearances of its name in the sagas of Icelanders. Then, we classify these occurrences based on the way the weapon is described or used, and try to use these statistics to compare the weapon with the archaeological artefacts or with the knowledge about later pole-weapons.

We then list the possible archaeological candidates for the weapon from the Viking Age to the 13th century, and, comparing these candidates to the descriptions in the sagas and the literary context, we try to find the most likely type of object corresponding to the weapon's name.

II. HÖGGSPJÓT

II.1. Literary occurrences

II.1.1. Etymology

The etymology and meaning of the word *höggspjót*[8] *are quite clear. The two roots here are the noun* spjót, *which is the most common word to denote a spear*[9]*, and the verb* höggva.

The verb *höggva* means "to strike, to smite"[10]. With a weapon or tool, it takes the meaning "to cut", hence the term *höggvapn* (cutting weapon, as opposed to a thrusting weapon – *lagvapn*)[11]. It is worth noting that it is the verb used when cutting down a tree (*höggva upp tré*)[12], or when using an axe. The "cut" implied by this verb is therefore about chopping, not slicing.

We have the impression of a weapon being closely related to a spear, but still being able to chop like an axe. Given this etymology, we will use the translation "hewing spear" for this weapon.

II.1.2. Appearance in sagas

The *höggspjót* appears sporadically in various sagas. Unfortunately, this corpus is quite small, and not very specific about the shape or the use of the weapon:

---

[8] We use the standardized orthography for Old Norse, with *ö* designating the long open [ɔ] sound, often also written ǫ.

[9] Cleasby and Vigfusson, *An Icelandic-English Dictionary*.

[10] Zoëga, *A Concise Dictionary Of Old Icelandic*.

[11] Ibid.

[12] Ibid.

- In Egils Saga (chapter 58), Egil is wielding a *höggspjót* in one hand, while carrying a shield in the other hand. The same weapon gets referred to as a *spjót* and a *kesja*[13].
- In Gísla Saga (chapter 2), Gisli uses a *höggspjót* to cut through a shield and its bearer[14].
- In Kormáks Saga (chapter 16), Bersi wields a *höggspjót* in one hand, and a parrying stick in the other hand[15].
- In Króka-Refs Saga (chapter 3), Refs takes a "big" *höggspjót*, and later uses it as a throwing spear[16].
- In Ljósvetninga Saga (chapter 12), Bjarni mentions his *höggspjót*. The same weapon is also referred to as a *skaftamunur* in Icelandic, translated as a "pike"[17]. The Old Norse form might have been **skaptamunr*, meaning a "shafted thing", i.e. a pole-weapon.
- In the same saga (chapter 19), Thorkel takes a *höggspjót* and wields it in two hands.
- In Víga-Glúms Saga (chapter 22), Glum is said to have a *höggspjót*, probably used in one hand.
- In Vopnfirðinga Saga (chapter 2), Svart makes a two-handed thrust with a "big" *höggspjót*[18].

The weapon is several times referred to as being big. It might be an indicator that a *höggspjót* is larger than a common spear, but it might just as well signify that the weapon described in the text is big even for a *höggspjót*.

We can see that this weapon appears to be used in one hand (with a shield or a parrying stick) as well as in two hands. It is similar to the way a simple spear can be wielded, and implies a reasonable weight.

The weapon is used to thrust, but also seems to possess an impressive cutting power, being able to chop through shield and man. Here again, we have the confirmation of a chopping motion, since slicing would have been rather ineffective against a wooden shield. It is worth noticing that it is the narrow "tail" of the shield which is said to be cut through[19], clearly implying a kite-shaped shield and a 13th century context for Gísla Saga (Fig. 2b, Fig. 7a).

---

[13] Appendix 10, 11 and 12.
[14] Appendix 15.
[15] Appendix 17.
[16] Appendix 18.
[17] Appendix 19.
[18] Appendix 20.
[19] Appendix 15.

Figure 2: Example of 13th century strapped shields: round targe (**a**), and transition from a large kite shield (**b**) (here worn on the back) to a smaller heater shield (**c**). Based on the Maciejowski Bible, ca. 1245 (New York, Morgan Library, Ms. M. 638, f° 9v, 10v and 10r).

II.2. Archaeological candidates

Given the name of the weapon, we focus our search for archaeological candidates on spears and spear-like pole-arms, and do not look at any kinds of axes.

II.2.1. Spears

Let us first focus on spears, i.e. thrust-centric pole-weapon with a sharp, symmetrical blade. In almost any era since the Bronze Age, it is possible to find spears that are able to cut: one just needs to make a spearhead large and broad enough.

If we look at the Viking Age, we can find numerous examples of such spears, which are usually large specimens of Petersen types B and C[20]. Such large winged spears became popular during the Migration Era among the Germanic people, and can be found in Scandinavia as well as in continental Europe (Fig. 3 and 4).

These spearheads have blades broader than 5 cm, which is the typical breadth of a Viking-age sword. The curved shape of their blades makes them good slicing weapons, allowing them to turn a near-missed thrust into a deep cut. Their weight can reach from over 500 g (Fig. 3a) to almost 2 kg (Fig. 4a). Combined with the leverage provided by a long shaft, this also gives to such spears the ability to chop powerfully.

Such spears can be found until the very end of the Viking Age; other types of broad and heavy spears retain these slicing and chopping capacities in later medieval times (Fig. 6b and 6c).

---

[20] Petersen, *De Norske Vikingesverd*, pp. 23-24.

Figure 3: Large Viking spearheads with a cutting capacity. **a**: *41 cm long spearhead with 6.8 cm wide blade, (Stockholm, Statens Historiska Museet, catalogue nr. SHM 7571:256 (obj. 450765)), photograph:* © *Gabriel Hildebrand,* **b**: *53 cm long spearhead with 6.7 cm wide blade, (Stockholm, Statens Historiska Museet, catalogue nr. SHM 34000:Bj 850 (obj. 372011)), photograph:* © *Christer Åhlin. Reproduced with permission of the institution.* **c**: *spearhead, ~70 cm long, ~9 cm wide (Copenhagen, National Museum), own picture and estimations.* **d**: *spearhead, ~60 cm long, ~7 cm wide blade (Busdorf, Haithabu Museum), own picture and estimations.*

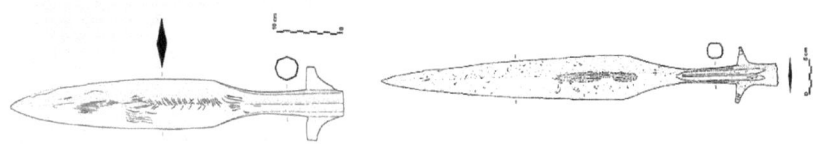

Figure 4: Other Viking-age spearheads. **a**: *Frankish 50.2 cm long spearhead with 7.2 cm wide blade, ~9th century, (Chalon-sur-Saône, Musée Denon, catalog nr. 93.34.5), and* **b**: *Frankish 58.7 cm long spearhead with 6.5 cm wide blade, 11th century, (Chalon-sur-Saône, Musée Denon, catalog nr. 67.4.2). Drawings by C. Michel. Reproduced with permission of the institution.*

II.2.2. Glaives

Among other types of pole-weapons, the one with the closest shape and use to a spear is the glaive. If we describe a spear as a dagger on a pole, then a glaive would be a knife on a pole: single edged, and designed as much to cut as to thrust.

Examples of glaives start to be seen in the 13th century – and would have therefore been contemporary to the authors of the sagas.

Figure 5: *Illustrations of 13th century pole-weapons. Panels* **a** *and* **b** *show a large-bladed glaive or falchion. The weapon is always used two-handed, but can be long- or short-shafted, used either on foot or on horseback. Panels* **c** *and* **d** *show a smaller glaive, which almost looks like half of a normal spearhead, except that is has a clearly curved cutting edge. Other shown weapons are spears, axes, maces, and what seems to be a mail-piercing pike similar to a later ahlspiess*[21] *(***a** *and* **d***). Based on the* Maciejowski Bible, *ca. 1245 (New York, Morgan Library, Ms. M. 638, f° 10r, 42r, 15r and 27v).*

Early examples of glaives appear in several folios of the anonymous *Maciejowski Bible* from ca. 1245 (Fig. 5). The first kind of glaive (Fig. 5a, 5b) appears on folios 10r, 10v and 42r. It is something half-way between a huge falchion and a glaive. The blade is extremely large, and the shaft is sometimes very short. The second kind appears on folios 15r, 16v, 17r, 27v, 43r and 43v, and is the exact opposite, with long and thin shafts and small blades. Surprisingly, the blade is always backwards when the weapon is used on horseback, indicating that the horsemen did not use it for cutting.

It is reasonable to think that intermediate-sized glaives had started emerging by the same time. Fig. 6a depicts a later (15th century) glaive, which would have such an intermediate size: a blade about 60 cm long on a ~2 m shaft.

---

[21] Oakeshott, *European Weapons and Armour*, p. 52

II.3. Interpretation

An important hint to understand the nature of the studied weapons might come from later sources on combat with pole-weapons.

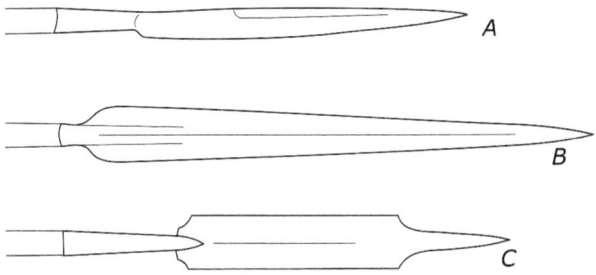

Figure 6: Examples of late medieval cut-and-thrust pole-weapons that are most closely related to the spear, based on museum examples (to scale). **a**: *a late 15th century glaive, similar to the older weapons seen in Fig. 5.* **b**: *a large 15th century spear.* **c**: *a broad-bladed ox-tongue spear from the late 15th century. Weapons such as* **b** *and* **c** *evolved into partisans during the Renaissance.*

Let us focus on the fact that the *höggspjót* can be used either two-handed, or one-handed with a parrying device (stick or shield) in the other hand. In later medieval and Renaissance fencing treatises, fighting with a pole-weapon and a shield is rarely described, but when it is the case, the weapon is always a spear, or a spear-like (symmetrical) weapon[22]. One could argue that the fencing treatises being often more duel than battle-oriented, it is not surprising to see few mentions of typically battlefield weapons such as the bill, the glaive... and that the use of the shield is less needed in a duelling context. This would be true, but the fact that only spears (light or heavy) are used in conjunction with a shield is overwhelmingly supported by pictorial evidences. The one-handed use of a pole-weapon such as a glaive or a halberd is extremely rarely, if ever, represented in artwork.

The reason for this is mechanically quite simple: to deliver an effective cut, one needs to apply enough torque on the handle of the weapon – which would not be possible with the strength of a single wrist and the large leverage of a pole-weapon. Therefore, if used one-handed, a pole-weapon can only be used effectively to thrust or to slice (draw-cut)[23].

The use of the *höggspjót* can be very well compared with the use of the partisan[24]: we have in both cases a heavy spear-like weapon with a cutting capacity, which can be used two-

---

[22] For example in Achille Marozzo, *Opera Nova*, (book 4, chap. 179), in *Die Blume des Kampfes* (Vienna, Österreichische Nationalbibliothek, Cod. 10799) or in *Gladiatoria* (Cracow, Biblioteka Jagiellońska, MS Germ. Quart. 16).

[23] Achille Marozzo, *Opera Nova*, book 4, chap. 179, introduction.

[24] Ibid., chap. 179 and 180.

handed or with a shield. The length, width and weight of partisans are also similar to the spears in Fig. 3 and 4.

It seems therefore reasonable to conclude that *höggspjót* is a word used to describe a large spear with a cutting capacity – as the name says it, a "hewing spear". Like any spear, it would be used mostly for thrusting, and could sometimes be used for slicing, be it one- or two-handed. Its specificity (and hence its name) compared to smaller spearheads would be its ability to chop (*höggva*) effectively when used two-handed.

III. ATGEIRR

III.1. Literary occurrences

III.1.1. Etymology

The word *atgeirr* is older that the Viking Age, and cognates can be found in Old English and other Germanic dialects (*atiger, setgare, aizger*), deriving from the Germanic root *gar* (in Old Norse *geirr*), meaning a spear[25]. In earlier Germanic languages, *gar* and *setgar* rather designates a heavy spear (as opposed to a light javelin), while *geirr* is just a common name for any spear in Old Norse[26]. Therefore, we are encouraged to think of a weapon closely related to a spear – something long-shafted and thrust-oriented.

The main question is to know what special meaning the prefix *at-* is giving to this word.

A first interpretation is to see it as deriving from the Latin *ad-*, which would be used in this case as an intensive[27]. In this scope, *atgeirr* can be interpreted meaning a "very spear", an "excellent spear".

When comparing with other Old Norse words, we can also notice that the prefix *at* often gives a martial meaning to words.

It derives from the word at (f.): *poet.* collision, clash, fight[28]. We can find this martial meaning in many words such as *at*ferð, *at*ganga (and *at*gangr), *at*hlaup, *at*laga, *at*ras, *at*reið, *at*róðr, *at*sókn, *at*vígi, which all mean "(go, ride, row to) attack", "(to) fight"[29].

In this context, we can understand the word *atgeirr* as denoting a "battle spear" – as opposed to a light javelin or a hunting spear, it underlines the man-killing character of the weapon, which is depicted in Brennu-Njáls saga as almost having a blood-lust on its own.

---

[25] Keller, *The Anglo-Saxon Weapon Names*, p. 21.
[26] Zoëga, *A Concise Dictionary Of Old Icelandic*.
[27] Keller, *The Anglo-Saxon Weapon Names*, p. 130.
[28] Cleasby and Vigfusson, *An Icelandic-English Dictionary*.
[29] Ibid.

Last but not least, the word *atgeirr* was kept in use in the Icelandic language and took the meaning of a regular European halberd (Fig. 1).

III.1.2. Appearance in sagas

The *atgeirr* appears in three different sagas: most prominently in Brennu-Njáls Saga, but also in the Laxdœla Saga and the Eyrbyggja Saga.

It is interesting to note that these three sagas are closely related. They all focus on events which historically happened around the same time (late 10th and early 11th century), and feature several characters in common, among which the famous Snorri Goði. The three sagas were written in the mid to late 13th century. Eyrbyggja Saga probably dates back to prior 1264[30], Laxdœla Saga to about 1230 – 1260[31], and Brennu-Njáls Saga was probably first written between 1270 and 1290[32].

It is likely that the (unknown) author of Eyrbyggja Saga knew the text of Laxdœla Saga, and that the author of Brennu-Njáls Saga knew the two previous ones. It is therefore possible that the author of Brennu-Njáls Saga chose from the weapons mentioned in the two older sagas the name he saw most fitting for the fearsome weapon that became central to Gunnar Hámundarson's story.

We therefore assume that the authors of the three sagas had the same weapon in mind when using the word *atgeirr*.

- **Brennu-Njáls saga**

It is in this saga that the *atgeirr* achieved fame. The weapon's name is mentioned no less than 51 times, with about 69% of these appearances happening in the context of a fight or battle. The *atgeirr* of this saga is obviously a very special weapon. Save for its first appearance and a mention as "Gunnar's *atgeirr*", 49 times out of 51 is it mentioned in a definite form, as "the *atgeirr*" (*atgeirinn*)[33]. In contrast, even weapons as important as swords are often usually in an indefinite form (e.g. "Sigmund was girded with a sword"[34]) unless they have a name or a special context attached to them. This proves how unique the *atgeirr* is. It is also explicitly mentioned as being a magical weapon. In the first two occurrences where the weapon (then belonging to Hallgrim) is mentioned (chapter 30), it is explained how it has been enchanted - one of its powers being a loud ringing of the blade foretelling killings[35]. Later in the saga, this prophetic ringing is mentioned again

---

[30] Mallet, Scott, et al. *Northern Antiquities*, p. 517.

[31] Sveinsson (ed.), *Laxdæla Saga*, p. xxv.

[32] Gylfason (ed.), *Njál's Saga*, Introduction, p. XIII.

[33] e.g. Appendix 4 and 5.

[34] Appendix 3.

[35] Appendix 2.

(chapter 54), and in one occurrence, blood appears out of nowhere on the blade, as another sign of upcoming bloodshed (chapter 72).

- **In the other sagas**

The *atgeirr* appears also in one scene of each of the older sagas.

In Eyrbyggja Saga (chapter 26), it is mentioned three times in Svart's failed attempt to murder Snorri Goði. Each time, it is mentioned as a thrusting weapon.

In Laxdœla Saga (chapter 64), Hardbein thrusts an *atgeirr* through Thorstein's iron skull-cap. This might show how powerful the weapon was, might be a literary exaggeration, or might be a realistic event of a spear made of good steel (a "very spear") cracking the iron of a poor quality skull-cap.

III.1.3. Use as a weapon

In none of the sagas is the *atgeirr* described. However, more information can be derived from the description of its use, in combat or otherwise.

Apart from using it in combat, Gunnar uses the *atgeirr* twice to vault himself onto his saddle (chapters 54 and 74). This is a good indicator of the geometry of the shaft.

To vault oneself high enough, there are two options. The first is to push downwards, ideally on a horizontal surface, if said surface is lower than shoulder-high – this would be possible by using e.g. the butt of a two-handed axe as the handle of a (tall) walking stick. The other option is to pull oneself up on a shaft higher than shoulder-high – this option matches more a shaft as long as a spear. Given our assumptions on the weapon, we keep the second option, and therefore conclude that Gunnar's *atgeirr* is as long-shafted as a (long) spear, meaning that the socket of the blade is at or above eye-level.

Table 1 summarizes all the fighting moves related to an *atgeirr* in the three sagas.

The first element that we will derive from these statistics are the guards used for this weapon.

Quite often, the fights are short or unexpected and are not described in details, so that it is difficult to know how the protagonists are equipped, and therefore if the *atgeirr* is used in one or two hands (16 cases out of 39). In the cases were we can guess how the weapon is held, we see that it is almost as often used one-handed as two-handed (12 vs. 11 cases).

It is worth mentioning that in the case of a one-handed use, Gunnar is described either wielding the *atgeirr* and a shield, or the *atgeirr* in one hand and a sword in the other one. It even happens that these two configurations are described in the same fight, somewhat inconsistently, since it is unclear how the Gunnar could sheathe / unsheathe his sword or discard / grab his shield at such a pace (chapter 54).

Move	One-handed	Two-handed	Unknown	Total
Thrusting	4	6	5	15
Cutting	1	0	1	2
Lifting[36]	1	2	1	4
Shooting[37]	2	0	0	2
Parrying	1	0	1	2
Twisting[38]	0	1	0	1
Holding[39]	0	2	6	8
Other[40]	3	0	2	5
Total	12	11	16	39

Table 1: Statistics of the use of an atgeirr *in combat in Brennu-Njáls, Eyrbyggja and Laxdæla Sagas. The number of hands holding the weapon is either explicitly mentioned in the saga, or derived from the context (used with a shield, another weapon, etc.)*

When holding the weapon one-handed, and assuming that it is wielded more or less like a spear, another question arises about the guard, since three possible positions are depicted in artwork throughout history for the one-handed spear: the overarm, underarm and couched guards (Fig. 7). In two situations, we can guess what the guard of the protagonist is:

- when Gunnar shoots (thrusts or throws) the *atgeirr* through a enemy shield and its bearer in what seems to be a downward blow, we can guess the use of an overarm guard[41],
- when Gunnar lifts an impaled Egil on the *atgeirr* with a single arm (chapter 63): the scene is quite obviously a literary overstatement, magnifying Gunnar's strength, but this feat can be marginally reasonable if a pivot point is provided by the armpit to use the shaft of the weapon as a lever. The blow might have been delivered from a couched or underarm guard, and the lifting is done in the couched guard.

The second, and probably most important element that we can study is the kind of blows delivered by this weapon. We therefore disregard here the actions of parrying or simply holding the weapon, which leaves us with 29 actions out of 39.

---

[36] Lifting an impaled opponent.
[37] Thrusting or throwing?
[38] Twisting the blade in the wound.
[39] Holding, grabbing, raising, aiming…
[40] Fighting, killing, running through.
[41] Appendix 5.

Figure 7: Spear and shield guards for infantry: overarm, underarm and couched spear.
a: Bayeux Tapestry, *11th century, with special authorization of the city of Bayeux.*
b: Achilles fighting Hector, *greek volute crater, (London, British Museum, catalog nr. 1848,0801.1). © British Museum (CC BY NC SA 4.0).*
c: Bible d'Étienne Harding, *ca. 1109-1111 (Dijon, Bibliothèque municipale, Ms. 14,. f°13v). Reproduced with permission of the institution.*

We notice first that it is unclear from the text whether the verb "shooting" (*skjóta*) designates the action of throwing or thrusting the weapon. This verb applies to archery (*skjóta af boga* ▢ shooting a bow[42]), which could imply a meaning of throwing in the case of a pole-weapon, but it is also used for any quick forward motion (*skjóta skildi fyrir sik* ▢ to put a shield before oneself[43]), so a thrust is a possible option too. In the case of the *atgeirr*, it seems that the weapon is immediately recovered and used again, which might prove a thrusting motion[44]. It is also consistent with the fact that a throw and a thrust from the overarm guard are basically the same motion.

Leaving aside the few occurrences where we are just told that the opponent is "killed", "run through" or receives his "death blow", etc. (5 cases out of 29), and the specific motions of twisting the blade (1 occurrence) and lifting the impaled opponent (4 occurrences), we can see that we are left with an overwhelming majority of thrusts. "Thrusting" and "shooting" occurs 17 times, whereas "cutting" only two times. Out of these two cuts, one is a cut through a spear shaft (chapter 79), and the other one is actually likely to be a cut made with a sword, since it occurs in a situation where Gunnar is fighting with the *atgeirr* in one hand and a sword in the other hand[45]. It is not obvious from the text whether the cut is made by the *atgeirr* or the sword, but the fight happens right after a scene where Gunnar describes a premonitory dream where he "cuts with his sword and thrusts with the *atgeirr*" (chapter 62).

---

[42] Zoëga, *A Concise Dictionary Of Old Icelandic.*
[43] Ibid.
[44] e.g. Appendix 5.
[45] Appendix 6.

Therefore, if we limit ourselves to wounding blows that are described accurately, we end up with 100 % of thrusts.

III.2. Archaeological candidates

Given its uses in battle and the strongly spear-related name, the *atgeirr* might be the same kind of weapon as the *höggspjót* (see section II.2).

The *atgeirr* being almost exclusively used for thrusting, we could have assumed that the weapon could be any type of spear. However, the instance where the *atgeirr* manages to cut (*höggva*) through a spear shaft indicates that it must have had a substantial blade.

The lifting of impaled opponents also gives a hint about the geometry of the blade, which prevents the body from sliding down the shaft: either the spear must be quite broad, or, even better, it must have wings on the socket (Fig. 3). Therefore, glaive blades do not make as good candidates as certain types of spears.

III.3. Interpretation

An important thing to note about Brennu-Njáls Saga is that it is very strongly set in a 13th century context[46]. Apart from the details about customs and clothing, one of the most obvious indicators of this setting is the all-around presence of kite shields (Fig. 2b). The same goes for Laxdœla Saga, with the mention of kite shields as well as an iron skull-cap, which is a type of helmet that appeared only in the 12th century[47]. Therefore, the author might have had a 13th century weapon in mind when writing about the *atgeirr*.

However, one has to keep in mind that in Brennu-Njáls Saga, the *atgeirr* is clearly a unique weapon, at least due to its magical properties. It is therefore likely that the shape of the *atgeirr* would be unusual as well: the weapon could be either foreign, or ancient – which would be consistent with the old Germanic origin of the word.

We must therefore consider three options: the *atgeirr* of Brennu-Njáls Saga might be a normal, 13th-century Icelandic weapon, given a special name to emphasize its uniqueness, or a foreign, unusual weapon, or an ancient weapon, that would be anachronistic in a 13th century context.

The fact that an *atgeirr* is casually mentioned in other sagas would tend to rule out the hypothesis of a foreign weapon – one would expect the authors to dwell more on the description of such a rare weapon, like the author of Brennu-Njáls Saga does when the *atgeirr* is first mentioned in the hands of Hallgrim.

The *atgeirr* is therefore most likely a type of spear that was at least to some extent known to 13th century Icelanders. And, even though it contradicts the later meaning of the word *atgeirr* as a regular halberd, and even though the supposed uniqueness of the *atgeirr* in

---

[46] Sigurðsson, *The Medieval Icelandic Saga and Oral Tradition*, pp. 301-303.

[47] Nicolle, *Knight of Outremer, 1187-1344*, p. 51.

Brennu-Njáls Saga makes it difficult to give an assertive conclusion, the best option for the *atgeirr* of the sagas, given its use, would be a large hewing spear, most probably with wings.

IV. KESJA

IV.1. Literary occurrences

IV.1.1. Etymology
The word *kesja* has the least obvious etymology. It is supposed to derive from (or share a common origin with) the Celtic (Gaulish) word *gæsum*, which means a javelin, or throwing spear. The word *gæsum* might also share a common origin with the word *geirr* – "spear"[48].

Given the distance in space and time between 1st century Gaul and 13th century Iceland, we will only assume a vague relationship between the objects these two words designate, just like the words "javelin" and "gavelock" (iron bar or lever, in some modern English dialects[49]), while sharing a common Germanic origin, ended up meaning quite different things, after centuries of linguistic evolution and semantic drift.

We will therefore only assume a *kesja* to be a shafted weapon, without any other specification.

IV.1.2. Appearance in sagas
As opposed to the other weapons studied here, the *kesja* appears almost exclusively in one saga, namely Egils Saga Skalla-Grímssonar. There is also a single occurrence of a *kesja* in Ljósvetninga Saga (in which Gudmund "plunges" it into Rindil, without other details ☐ chapter 20).

The appearances of the *kesja* in Egils Saga are extremely diverse, showing a large range of situations, uses, and we are even provided with a detailed description of the weapon. Egil is by far the character most often mentioned wielding a *kesja*, but he is not the only one.

- Four times, a *kesja* is mentioned as an element of the panoply of a warrior, usually consisting of a shield, a sword and a *kesja* (as well as a helmet and sometimes a mail shirt). In one case, the *kesja* belongs to Thorolf (chapter 53), in the other cases, to Egil. Sometimes Egil has the sword tied to the wrist instead of having it sheathed[50].
- Egil breaks off the head of his *kesja* to pack it in a bundle with his other weapons (chapter 45).

---

[48] Cleasby and Vigfusson, *An Icelandic-English Dictionary*.
[49] Webster et al., *Webster's dictionary*.
[50] e.g. Appendix 13.

- Thorolf's *kesja* is described as being a *brynþvari* (chapter 53).
- Thorolf uses his *kesja*, here referred to as a *spjót* ("spear"), two handed, for cutting and thrusting (chapter 53).
- Thorolf's *kesja* pierces a mail shirt (chapter 53). The impaled opponent is lifted on it and the weapon is stuck in the ground to keep him aloft. In the same sentence, the *kesja* is referred to as a *spjót*[51].
- Thorolf is killed when many *kesjur* are drawn against him / thrust at him (chapter 54).
- Egil fights with his *kesja* in one or two hands.
- Egil and Berg-Önund throw *kesjur* at each other, the weapons are deflected by the shields or get stuck in it. The weapon is here again referred to as a *spjót* (chapter 58).
- Egil shoots (throws or thrusts?) his *kesja* through shield and man.
- Egil uses his *kesja* in a naval battle (chapter 70).

The description of Thorolf's *kesja*, referred to as a *brynþvari* ("mail-stick" or "mail-spear"), is very interesting. The Old Icelandic text can be translated in the following way (based on [52] and [53]):

> *Kesju hafði hann í hendi. Fjöðrin var tveggja álna löng ok sleginn fram broddr ferstrendr, en upp var fjöðrin breið, falrinn bæði langr ok digr, skaftit var eigi hæra en taka mátti hendi til fals ok furðuliga digrt. Járnteinn var í falnum ok skaftit allt járnvafit. Þau spjót váru kölluð brynþvarar.*

> He had a *kesja* in his hand; the blade was two ells long, and forged to a four-edged point, but at its base the blade was broad. The socket was both long and thick. The shaft was not longer that what was needed to be able to grasp the socket with the hand, and was exceedingly thick. There was an iron spike in the socket, and the shaft was all bound with iron. Such spears were called *brynþvarar*.

(Egils Saga, chapter 53)

---

[51] Appendix 9.
[52] Edwards and Pálsson (eds.), *Egil's Saga*, chap 53.
[53] Zoëga, *A Concise Dictionary Of Old Icelandic*.

IV.1.3. Use as a weapon

Table 2 summarizes the uses of the *kesja* in combat.

Move	One-handed	Two-handed	Unknown	Total
Thrusting	1 (2?)	2	Many	2 (3?) + many
Cutting	0	1	0	1
Lifting[54]	0	0	1	1
Throwing	2 (3?)	0	0	2 (3?)
Fighting	1	1	1	3
Total	4	4	2 + many	10 + many

Table 2: Statistics of the use of a kesja *in combat in Egils and Ljósvetninga Sagas. The number of hands holding the weapon is either explicitly mentioned in the saga, or derived from the context.*

We can see that the weapon is rarely used for cutting, that it can be used in one or two hands (e.g. with the shield carried on the back), and from what is described, it is used both for thrusting and throwing – which is consistent with the fact that *spjót* ("spear") is used several times as a synonym for the weapon.

The seldom use of cuts is, in turn, consistent with the fact that the weapon is once referred to as a *höggspjót* (Egils Saga, chapter 58).

IV.2. Archaeological candidates

As Table 2 shows, the *kesja* can be used in a variety of different ways, including throwing, thrusting, cutting... We could therefore assume the same candidates for the *kesja* as we did for the *höggspjót* and the *atgeirr* – which would be consistent with the hypothesis by Cleasby & Vigfusson[55] that the *höggspjót*, the *kesja* and the *atgeirr* would be the same thing.

However, a heavy hewing spear does not make a very good candidate for a throwing weapon[56]. Besides, the description of a *kesja* in chapter 53 of Egils Saga can provide us with several other archaeological candidates.

A first interpretation of this description is that the *kesja* has a long, sturdy point, with a broad blade at its base (an axe blade?) and another spike at the socket (a back spike?) – it would then look just like an early halberd (Fig. 1).

Another interpretation is that of a spear blade with a narrow point that is flaring out quite significantly, perhaps like Fig. 3c or like the ox-tongue spear from Fig. 6c. The iron spike in the socket could then either be a crossbar, like one would have on a boar-spear (Fig. 11), or, simply, the nail or rivet which is used to attach the socket of the *kesja* to the shaft.

---

[54] Lifting an impaled opponent.

[55] Cleasby and Vigfusson, *An Icelandic-English Dictionary* .

[56] Although Achille Marozzo mentions the throwing of partisans (*Opera Nova*, Bologna, book 4, chapter 179, 8th play).

Finally, the four-edged point of the *kesja* blade can be reminiscent of what was most likely called a *brodd-spjót*: "a spear ending in a four-edged point"[57, 58]. These *brodd-spjót* can have referred to slender, high-ridged spears (Fig. 8c), or to even more specific mail-piercing blades, examples of which survive from the Vendel Age, one to three centuries before the Viking Age (Fig 8a and 8b). If it was not for its size (less than 40 cm instead of two ells – about 98 cm!), the shape of the spearhead on Fig. 8b could have matched perfectly the description from the saga.

Figure 8: Scandinavian spearheads with a four-edged point. a: strongly hollow-ground Vendel age mail-piercing spearhead, (Stockholm, Statens Historiska Museet, catalog nr. SHM 1209 (obj. 371669)), photograph: © Jenny Nyberg, b: high-ridged Vendel age mail-piercing spearhead widening at its base, (Stockholm, Statens Historiska Museet, catalog nr. SHM 1209 (obj. 371670)), photograph: © Jenny Nyberg, c: high-ridged Viking age slender spearhead, (Stockholm, Statens Historiska Museet, catalog nr. SHM 34000:Bj 708 (obj.467387)), photograph: © Ulrik Skans. Reproduced with permission of the institution.

IV.3. Interpretation

The interpretation of the *kesja* as something very similar to a later halberd is tempting, but we have to reject it for a number of reasons.

First and foremost, halberds like those on Fig. 1 did not start emerging before the very end of the 14th century. Therefore, such weapons would have been unknown not only to the protagonists of the saga, set in the 9th and 10th centuries during the reigns of Harald

---

[57] Zoëga, *A Concise Dictionary Of Old Icelandic*.

[58] Falk, *Altnordische Waffenkunden*, p. 68.

Fairhair and Eirik Bloodaxe, but also to the author of the saga, writing it in the 13th century.

For a 13th century context, H. Falk suggests that the *brynþvari* might be a variant of *bryntroll* (see Sect. VI.1.), and would be a kind of double-bladed axe with a four-edged point on top[59], which makes it akin to a halberd. However, another reason to discard the halberd as a viable candidate is the use of the *kesja* as a throwing weapon in conjugation with a shield – which seems quite a ridiculous way to use a halberd.

Finally, in the description in chapter 53, the head of the kesja is referred to as a *fjöðr*. The word *fjöðr* primarily means "feather" or "quill"[60], but can also designate a spearhead – obviously due to its feather-like shape. Therefore, this word is extremely unlikely to be used to describe something like a halberd or bill blade. It is also consistent with the fact that weapons called *kesja* are often also referred to as spears (*spjót*).

We are thus left with the option of different types of spears.

An indicator of the spears to look at is the historical setting of the saga. Unlike Brennu-Njáls Saga, which mostly featured 13th century elements, Egils Saga shows an attempt of the author to be more historically accurate about the period it is describing.

It can be seen from the shields appearing in the text: not a single kite shield is explicitly mentioned, moreover, Egil's panoply is indifferently described as consisting of a *kesja*, sword and shield, or a *kesja*, sword and buckler, or a *höggspjót*, sword and shield. Either we assume that Egil changes weapons (but that would be inconsistent with the author writing about his "customary weapons"[61]), or we conclude that these different words can refer indifferently to the same objects. In that case, calling the same object a shield and a buckler can show that the author has in mind a round, centre-gripped shield, which would be a larger version of a 13th century buckler (Fig. 9). Besides, in chapter 53, the author insists on the fact that the warriors are all equipped with their "Norse shields and Norse weapons"[62] – as if to emphasize the contrast with the 13th century weapons known to his readers. The fact that the fighters very rarely wear mail in the saga, even during pitched battles, is also an indicator of an older time period.

---

[59] Falk, *Altnordische Waffenkunden*, p. 111.
[60] Zoëga, *A Concise Dictionary Of Old Icelandic*.
[61] Appendix 7 and 10.
[62] Appendix 8.

Figure 9: Example of boss-held round shields from the Viking Age to the 13th century.
a: *Viking shield (usual size 80 □ 90 cm)⁶³ from the Gokstad ship burial, 9th century, (Oslo, Kulturhistorisk Museum, catalog nr. C10390b), photograph: © Eirik Ingens Johnsen (CC BY NC SA 4.0). Reproduced with permission of the institution.* **b**: *Bucklers used in combat, late 13th century, Liber de Arte Dimicatoria, ca. 1320 (Leed, Royal Armouries, MS I.33, f° 11r), © Board of Trustees of the Royal Armouries.*

In that scope, later designs of weapons such as an ox-tongue spear, or a boar-spear with a crossbar being the "spike in the socket" are not necessarily the best candidates for the *kesja*.

An attempted reconstruction of Thorolf's *kesja* described in chapter 53 is presented on Fig. 10. It has the four-edged point of the *brodd-spjót*, and a blade wide enough to act as a *höggspjót* – since Thorolf also uses it for cutting. The "spike in the socket" is represented as a simple nail, and the socket diameter, 4 cm, is indeed "exceedingly thick" for a spear. Overall, it looks a lot like an oversized specimen of the spear on Fig. 8b.

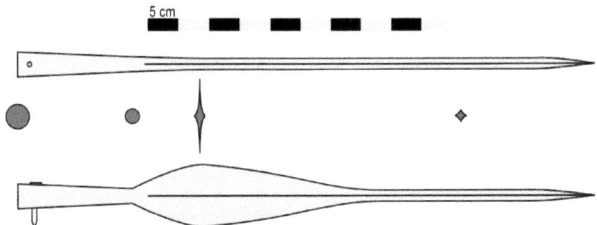

Figure 10: A hypothetical reconstruction of the kesja as described in Egils Saga: blade profiles and cross-sections.

This particular *kesja* gets referred to as a *brynþvari*. We understand that the description that was given is therefore not a description of any *kesja*, but of a specific type thereof. The question arises then to know what a *kesja* refers to in general.

The first option is that a *kesja* is a mail-piercing spear, a bit like the *brodd-spjót*. It might be, for example, that if the spear only has a four-edged (hollow-ground) point, it is a *broddspjót* (Fig. 8a, 8c), but if its blade it widening, then it is a *kesja* (Fig. 8b, 10). And if the said

---

[63] Short, *Viking shields*.

kesja is unusually big, like the one described in chapter 53, then it is called a *brynþvari*. In that case, the *kesja*, if small enough, can be used one-handed, for thrusting or throwing, and, if big enough, it can be used to deliver two-handed cuts – which corresponds to all the descriptions of this weapon in combat. However, it would be strange to use the name "mail-spear" only for the giant version, while the smaller versions are also perfectly suitable to burst the rings of a mail shirt.

The other option is to go for a broader meaning of the word *kesja*, and this is suggested by the scene of Thorolf's death, killed by many *kesjur*. If the *kesja* were a special and unusual type of weapon (be it a halberd, a mail-piercing spear or anything else), it would be unlikely that many warriors among Thorolf's enemies would have this kind of weapon, unless they had a good reason for it. In the battle that Thorolf fought with his *kesja* (chapter 53), it is explicitly mentioned that he was not wearing mail. It is therefore most likely that he was not wearing mail either on the following day (chapter 54), when he was killed. Therefore, his opponents had no reason to use mail-piercing spears against him, and the weapons they used in great numbers to kill Thorolf were probably of common nature. We can therefore suggest that the word *kesja* is yet another word to designate a spear, just like *spjót* and *geirr*. The *kesja*, being just a spear, can then be, depending on the context, a throwing spear, a hewing spear, a mail-piercing spear…

We favour the interpretation where *kesja* is a rare word to designate a spear, a word that was liked by the author of Egils Saga but rarely used by others.

This hypothesis is consistent with the fact that the *kesja* appears numerous times in the Heimskringla by Snorri Sturluson, who is likely also be the author of Egils Saga[64]. This corpus should be studied as well in order to provide a better understanding.

V. KRÓKSPJÓT

V.1. Literary occurrences

V.1.1. Etymology

The *krókaspjót*[65] or *krókspjót*[66] is yet another weapon deriving from a spear, as the name suggests.

It is a spear (*spjót*) which is characterized by its *krókar*. A *krókr* is a hook, or anything crooked[67]. It can also be the corner of a room, and it is suggested that a *krókr* could be a

---

[64] Einarsson, *A History of Icelandic Literature*, p. 140.
[65] Zoëga, *A Concise Dictionary Of Old Icelandic*.
[66] Cleasby and Vigfusson, *An Icelandic-English Dictionary*.
[67] Ibid.

barb[68], given its occurrence in the words *krókspjót* and *krókör*, which would then be a "barbed spear" and a "barbed arrow". The interpretation in e.g. favoured by Hjalmar Falk[69], although he admits that barbed spears are much more common in the Iron Age (Vendel Age) than in the Viking Age and later times.

Another interpretation is that the *krókar* would in fact designate the "wings", or "lugs"[70], which are often seen on the sockets of Migration era to Viking era Germanic spearheads, and survived in later medieval boar-spears either in the same "winged" shape, or as a crossbar (Fig. 11). This makes sense if we consider the *krókspjót* as a "hooking spear" – and one of the primary functions of the wings on spearheads was to hook, be it to take away the shield of the opponent or to catch his spear shaft or limb. In that case, the "hooking arrow" (*krókör*) would be hooking flesh, and the "hooking spear" (*krókspjót*) would be hooking shields and spear shafts.

Figure 11: 13th century boar-spear. Based on the Maciejowski Bible, *ca. 1245 (New York, Morgan Library, Ms. M. 638, f°27r).*

The two main candidates for the *krókspjót* are therefore Viking Age winged spears (or 13th century boar-spears) and barbed spears – we will try to distinguish between the two thanks to the sagas and the archaeological artefacts.

V.1.2. Appearance in texts

The *krókspjót* is referred to sporadically in various sagas, not necessarily linked to one another. The name of the weapon is inconsistently translated as a "spear", a "halberd", a "barbed spear", etc.

- In Bjarnar Saga Hítdælakappa (chapter 18), Björn has a *krókspjót* in his hand, a shield at his side and a sword at his belt. The context of the saga is clearly from the 13th century.
- In Egils Saga (chapter 86), an unnamed chieftain comes to the *thing*[71] carrying richly adorned equipment, consisting of a shield with golden decorations and an ornamented *krókspjót* with a gilt socket.
- In Fóstbræðra Saga (chapter 2), Jöd makes a thrust with a *krókspjót*, which is also referred to as a *spjót*[72]. In the same saga, Snorri uses in two hands a large *krókspjót* (chapter 12).

---

[68] Zoëga, *A Concise Dictionary Of Old Icelandic.*
[69] Falk, *Altnordische Waffenkunden*, p. 69.
[70] Short, *Viking Spear.*
[71] The Þing (or *thing*) is the ancient Scandinavian form of legislative assembly.
[72] Appendix 14.

- In Laxdœla Saga (chapter 21), Olaf has a high-status set of weapons, among which a decorated *krókspjót*, a shield and a sword at his belt.
- In the same saga (chapter 37), Eldgrim, wearing mail, brandishes a *krókspjót* in one hand, while having a shield in the other hand and a sword at his belt.
- In Grettis saga (chapter 19), Gretti picks up old Kar's large *krókspjót* from the wall where it was hanging, and uses it in a two-handed thrust that is able to pierce two men, with the blade buried in their bodies up to the *krókar*.
- In Þórðar Saga Hreðu (chapter 7), Indridi is mentioned twice having a very large *krókspjót* in his hand, along with a red shield and a sword.

We see that the *krókspjót* are usually large (or, like in the case of the *höggspjót*, that the described weapons are big even for a *krókspjót*). They are most often used in one hand, with a shield, and are primarily thrusting weapons. It also seems unusual for a large spear not to have *krókar*: in Grettis Saga, we learn that Gretti has a large spear, with a silver inlaid socket, but with no *krókar* – which seems to be worth mentioning for the author[73]. Such a spear might have looked exactly like Fig. 3c.

In the case of the *krókspjót*, we can also look at an occurrence in a Scandinavian text unrelated to the Icelandic sagas. In the Norwegian Gulathing Law, written in the 13th century, we can find the following statement[74]:

> En þat er hit þriðia misvigi ef maðr er lostenn krocoro. æða krocspiote. oc þarf at skera til.

which can translate as[75]:

> The third [form of] dishonourable man-slaying is wounding a man with a barbed arrow or barbed spear, so that [the head] has to be cut out.

This text clearly draws a parallel between the vicious wounds inflicted by a *krókör* or *krocoro* ("barbed arrow") and a *krocspiote*. A similar situation is described with a barbed arrow in Fóstbræðra saga (Flateyjarbók), when the arrow cannot be removed without damaging the surrounding flesh, because of the barbs.

V.2. Archaeological candidates

There are archaeological artefacts to support both the winged spear and the barbed spear hypothesis.

As mentioned, the winged spears, of Petersen types B, C and D[76], were very common before, during and even after the Viking Age. They came in various blade sizes and shapes,

---

[73] Appendix 16.

[74] Keyser and Munch (eds.), *Norges Gamle Love Indtil 1387*, p. 80.

[75] Larson, *The Earliest Norwegian Laws*, p. 160.

[76] Petersen, *De Norske Vikingesverd*, p. 23-26.

larger specimens can be seen on Fig. 3. During later Middle-Ages, it remained common for spears to have wings, lugs, hooks or crossbars, which served similar purposes as for Viking Age spears.

As for barbed spearheads, several artefacts survive as well from the Viking Age. Most of them are tanged spearheads (Petersen type L[77]), as seen on Fig. 12a. An example of a socketed barbed spearhead has also been found in Birka, Sweden (Fig. 12b), which bears a striking similarity to the earlier Germanic (Vendel Age) *ango*.

However, there is no evidence that these barbed spears where used as weapons of war, as it is attested for the *ango*. They were maybe fishing or whaling harpoons. Moreover, none of these barbed spears, be it tanged or socketed, could be described as large, decorated, gilt, etc. as mentioned in the sagas. After the Viking Age, barbed spears and javelins remained in use in Medieval Europe (probably due to the vicious wounds inflicted and to the hooking opportunities), shifting between tanged and socketed designs, and bearing one or two barbs[78]. It is therefore most likely that such weapons existed in the 13th century, and were directly related to earlier and later barbed spears.

V.3. Interpretation

Given that neither the texts nor the archaeology can provide us with a unifying theory, our hypothesis is that of a semantic drift.

The studied texts date back to the 13th century, while the studied families of weapons emerged as soon as in the 7th century. After its colonization, Iceland remained linguistically quite isolated, while Norway got more and more links with the rest of Europe, so that the Norwegian language drifted more quickly from Old Norse than Icelandic did. In modern Norwegian, *krok* still means a hook (more specifically a fishing hook), but the meanings of *krókspjót* and *krocspiote* might have already diverged by the 13th century.

---

[77] Ibid., p. 33-34.
[78] See, e.g., *Die Blume des Kampfes* (Vienna, Österreichische Nationalbibliothek, Cod. 10799), f° 190r.

*Figure 12: Examples of barbed spears from the Viking age. **a**: a tanged spearhead (harpoon?), Petersen type L, (Stockholm, Statens Historiska Museet, catalog nr. SHM 22293:2 (obj. 107519)), photograph: © Iliali Asp, **b**: a rare socketed spearhead (ango?), (Stockholm, Statens Historiska Museet, catalog nr. SHM 34000:Bj 596 (F101) (obj. 449486)), photograph: © Ny Björn Gustafsson. Reproduced with permission of the institution.*

On the Icelandic side, we have the description of a weapon which is quite common, often quite large, and can be a high-status weapon, worthy of a chieftain or king, and which is often gilt or otherwise ornamented. We even learn that it is uncommon for large spears (obvious weapons of war) not to have *krókar* – not to be a *krókspjót* – which is in perfect agreement with the winged spears that can be found commonly before, during and after the Viking Age. The scene where Gretti pierces two men with a *krókspjót* up to the *krókar* is also very consistent with a winged spear, since a secondary use for the wings (or primary, in the case of a later boar-spear) was to prevent over-penetration of the blade in the body of the enemy.

On the Norwegian side, we have a description which matches perfectly a barbed spear, or harpoon, through the wounds it inflicts. None of the known barbed spears are large or ornamented, and it is difficult to imagine a harpoon (or even an *ango*) as a high-status symbol. Besides, the *ango* demonstrate that the main use of a barbed spear is as a throwing weapon, while the *krókspjót* in the sagas are mostly used for thrusting and are sometimes used two-handed.

We therefore come to the conclusion that, while etymologically close, the *krókspjót* mentioned in the sagas and the *krocspiote* appearing in the Gulathing Law designate different objects, the former being the characteristic Viking winged spear (Fig. 3) or, in a 13th century context, a boar-spear, and the latter a barbed spear or harpoon.

VI. OTHER WEAPONS

VI.1. Bryntroll

The *bryntroll* (or *bryntröll*, although this spelling might be incorrect[79]) is another weapon of unknown nature. It is suggested that it might refer to the same weapon as the *brynþvari*[80, 81], which is a type of *kesja* (see IV.3).

Etymologically, a troll is "a monstrous, evil-disposed being"[82]. The word took the metaphorical meaning of anything fiendish, so that an X-troll would be "an enemy, a destroyer of X"[83]. In our case, the *bryntroll* is the enemy, the destroyer of the *brynja* – the byrnie, or mail shirt. This name might therefore be a *kenning*, a poetical metaphor characteristic of Nordic poetry, but kennings for weapons are far less common in sagas than is skaldic poetry. It is also worth underlining that the word *bryntroll* was kept in use in the Icelandic language and took the meaning of a regular European halberd (Fig. 1).

We therefore have the mention of a weapon the purpose of which is to destroy (or, at least, bypass) mail.

And this is exactly what the weapon does in the sagas:

- In Egils Saga, Kveldulf raises a *bryntroll* and cuts (*höggva*) at Hallvard (chapter 27). The cut goes through the helmet and into the head, burying the blade up to the shaft. The blade gets stuck in the skull, so that when tugging it back, Kveldulf swings Hallvard's body to the other side.
- In Harðar Saga Og Hólmverja (chapter 28), Hörd is wounded by a *bryntroll*.
- In Laxdœla Saga (chapter 37), Hrut owns a gold inlaid *bryntroll*, which is a royal gift. He uses it to kill Eldgrim from behind, by raising and "driving" (*setja*) the *bryntroll* between his shoulders, splitting the mail shirt. The *bryntroll* then "runs through the chest".
- In Valla-Ljóts Saga (chapter 2), Ljot owns an inlaid *bryntroll*. He carries it when he is in a good mood, as opposed to the sharp-horned axe he carries when in a killing mood. Ljot uses the *bryntroll* to keep attackers at bay during an ambush, and to deflect a spear thrown at him (chapter 8).

We can see that as opposed to the previously studied weapons, the *bryntroll* mostly cuts, and impressively so. Besides, it seems to be used two-handed, since no shield is mentioned

---

[79] Cleasby and Vigfusson, *An Icelandic-English Dictionary*.
[80] Zoëga, *A Concise Dictionary Of Old Icelandic*.
[81] Falk, *Altnordische Waffenkunden*, p. 111.
[82] Zoëga, *A Concise Dictionary Of Old Icelandic*.
[83] Cleasby and Vigfusson, *An Icelandic-English Dictionary*.

in any of its appearances. And, given that the weapon is buried "up to the shaft" when delivering a cut, the blade must be mounted so that the shaft is behind the blade. We might therefore finally have something closer to a long-shafted axe – even more so that in Egils Saga and Laxdœla Saga, other weapons like the *höggspjót*, the *atgeirr*, the *kesja* and the *krókspjót* are mentioned, but never compared to the *bryntroll*.

However, the *bryntroll* is supposed to be contrasting with Ljóts sharp-horned axe. If we suppose this axe to look like a Danish axe or a later large battle axe (Fig. 13), then the *bryntroll* must have had quite a different look. We must think then of another pole-weapon that is not a spear.

Figure 13: Axes from the Viking Age to the 13th century.
a: large Viking axe-head ("Dane axe"), 10th-11th century, (London , British museum, catalog nr. 1891,0905.8), © British Museum (CC BY NC SA 4.0).
b: Norman two-handed axe, direct descendent from the previous one. Bayeux Tapestry, late 11th century, with special authorization of the city of Bayeux.
c: 13th century long-shafted battle axe – the shape is more crescent-like, the size of the blade and length of the shaft have increased. Based on the Maciejowski Bible, ca. 1245 (New York, Morgan Library, Ms. M. 638, f° 35r). Similar one-handed axes are shown as well (Fig. 5b).

Apart from various spears and axes, there is no evidence of other pole-weapons in the Viking Age, therefore, if the *bryntroll* is neither spear nor axe, it is either an unknown weapon (so rare that no archaeological artefact had survived to modern days), or it has to be an anachronistic weapon, known to the 13th century authors, but posterior to the Viking Age. The hypothesis of a rare (or foreign, or later) weapon is favored by Hjalmar Falk[84], who sees the *bryntroll* as a double-bladed axe or a twybill.

Given the feats the *bryntroll* achieves, a possible candidate among 13th century weapons could also be a huge-bladed glaive or falchion (Fig. 5a, 5b). This weapon is shown in one instance cutting in half a mail-clad knight, which is probably an exaggeration of the artist, but is by far the most impressive cut depicted in the whole Maciejowski Bible manuscript[85].

---

[84] Falk, *Altnordische Waffenkunden*, p. 111.
[85] Anonymous, *Maciejowski Bible*, Ms. M. 638, ca. 1245, f° 10v.

However, in this case we are just guessing what a *bryntroll* might have looked like, and we can give no assertive conclusion on this weapon.

VI.2. Fleinn

The last weapon we will study here is the *fleinn*. This word seems to designate a pole-weapon with a cutting and thrusting capacity.

The meaning of the word is unclear, because of its rarity. The Old Icelandic *fleinn* has an equivalent in Ancient Swedish with *flán*. The possible meanings of the word include "a bayonet-like pike", "the fluke of an anchor" or "a kind of shaft, a dart" (mostly for the Swedish counterpart)[86].

If we venture out of the martial context, the interpretation as a "shaft" might be reinforced by the word *flann-fluga* ("a woman who runs away from her wedded husband")[87]. The male counterpart of *flann-fluga* is *fuð-flogi* ("a runaway from his betrothed bride"), which derives from the word *fuð* – "cunnus"[88]. Therefore, if the *fuð-flogi* is "fleeing the cunt", it makes sense to see the *flann-fluga* as being "fleeing the shaft".

If we leave aside the "bayonet-like pike" because it might narrow down our interpretation, we are left with a word designating something similar to a shaft (or fluke, or dart). This is coherent with the interpretation of Hjalmar Falk[89], who sees the *fleinn* indifferently as a throwing spear or an arrow.

The *fleinn* appears only three times in the Icelandic Sagas. This rarity makes it even more difficult to obtain a statistical analysis of the contexts in which this weapon is mentioned.

In Brennu-Njáls Saga (chapter 30), Kolskegg throws a *fleinn* at Karli's ship[90] but it seems to refer here to the fluke of an anchor, or grapnel. In Grettis Saga (chapter 66), Gretti fights a giant who is said to be wielding a *fleinn*, described as a *heftisax*, a weapon with which he can cut and thrust. Finally, in Heiðarvíga Saga (chapter 33), in a situation where peace must be kept, the author uses the expression "no *fleinn* shall be reddened", referring broadly to all weapons.

---

[86] Cleasby and Vigfusson, *An Icelandic-English Dictionary*.
[87] Ibid.
[88] Ibid.
[89] Falk, *Altnordische Waffenkunden*, p. 66.
[90] Appendix 1.

Assuming that a *fleinn* is always the same thing as a *heftisax* (literally, a "hafted sax") is probably a mistake, and the reason why the word was said to have the meaning of a "bayonet-like pike"[91]. The interpretation of the *heftisax* as a bayonet-like pike makes sense – one can imagine a sax being affixed to the end of a pole, providing a primitive glaive. This construction would even be reminiscent of the much later *svärdstav*, used by Swedish militias around the year 1500[92] – although assuming a lineage between the two weapons would be far-fetched.

In the sentence "no *fleinn* shall be reddened", the word also seems to be used as a generic name for weapons. It is unlikely that a word usually designating a very specific pole-weapon would be used in this context. We might think that *fleinn* is then a rare synonym for *vapn* ("weapon"), but this takes us a bit too far, because we are losing the "shaft, fluke, dart" meaning of the word. A middle way is to point out the fact that the most common weapon on most of the battlefields from the Viking Age to the 13th century was by far the spear (light or heavy, winged or not...). Saying "no spears shall be reddened" would probably sound to a 13th century reader just as "no guns shall be fired" would sound to us – we don't need to know that throwing grenades and stabbing with bayonets is forbidden as well to understand the meaning of peace implied by the sentence.

In this scope, it seems reasonable to conclude that the word *fleinn* is simply yet another (rare) word to refer to a spear, or to a shafted weapon in general □ maybe including even light javelins and arrows.

VII. CONCLUSION

As we have shown, the rarer pole-weapons of the Icelandic Sagas should not be called "halberds" without a reason. Based on the correlations between the text, the artefacts and their uses in combat, we can propose a range of new interpretations for the weapons studied in the article:

- the *höggspjót* is simply a "hewing spear", and it corresponds to any large spear with a good cutting capacity. Such a spear would be used mostly for thrusting, but occasional slicing or chopping motion can be effective too, which makes it similar in its wielding to a later partisan.
- for the *atgeirr*, the translations "battle-spear" or "overspear" (to emphasize the uniqueness of the weapon) should be preferred to the word "halberd". Although it is not fully clear what archaeologically the *atgeirr* was, its geometry and use (prevalent thrusts and occasional cuts) show that it was probably a specimen (or subtype) of hewing spear.

---

[91] Cleasby and Vigfusson, *An Icelandic-English Dictionary*.
[92] Dolstein, *Landsknecht's diary*, ca. 1502.

- the *kesja* appears in such a variety of situations that is probably refers to a broad category of objects as well, including throwing spears - hewing spears and mail-piercing spears - such as the *brynþvari*. It is most probably another word for "spear", but a rare one, of ancient origin. Translators might try to use obsolete English synonyms for "spear" to translate this word, like e.g. "gar".
- the *krókspjót*, in the context of the sagas, is most likely a "winged spear", rather than a "barbed spear" □ it refers to large-bladed, often ornate weapons, and the wings (*krókar*) can be used for hooking motions, as well as for avoiding a too deep penetration of the spear into the opponent's body.
- the *bryntroll* is the least understood weapon of all. It is predominantly a cutting pole-weapon, while being quite distinct from an axe. Any reader would understand that a "mail-troll" in fearsome weapon able to split a mail shirt, but further research on closely related names (*brynfagð*, *brynþvari*) in other texts would be needed to better grasp the nature of this pole-arm, which is in any case a post-Viking-age weapon.
- the *fleinn* seems to refer to the general concept of a shafted weapon, be it a spear, a javelin or an arrow. Depending on the context, it would be probably best rendered as simply a "spear", or a "pole-wepon", etc.

Further and better understanding of these weapons could be provided by an expanded literary study. An even larger corpus of Old Icelandic (Old Norse) texts dating from the Viking Age to the 13th century - skaldic poetry, and sagas such as the King's Mirror (Heimskringla), the Sagas of Kings, the Legendary Sagas - could be analysed, and compared to texts in other languages about the same period (such as the Gesta Danorum by Saxo Grammaticus, Frankish and Anglo-Saxon chronicles, Arabic travel impressions, etc.). We would also benefit from a more systematic study of archaeological artefacts from the Viking Age to the 13th century, which could provide a more complete classification of pole-weapons. However, this would be enough work for a thesis – in contrast, this short article was made possible only thanks to the fantastic preliminary work done by William R. Short[93].

Acknowledgements

First and foremost, I want to thank my comrades and mentors, Thomas Mainguy and Romain Wenz, for the fruitful conversations we had, the ideas and insight they provided, and their spontaneous offer to proof-read this paper.

I want to thank heartily Mr. Gilles Martinez for providing me with illustrations and invaluable information about spear fighting.

---

[93] Short, *Arms and Armor in Sagas*.

I would also like to thank Mrs. Katarina Nimmervoll and Mr. Gunnar Andersson from the Stockholm Historiska Museet for helping me with the archaeological part of my research.

BIBLIOGRAPHY

Primary sources

Anonymous, *Bandmanna saga, Bárðar saga Snæfellsáss, Bjanar saga Hítdælakappa, Brennu-Njáls saga, Droplaugarsona saga, Egils saga Skallagrímssonar, Eiríks saga rauða, Eyrbyggja saga, Finnboga saga ramma, Fljótsdæla saga, Flóamanna saga, Fóstbræðra saga, Gísla saga Súrssonar, Grettis saga, Grænlendiga saga, Grænlendiga þáttur, Gull-Þóris saga, Gunnars saga Keldugnúpsfífls, Gunnlaugs saga ormstungu, Hallfreðar saga, Harðar saga ok Hólmverja, Hávarðar saga Ísfirðing, Heiðarvíga saga, Hrafnkels saga Freysgoði, Hænsna-Þóris saga, Kjalnesinga saga, Jökuls þáttur Búasonar, Kormáks saga, Króka-Refs saga, Laxdæla saga, Ljósvetninga saga, Reykdæla saga ok Víga-Skútu, Svarfdæla saga, Valla-Ljóts saga, Vatnsdæla saga, Víga-Glúms saga, Víglundar saga, Vopnfirðinga saga, Þórðar saga hreðu, Þorsteins saga hvíta, Þorsteins saga Síðu-Hallssonar, Ölkofra saga*, 13th century, ed. by Bragi Halldórsson et al. (Reyjavík: Mál og menning, 1998).

Anonymous, *Gulaþingslög*, 13th century, ed. by R. Keyser and P. A. Munch (*Norges Gamle Love Indtil 1387*, Christiania: Chr. Gröndahl, 1846), translated by L. M. Larson (*The Earliest Norwegian Laws*, Oxford: Oxford University Press, 1935).

Achille Marozzo, *Opera Nova*, Bologna, 1536.

Paul Dolstein, *Landskecht's diary*, 1502 (Weimar: ThHtStAW Ernestinisches Gesamtarchiv, Reg. S fol. 460).

Pictorial sources

Anonymous, *Bayeux tapestry: La telle du conquest*, ca. 1077 (Bayeux, 0.5 m x 68.38 m embroidered cloth).

Anonymous, *Maciejowski Bible*, ca. 1245 (New York: Pierpont Morgan Library, Ms M. 638).

Secondary sources

Cleasby, Richard and Vigfusson, Gudbrand, *An Icelandic-English Dictionary* (Oxford: At the Clarendon Press, 1874).

Einarsson, Stefán, *A History of Icelandic Literature* (Baltimore: Johns Hopkins Press, 1957).

Falk, Hjalmar, *Altnordische Waffenkunde* (Kristiania: Dybwad i Komm., 1914).

Gylfason, Þorsteinn, *Njál's Saga*, Introduction (Ware: Wordsworth Classics, 1998).

Hreinsson, Viðar, editor, Attwood, Katrina C., translator, *The Complete Sagas of Icelanders* (Reykjavík: Leifur Eiriksson Publishing, 1997).

Keller, May L., *The Anglo-Saxon Weapon Names Treated Etymologically and Archæologically* (Heidelberg: Carl Winter's Universitätsbuchhandlung, 1906).

Mallet, Paul Henri, Scott, Walter et al., *Northern Antiquities: Or, An Historical Account of the Manners, Customs, Religion and Laws, Maritime Expeditions and Discoveries, Language and Literature of the Ancient Scandinavians* (London: H. G. Bohn, 1847).

Nicolle, David, *Knight of Outremer, 1187-1344* (Oxford: Osprey Publishing, 1996).

Oakeshott, Ewart, *European Weapons and Armour: From the Renaissance to the Industrial Revolution* (Oxford: Boydell Press, 2012).

Petersen, Jan G.T. *De Norske Vikingesverd*, (Kristiania: Dybwad i Komm., 1919).

Short, William R., *Viking Age Arms and Armor: Viking Shields*, <http://www.hurstwic.com/history/articles/manufacturing/text/viking_shields.htm>, accessed 3 March 2016.

Short, William R., *Viking Age Arms and Armor: Viking Spear*, <http://www.hurstwic.com/history/articles/manufacturing/text/viking_spear.htm >, accessed 3 March 2015.

Short, William R., *A Listing of References to Arms and Armor in the Sagas of Icelanders*, <http://www.hurstwic.com/library/arms_in_sagas>, and references therein, accessed 3 March 2015.

Sigurðsson, Gísli, *The Medieval Icelandic Saga and Oral Tradition: A Discourse on Method* (Cambridge: Harvard University Press, 2004).

Sveinsson, Einar Ól, *Laxdæla saga*, preface (Reykjavík: Hið íslenzka fornritafélag, 1934).

Webster, Noah et al., *Webster's international dictionary of the English language* (Springfield: G. & C. Merriam Co, 1913).

Zoëga, Geir T., *A Concise Dictionary Of Old Icelandic* (Oxford: At the Clarendon Press, 1910).

APPENDIX

Citations from the Sagas of Icelanders showing particularly interesting appearances of the studied pole-weapons. The (modern) Icelandic text is given along with a proposed translation.

1. Brennu-Njáls Saga, chapter 30:

   Kolskeggur þreif upp akkeri og kastar á skip Karls og kom fleinninn í borðið og gekk út í gegnum og féll þar inn sær kolblár.

   Kolskegg snatched up a grapnel and cast it at Karli's ship, and the fluke fell inside the hold, and went out through one of the planks, and in rushed the coal-blue sea.

2. Brennu-Njáls Saga, chapter 30:

   Hallgrímur hefir atgeir þann er hann hefir látið seiða til að honum skal ekki vopn að bana verða nema hann. Það fylgir og að þegar veit er víg er vegið með atgeirinum því að svo syngur í honum áður að langt heyrir til.

   Hallgrim had an *atgeirr* on which he had put a spell, to the effect that no other weapon that this could kill him. Another thing is that it is known at once when a man is to be slain with the *atgeirr*, for something sings in it so loudly that it may be heard a long way off.

3. Brennu-Njáls Saga, chapter 45:

   Sigmundur hafði hjálm á höfði sér og skjöld á hlið og gyrður sverði og hafði spjót í hendi.

   Sigmund had a helmet on his head and a shield at his side and was girded with a sword and had a spear in hand.

4. Brennu-Njáls Saga, chapter 54:

   Gunnar mælti til þeirra: "Nú er að verja sig. Er hér nú atgeirinn."

   Gunnar said to them: "It is time to defend yourselves. Here is the *atgeirr*."

5. Brennu-Njáls Saga, chapter 63:

   Litlu síðar skýtur Gunnar til Barkar atgeirinum og kom á hann miðjan og í gegnum hann og niður í völlinn.

   Shortly after, Gunnar shot the *atgeirr* at Bork, it went through him at the waist and then into the ground.

6. Brennu-Njáls Saga, chapter 63:

   Gunnar sér þetta og varpar sér skjótt til höggs við Austmanninn og sníður hann í sundur í miðju.

   Gunnar saw this and threw himself at the Easterner with a hacking blow and cut him in two at the waist.

7. Egils Saga, chapter 43:

   Egill hafði vopn sín, sverð og kesju og buklara.

   Egil had his weapons, a sword, a *kesja* and a buckler.

8. Egils Saga, chapter 53:

Allt lið þeirra hafði norræna skjöldu og allan norrænan herbúnað.
All of them had their Norse shield and all Norse weapons.

9. Egils Saga, chapter 53:

   Síðan lagði hann spjótinu fyrir brjóst jarlinum, í gegnum brynjuna og búkinn, svo að út gekk um herðarnar, og hóf hann upp á kesjunni yfir höfuð sér og skaut niður spjótshalanum í jörðina, en jarlinn sæfðist á spjótinu, og sáu það allir, bæði hans menn og svo hans óvinir.

   Then he thrust the spear at the earl's chest, through the mail-shirt and the body, so that it came out between the shoulder blades. He lifted him on the *kesja* over his head, and stuck the spear-butt into the ground. Everyone saw that the earl died on the spear, both his men and his enemies.

10. Egils Saga, chapter 58:

    Egill hafði vopn sín, þau er hann var vanur að hafa, hjálm og skjöld, gyrður sverði, höggspjót í hend.

    Egil had his customary weapons, a helmet and shield, a sword at his girdle, a *höggspjót* in his hand.

11. Egils Saga, chapter 58:

    Egils spjót kom á miðjan skjöldinn og gekk í gegnum langt upp á fjöðrina.

    Egil's spear hit the middle of the shield and the whole length of the spear blade penetrated it.

12. Egils Saga, chapter 58:

    Egill snerist í móti þeim; hann skaut kesjunni að Fróða og í gegnum skjöld hans og í brjóstið, svo að yddi um bakið.

    Egil turned to face them; he shot his *kesja* at Frodi, through his shield and his chest, so that the point came out through his back.

13. Egils Saga, chapter 66:

    Gekk Egill fram og hafði hjálm á höfði og skjöld fyrir sér og kesju í hendi, en sverðið Dragvandil festi hann við hægri hönd sér.

    Egil came forward with a helmet on the head, a shield in front of him and a *kesja* in hand, and he had his sword Slicer tied to his right hand.

14. Fóstbræðra Saga, chapter 2:

    Jöður hafði krókaspjót í hendi. Hann snarar þá að Hávari og leggur spjóti í gegnum hann.

    Jöd had a *krókspjót* in hand. He turned suddenly to Havar and thrust the spear through him.

15. Gísla Saga, chapter 2:

    Gísli hjó í móti með höggspjóti og af sporðinn skildinum og af honum fótinn.

    Gisli struck back at him with his *höggspjót*, both through the tail of the shield, and through his leg.

16. Grettis Saga, chapter 48:

Hann hafði hjálm á höfði og gyrður saxinu og spjót mikið í hendi og öngvir krókarnir á og var silfurrekinn falurinn á.

He had a helmet and was girded with a sax, and he had a large spear in his hand, with no barbs but with a silver-inlaid socket.

17. Kormáks Saga, chapter 16:

    Bersi hafði höggspjót í hendi og staf í annarri en Halldór Hvíting.

    Bersi had a *höggspjót* in one hand and a staff in the other, and Halldor had [the sword] Hviting.

18. Króka-Refs Saga, chapter 3:

    Hann tekur ofan höggspjót mikið. [...] Refur gengur nú úr garði og fer á þá leið að hann skýtur spjótinu fyrir sig og hleypur þar eftir

    He took down a large *höggspjót*. [...] Ref went out of the farm and went along the road, throwing the spear ahead of himself and running after it.

19. Ljósvetninga Saga, chapter 12:

    [...] þú og sagðir hann eigi vera mundu meira en annarrar handar mann gilds manns og kvaðst hann hafa hálfþynnu eina í hendi en mig höggspjót gilt á hávu skafti. En eg em nú minni höfðingi en þú og sýnist mér sem hann muni eigi þar lengi gengið hafa skaftamuninn.

    [...] and you said that he was only half a real man and had only a small axe while I had a long-shafted *höggspjót*. I am lesser a chieftain than you, but I think that it didn't take him long to make up the difference between an axe and a pole-weapon.

20. Vopnfirðinga Saga, chapter 2:

    Svartur hljóp að honum og leggur til hans með höggspjóti miklu.

    Svart ran at him, and thrust at him with a large *höggspjót*.

DOI 10.1515/apd-2016-0006

Two late flying prints informing on the artist involved in the *Opera Nova* of Achille Marozzo and on the date of an original (lost) edition?

Roberto Gotti, Museum of Martial Arts (Botticino) and Daniel Jaquet, Max Planck Institute for History of Science (Berlin), djaquet@mpiwg-berlin.mpg.de

At least two editions and six reprints of the work of Marozzo are known today (cf. Bibliography). The first edition of this masterpiece of the "Bolognese tradition" is the one of Modena in 1536. However, Gelli mentions in his bibliography a prior edition, "similar to the edition of Modena", dated 1517 and kept in the R. Biblioteca Pisana.[1] This first edition, if it ever existed, was never found again – or at least never mentioned in publication other than by referring to Gelli.[2]

Since the monograms found in the 1536 edition cannot lead to the firm identification of the artist(s) involved in the xylographies, the discovery of two late 17th c. flying prints examined here might lead to the identification of the date of an unknown edition prior to the Modena 1536 edition and of the artist involved in the engravings.

I. THE LATE FLYING PRINTS, THE MONOGRAM AND THE DATING

The two flying prints reproduce illustrations matching those from the 1536 edition of the *Opera Nova* of Achille Marozzo, in dimensions and details (Fig.1). The first (*dell'abbattimento di pugnale e cappa*) measures 120x121mm, with a printing surface of 111x108mm; the second (*vigesima prima presa*) measures 174x172mm, with a printing surface of 130x128mm. Both xylographies are printed on late 17th, possibly early 18th c. paper after examination of its quality (wire-lines and type of grain). It bears no other illustration, nor printed or manuscript text. When compared to the original xylographies, on the first flying print on the lower left register, the monogram "HsP" is added, and on the other at the same location, the date "1529" (see details, Fig. 1). The wood blocks used to produce those prints appear to be the originals, bearing use-wear marks in the different editions of the work throughout the 16th (Fig. 2) up to the early 18th c., as can be documented with the book of Giuseppe Colombani in 1711 (Fig. 3, see discussion below).

---

* We are indebted to Mr and Mrs Terminiello for their revisions and suggestions.

[1] His brief description: "Carte 181; di cui l'ultima non numerata. Le tavole sono simili a quelle dell'edizione modenese". Gelli, *Bibliografia Generale della scherma*, p. 130.

[2] Opinion shared with Sodini, see her introduction in the anastatic reproduction of the 1568 edition, p. 18, note 24.

The added monogram of the artist and the date could have been marked on the back or the side of the original wood blocks. While potentially using these in the late 17th or early 18th c. to produce the flying prints, the patron might have asked the printer to reproduce the monogram on the print; or the printer chose to add the monogram and the date to the print. It is also possible that this information was known by the last owner of the wood blocks.

II. ILLUSTRATING *OPERA NOVA* IN ITS DIFFERENT EDITIONS

Little research has been done on the involvement of the artists in the realisation of the first editions of Achille Marozzo,[3] while more is known about the artists of the new copper etchings of the second editions in 1569 and 1615.[4] The monograms on the twenty-four xylographies on eighty-two existing of the 1536 edition are inconsistent (*b.R., .b., b,* see occurrences on Fig.1, 2 and 3). According to nineteenth century reference works of Nagler, followed by Benezit, the monogram *b.R* might be attributed to the Italian engraver Francesco Barratini, while Drugulin postulates an attribution to Giovani Britto.[5] This can obviously be challenged, as noted by Sodini, who hypothesises a German origin (or influence at least) for those illustrations.[6]

On Fig. 2, the same plates in the four editions of the 16th c are displayed. The added monogram "HsP" and the added date "1529" are not present in the other editions. The woodcuts used for the late 17th c. flying prints appear to be the same as the originals, but consumed over time. Use-wear traces can be observed throughout the editions, up until 1711, where Giuseppe Colombani printed his small treatise on swordsmanship, using four of the original plates to illustrate his book (Fig. 3).[7] As in the flying prints, one can observe the use-wear trace, like the enlargement of lines due to use, the damage in the margins

---

[3] See mainly Sodini, "introduction", pp. 11-53, esp. 20-23. Nothing on the artists in the following: Gelli, *L'arte dell'armi*, pp. 76-85; Castle, *Schools and Masters*, pp. 34-45; Spotti, *A Fil Di Spada*, p. 142; Anglo, *The Martial Arts*, p. 135-137; Mondschein, "The Italian Schools of Fencing".

[4] The Venetian printer Antonio Pinargenti worked with Giovan Battista Fontana, probably in collaboration with the brothers Giulio for the 26 new copper etchings for his edition. The same brothers were involved in the new etchings for the second edition of Camillo Aggrippa from the same printer. See Sodini, "introduction", pp. 31-38.

[5] Benezit, *Dictionnaire critique et documentaire des peintres*, vol. 1, p. 720 and Nagler, *Die Monogrammisten, und diejenigen bekannten...*, p. 712 (n°1612) and pp. 876-877 (n°2040).

[6] "Osservando la molteplicità dei personaggi e delle loro espressioni, la foggia degli abiti e il tratto delle incisioni su legno dell'Opera Nova, si potrebbe anche ipotizzare che il loro autore fosse di origine tedesca, o quanto meno, influenzato da maestri ultramonti." Sodini, "introduction", p. 21.

[7] The author actually does not use the plates in his technical discourse, it appears to serve merely as illustration technically unrelated to the content of his small book. On the author, see the notice of Lasagni, *Dizionario biografico* and the commented transcription and translation published online by Terminiello, "L'Arte maestra".

due to use and possibly transport or the worm holes bored into the wood (see examples on Fig. 4).

III. HANS SEBALD BEHAM

The monogram on the flying print is the one of Hans Sebald Beham (1500-1550). He was a German engraver (*Formschneider*), trained under Albrecht Dürer and he opened his own workshop as a master engraver in Nurnberg in 1524.[8] He changed his monogram ᛭ᛒ (HsB, 1518-1530) to ᛭ᛈ (HsP, 1531-1550) when he moved from Nurnberg to Frankfuhrt am Main in 1532 (P reflects the Franconian pronounciation of "B").[9] This change matches the date 1529 found on the flying print. He is mostly known for his peasant festival imagery, but produced more than 250 engravings, 18 etchings and 1500 woodcuts. If he was involved in the making of an earlier edition of the *Opera Nova* of Achille Marozzo as suggested by the addition of his monogram on the late 17th c. flying print remains an hypothesis demanding further research. However, this would prove to be a relevant endeavour. Firstly, it follows the opinion of Sodini who believes in a German origin of the illustrations, and secondly, the younger brother of Hans Sebald, Barthel, did travel from München to Italy from 1528 on, where he died in 1540.[10]

IV. CONCLUSION

The reason why the added monogram and the date are to be found on the discovered flying print, kept today at the Museum of Martial Arts, Botticino, remains unclear. However, circumstantial evidence tends to prove that the wood blocks were still used in the early 18th c., and that they were indeed used to produce the flying prints. Moreover, the information implied regarding the date and the artist build an interesting scenario that may lead to the identification of an unknown edition prior to the Modena 1536 edition and of the artist involved in the xylographies. We therefore invite further research to be conducted to turn this potential scenario into a proper case study.

---

[8] On the master, see Stewart, *Before Brügel*, pp. 15-34; Koreny, "Unbekannte Holzschnitte von Hans Sebald Beham", pp. 207-214 and Zschelletzschky, *Die drei gottlosen Maler*.

[9] Pauli, *Hans Sebald Beham*, pp. 2-4. The discussion about the date and the hypothesis of Alfred Bauch (1897) is discussed in the references mentioned in the upper footnote.

[10] For Sodini's opinion, see footnote 5. For Barthel Beham, see Zschelletzschky, *Die drei gottlosen Maler*.

216 *Two late flying prints informing on the artist involved in the Opera Nova of Achille Marozzo*

Figure 1: Flying prints and detail of the added monogram and date

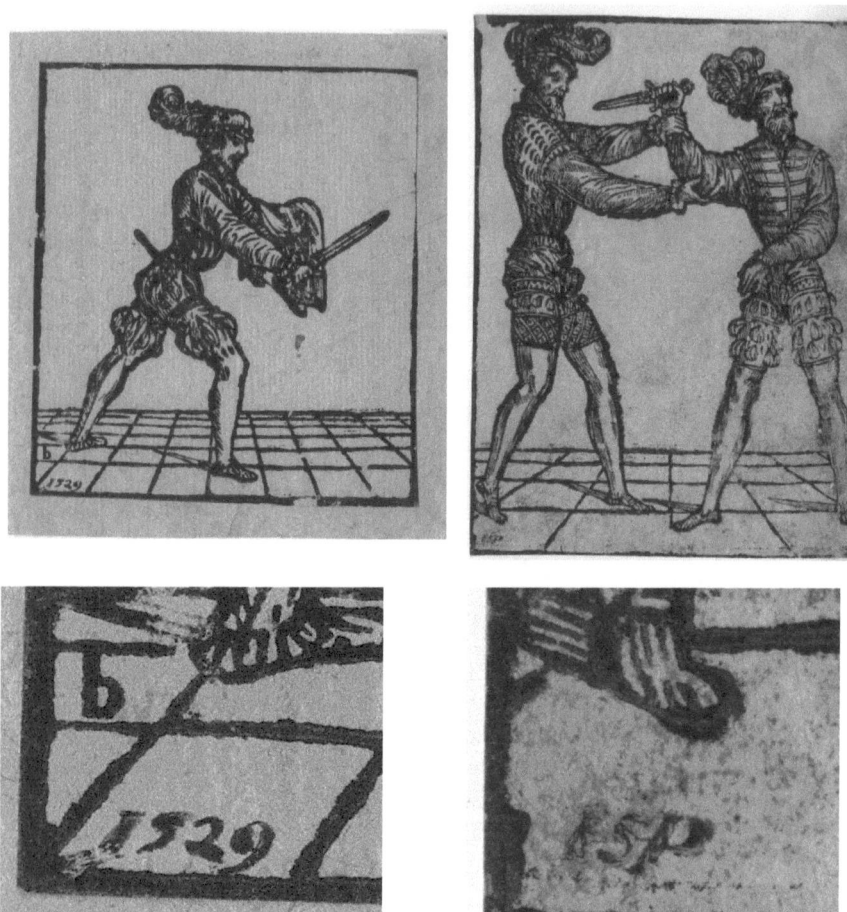

Legend: Flying prints, undated (17th c.). Corresponding to the xylographies of the 1536 Modena p. 18 (Lib. II, cap. 58: dell'abbattimento di pugnale e cappa) and p. 131 (lib. V: vigesima prima presa). Kept at the Museum of Martial Arts, Botticino. Reproduced with permission, photo T. Suazo.

Figure 2: Corresponding plates from the *Opera Nova* (different editions)

1536   1550   undated   1568

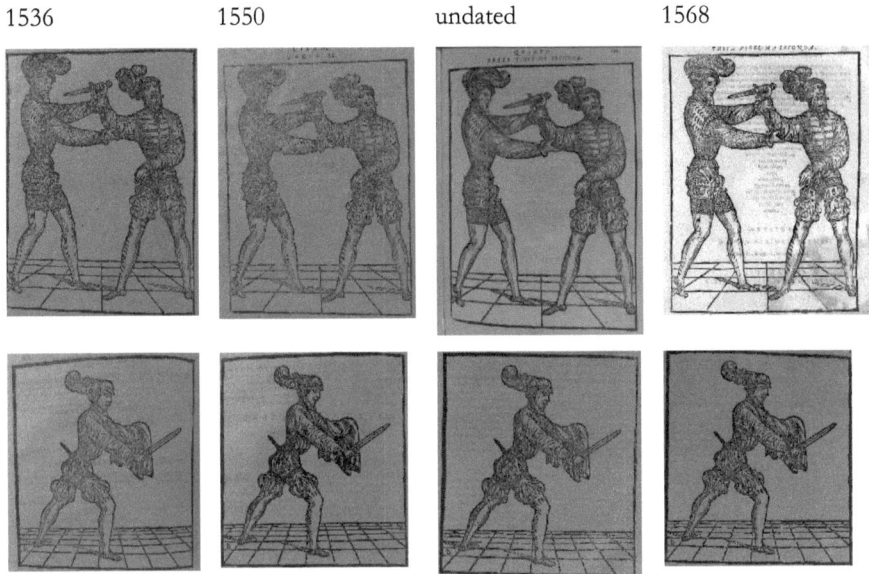

Legend: Achille Marozzo, Opera Nova, different editions (cf. Bibliography): p. 18 (Lib. II, cap. 58: dell'abbattimento di pugnale e cappa) and p. 131 (lib. V: vigesima prima presa). Kept at the Museum of Martial Arts, Botticino. Reproduced with permission, photo T. Suazo.

Figure 3: 1536 plates reproduced in the 1711 *L'Arte maestra* by Colombani

Legend: The four illustrations of the Giuseppe Colombani, L'Arte maestra, 1711 (cf. Bibliography). Kept at the Kelvingrove Museum, Glasgow (R.L. Scott collection). Reproduced with permission, photo Glasgow Museums Resource Centre.

Figure 4: Example of use-wear trace on the wood blocks

Example of a worm hole in the middle of the shin.

1568

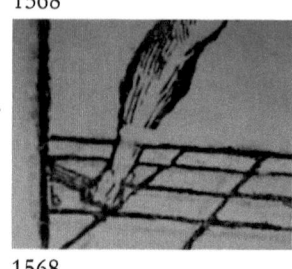

1711

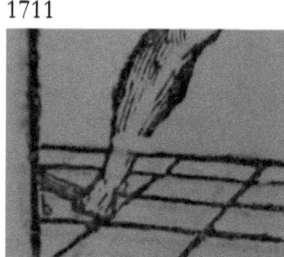

Example of ink feathering due to use (grid and shadow of the leg).

1568

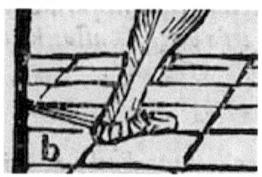

Flying print, undated (17th c.)

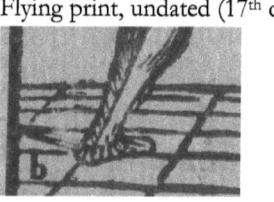

Legend: Details of captions from Fig. 1-3, corresponding bibliographical information and credits apply.

V. BIBLIOGRAPHY

V.1. Primary source

Achille Marozzo, *Opera nova chiamata duello, o vero fiore dell'armi de singolari abatimenti offensive, et difensivi... che tratta de casi occorrenti ne l'arte militare... e tratta de gli abatimenti de tutte l'armi... con le figure che dimostrano con l'armi in mano tutti gli effetti et guardie che possano far*, Mutinae, D. Antonii Bergolae, 1536.

Achille Marozzo, *Il duello. Libro di scherma*, s.l. (Bologna or Modena), s.d. (1540) – reprint of Modena edition.

Achille Marozzo, *Opera nova (chiamata duello, o vero fiore dell'armi de singolari abatimenti offensive, et difensivi... che tratta de casi occorrenti ne l'arte militare... e tratta de gli abatimenti de tutte l'armi... con le figure che dimostrano con l'armi in mano tutti gli effetti et guardie che possano far)*, Venetia, Gioane Padovano, 1550 – reprint of Modena edition.

Achille Marozzo, *Dei singolari abbattimenti offensive e difensivi nella disciplina Arte Militari libri 5*, Bologna, 1560 – reprint of Modena edition (cf. Orlandi, *Notizie*, p. 18).

Achille Marozzo, *Arte dell'armi di Achille Marozzo bolognese, maestro generale dell'arte de l'armi*, Venetia, heredi di Marchio Sesse, 1568. – reprint of Modena edition.

Achille Marozzo, *Arte dell'armi di Achille Marozzo, Bolognese, Ricorretto et ornato di nuove figure in rame*, Venetia, Antonio Pinargenti, 1568 (1569). – second edition.

(Sebastiano Marozzo), *Arte dell'armi di Achille Marozzo, Bolognese, Ricorretto et ornato di nuove figure in rame* Verona, 1615 – reprint of Venice edition.

Giuseppe Colombani, *L'arte maestra, di Giuseppe Colombani detto l'alfier Lombardo*, Venetia, il Miloco, 1711. – original work of the author, but with five plates reproduced from the Modena edition.

V.2. Secondary Literature

Achille Marozzo, *Arte Dell'armi: Venezia, Antonio Pinargenti, 1568*, anastatic reproduction with introd. of C. Sodini (Lucca: Pacini Fazzi, 2007).

Anglo, Sydney, *The Martial Arts of Renaissance Europe* (New Haven: Yale University Press, 2000).

Bénézit, Emmanuel, *Dictionnaire critique et documentaire des peintres, sculpteurs, dessinateurs et graveurs de tous les temps et de tous les pays*, augm. ed. – first ed. 1924 (Paris: Gründ, 1999)

Castle, Egerton, *Schools and Masters of Fence, from the Middle Ages to the Eighteenth Century* (London: G. Bell and sons, 1885).

Gelli, Jacopo, *Bibliografia Generale Della Scherma : Con Note Critiche, Biografiche E Storiche. Bibliographie Générale de L'escrime : Avec Notes Critiques, Biographiques et Historiques*, 2nd ed. (Milano: Hoepli, 1895)

Gelli, Jacopo, *L'arte dell'armi in italia* (Bergamo: Istituto italiano d'arti grafiche, 1906).

Koreny, Fritz, 'Unbekannte Holzschnitte von Hans Sebald Beham - Ein Unbeachtetes Nürnberger Künstlerkartenspiel', *Wiener Jahrbuch Für Kunstgeschichte*, 30-31 (1978), 207–14.

Mondschein, Ken, 'The Italian Schools of Fencing: Art, Science, and Pedagogy', in D. Jaquet, T. Dawson and K. Verelst (eds), *Late Medieval and Early Modern Fight Books* (Leiden: Brill, 2016 <under press>).

Nagler, Georg Kaspar, *Die Monogrammisten und diejenigen bekannten Künstler aller Schulen welche sich zur Bezeichnung Ihrer Werke eines figürlichen Zeichens, Der Initialen Des Namens, Der Abbreviatur...* (München: G. Franz, 1858).

Orlandi, Pellegrino Antonio, *Notizie degli scrittori bolognesi e dell'opere da loro stampate e manoscritte* (Bologna: Costantino Pisarri, 1714).

Pauli, Gustav, *Hans Sebald Beham. Ein kritisches Verzeichniss seiner Kupferstiche, Radirungen und Holzschnitte* (Strassburg: Heitz und Mündel, 1901).

Spotti, Alda, ed., *A Fil Di Spada: Il Duello Dalle Origini... Agli Ori Olimpici* (Roma: Colombo, 2005).

Stewart, Alison G., *Before Bruegel: Sebald Beham and the Origins of Peasant Festival Imagery* (Aldershot, England ; Burlington, VT: Ashgate, 2008)

Terminiello, Piermarco, "L'Arte maestra (The Master Art) by Giuseppe Colombani" (online: <http://schoolofthesword.com/Colombani%20 Transcription%20&%20Translation.pdf>, accessed 02 January 2016).

Zschelletzschky, Herbert, *Die 'drei gottlosen Maler' von Nürnberg: Sebald Beham, Barthel Beham und Georg Pencz: historische Grundlagen und ikonologische Probleme ihrer Graphik zu Reformations- und Bauernkriegszeit* (Leipzig: Seemann, 1975).

Jeffrey L. Forgeng, *The Art of Swordsmanship by Hans Lecküchner* (Armour and Weapons, 4), Woodbridge: Boydell and Brewer, 2015, 453p. ISBN 978-1-78327-028-6. Dimensions: 23.4 x 15.6 cm

Reviewed by Daniel Jaquet, Max Planck Institute for History of Science (Berlin), djaquet@mpiwg-berlin.mpg.de

Fourth volume of the new collection "Armour and Weapons" directed by Kelly DeVries, this translation of the Hans Lecküchner treatise on unarmoured combat with the *Langes Messer* ("Long knife", translated by the author as "Falchion") is another welcomed addition for reference work for Historical European Martial Arts studies. It follows a series of translations by the author, namely the translation of the anonymous *Liber de arte dimicatoria* (2003-2013) and Joachim Meyer, *Gründtliche Beschreibung...* (2006-2015), and several forthcoming titles. Currently the curator for Arms and Armours at the Worcester Art Museum and an Adjunct Professor at Worchester Polytechnic Institute, Jeffrey L. Forgeng is a great connoisseur of the Fight Book corpus and his contribution on the field of study is noteworthy[1]. He is one of the few undertaking the arduous task of translation of these technical texts, providing useful reference works for the practitioner and the scholar alike.

The volume offers an English translation (p. 1-432), preceded by a short introduction (p. ix-xxvviii), and followed by a Glossary with a German-English word list (p. 433-443), two Appendixes (Dedicatory Letter to Philip the Upright, p. 444-445; Table of the structure of the treatise with concordance to other texts, p. 446) and a bibliography (p. 447-453). The translation is accompanied by all images from the manuscript referred to as M (München, Bayerische Staatsbibliothek, Cgm 582), cropped to include only the pairs of fighters, in a rather small black and white format.

The introduction presents the author and its text (p. x-xii), places its work in the context of the other related bodies of technical literature (p. x-xii, xv-xviii, xx-xxi), identifying him as one of the "three chief authorities" of German Medieval art of fighting (p. ix, the two other being Johannes Liechtenauer and Master Ott). It also discusses the weapon (p. xii-

---

[1] Apart from his translations, see his research paperKiermayer, Alex, and Jeffrey Forgeng, "'The Chivalric Art": German Martial Arts Treatises of the Middle Ages and Renaissance', in The Cutting Edge: Studies in Ancient and Medieval Combat, ed. by Barry Molloy (Stroud: Tempus, 2007), pp. 153–67 and Forgeng, Jeffrey, 'Owning the Art: The German Fechtbuch Tradition', in The Noble Art of the Sword: Fashion and Fencing in Renaissance Europe 1520-1630, ed. by Tobias Capwell (London: Paul Holberton Publishing, 2012), pp. 164–75.

xviii), the manuscript tradition (p. xvii-xix), and proposes several caveats for the interpretation of the text (p. xxi-xxv). This introductive part provides the reader with clear and straight to the point elements. It works as a survey, flying over different issues, most of the time well referenced with the secondary literature discussing those – but lacking the critical description of the different theses of the latter, probably for the sake of brevity[2]. Noteworthy, as in his other publication[2], the translator tends to attribute alternative titles to Fight Books – mainly for compendiums –, based on the history of their ownership, rather than on the problematic authorial attribution[3].

The translation – without edition of the Middle High German text – is seeking to "present the fullest and clearest possible version of Lecküchner's techniques as documented in the two principal medieval sources" (p. xxvii). The translator provide the reader with variants from H, "when these might prove of interest", and with comparative samples to S[4], "just enough to sketch out this third, intermediate redaction [...]" (p. xxvii). Such choices enhance the value of the translation, but also diminish the value of such an editorial work for academic research purpose, since most of the editorial additions is not systematically done – or exhaustively indicated in a proper apparatus. He also discusses the philological tradition, stating that neither M nor H are direct author's productions and that the *urtext* on to M and H are probably based is today missing (p. xix). He comments as well on the copies or influences to later texts (up to 1679). A stemma codicum for a more clear visualisation or a more exhaustive table than the one on the appendix B (p. 446) would have been welcomed to support these complex connections and would have added value to the editorial work done. This is then neither a translation alone (of a unicum or a print, such as his previous translations), neither a critical edition, but somewhere in the middle[5].

---

[2] For example, little is said on the theses of Jan-Dirk Müller article analysing the content and the production of these treatises. Several footnotes listing almost exhaustively reference material are to be found, but with no critical discussion about these.

[3] E.g. "Starrhemberg" for Rome, Biblioteca dell'Accademia Nazionale dei Lincei e Corsiniana, Cod. 44 A 8 or "Balder" for Wolfenbüttel, Herzog August Bibliothek, Cod. Guelf. 78.2 Aug. 20. This is fine for compendia (e.g. also done by Rainer Welle for his 2014 edition of Augsburg, Universitätsbibliothek, Cod. I.6.4°.2, referenced as "von Baumann's Fechtbuch"), however it is less for other compendia referenced by the translator to one of the contributor or compiler (see bibliography, for "Dobringer, Lew, Speyer, Ringeck"). Since there is no distinction between the two methods for attributing titles, this is resulting in adding more confusion than clarity.

[4] Hans von Speyer, 1491. Salzburg, Universitätsbibliothek, M.I.29. Identified as a complete copy (p. xix-xx, reference to S in footnote 37).

[5] There is no critical edition available. Grzerogz Zabinski, Russ Mitchell and Falko Fritz offered in an online self-published document a synoptical edition of M and H, as well as English translation of the two versions. See Zabinski, Russel and Fritz, A Falchion / Langes Messer Fencing Treatise by Johannes Lecküchner (1482), 2012 (online <http://www.hammaborg.de/pdf/transkriptionen/leckuechner_cgm582/zabinski_mitchell_fritz_leckuchner.pdf>, accessed 08 September 2015), 636p. This work is not referenced in the reviewed book.

The practitioner will enjoy this book for the accessibility to the original material carefully translated, referenced according to folia and to the numbered *stücke* (combat sequences), with the illustration in regard to the text. The scholar will enjoy this book for the quality of the translation provided by a trusted author, but might be disappointed by some of the author's editorial choices, e.g. for not including the edition of the original text or for being not systematic in the apparatus when comparing versions and offering concordances.

Jaser, Christian and Israel, Uwe (Eds.), Zweikämpfer. Fechtmeister – Kämpen – Samurai [Duellists. Fencing masters - champions - Samurai]. Das Mittelalter: Perspektiven mediävistischer Forschung, Zeitschrift des Mediävistenverbandes 19/2 (2014). 211 p.

Walter de Gruyter GmbH,
ISSN: 0949-0345 · e-ISSN 2196-6869

Reviewed by Ingo Petri, Deutsches Archäologisches Institut (Berlin), ingopetri@gmx.de

Volume 19, issue 2 of the journal "Das Mittelalter. Perspektiven mediävistischer Forschung. Zeitschrift des Mediävistenverbandes" unites under its key topic "Duellists. Fencing masters - champions – Samurai" six articles from the fields of historical science, German philological medieval studies, Scandinavian studies, codicology and Japanese Studies. It is partly the outcome of the conference "Akteure des mittelalterlichen Zweikampfs zwischen Marginalisierung und Professionalisierung" [Actors of medieval duel between marginalisation and professionalization] in January 2012 in Dresden. All Articles are provided with an English summary, otherwise the book is, with the exception of Michael Wert´s English article, written in German.

The editors Christian Jaser and Uwe Israel provide an introduction to the topic and put the contributions of the book into this context (pp. 241-248). This is followed by a bibliography of selected publications on the topic (pp. 249-252). The major comprehensive publications of the last 130 years are presented while abstaining from publications of single sources.

In his article "Die Aufzeichnung des Nicht-Sagbaren. Annäherung an die kommunikative Funktion der Bilder in den Fechtbüchern des Hans Talhofer" [Recording the non-speakable. Approach to the communicative function of the pictures in the fighting books of Hans Talhofer] (pp. 253-301) Eric Burkart discusses the communication strategies of medieval fighting books and the purpose of integrated images. In a case study on the five 15th century manuscripts ascribed to Hans Talhofer the didactic use of images is examined, stating that images in Talhofer´s manuscripts fulfil the function of interpretative Glosses in other teachings in the tradition of Liechtenauer. Further he analyses what purpose the pictorial representations of the fencing master and his pupils serve and how their identification is made possible, being very critical about the representations of Talhofer, as identified in the research literature up to now and showing that the depictions in the manuscript Hs. XIX, 17-3 from Königseggwald are not the subsequent recording of a real judicial duel but an ideal image of "true fencing" after Talhofer´s teaching.Matthias Johannes Bauer´s article, *"Einen Zedel fechter ich mich ruem/ Im*

Schwerd vnd Messer vngestuem. Fechtmeister als Protagonisten und als (fach-)literarisches Motiv in den deutschsprachigen Fechtlehren des Mittelalters und der frühen Neuzeit" [*A Zedel fencer I boast to be/ In sword and knife impetuous*. Fencing masters as protagonists and as a (specialist) literary motif in the German-language fencing teachings of the Middle Ages and the early modern period] (pp. 302-325) investigates the group of fencing masters of the 14th to 16th century. He mainly addresses four questions: What terms are used to describe or distinguish between fencers in Early New High German sources? Is it possible to form groups or represent role models? To what extent are the fencers presented as contemporary or real figures and to what extent are they just a (specialist) literary motif, for example for certification or as evidence for authority? Could these literary motives be used for allegories of fencers? He mainly focuses on Talhofer and Kal, the former being only temporarily entrusted, the latter serving a long time at courts as "Schirrmeister" (stable master) and not as "Schirmmeister" (fencing master) as usually assumed. He concludes that fencing masters are fighting for reputation and are from a German philological point of view mainly a (specialist) literary motif respectively a topos.

Daniel Gehrt, "Turnier-, Fecht- und Ringbücher in den Bibliotheken der Ernestiner" [Tournament-, fencing- and wrestling books in the libraries of the Ernestinians] (p. 326-349) deals with the complicated ways of tradition of the tournament-, fencing- and wrestling treatises from the libraries of the Ernestinian dukes of Saxony. His main questions are which functional and symbolic meaning can be attributed to them, if they served as a practical guide in learning the knightly arts or if they had predominantly a representative function in the princely libraries and what motives were behind the documentation of own tournaments and the collecting of old fencing- and wrestling books. He shows that the books were acquired partly for the education of the princes but mostly served the representation of the dynasty and the memory of agonal achievements. At the end he gives a table of the handwritten tournament-, fencing- and wrestling books that were in the library in Gotha or that still are.

Sixt Wetzler analyses the different roles of the duellists in the Icelandic saga literature. In his article "Ehre, Schwert und das Recht. Zweikämpfe im alten Island" [Honor, sword and the law. Duels in Old Iceland] (pp. 350-379) he focuses on hólmganga and glíma, the specific Old Icelandic forms of duelling. He analyses the role of the personnel of the duel and of duelling as an access to social prestige. A secondary question is how seemingly non-ritualised forms of violence can be understood from the perspective of the duel's underlying ideological principles. Wetzler concludes, that hólmganga and glíma had many differences but that they had in common that they offered a way to improve, to back up or to restore the social position. Their performance was integrated into the public life and was subject to the control of the community, they controlled and situated violence in everyday life. Even unregulated fights were influenced by thought patterns and behaviours that the ritualised duels were based on.

In his article "*Infamis etiam campio non esse potest*. Kämpen in deutschen und italienischen Städten des Spätmittelalters zwischen Marginalität und Rechtspflege" [Champions in

German and Italian cities of the late Middle Ages between marginality and judicature] (pp. 380-406) Christian Jaser develops a new perspective on the role of medieval paid fighters (Lohnkämpfer). Opposite to their general stated lack of rights on the basis of account books and statutes of late medieval German and Italian cities he shows a change of their role towards a professional protagonist of legislation. He concludes that in German cities, the image of the travelling lawless champions is relativised by a fixed employment with stable monthly salary, in Italy the champion business appears as institutionalised with remuneration according to fixed tariffs, with regulated occupation of the duel and set requirements for the fighters. In the Italian duel literature of the late Middle Ages the champions are even redefined to lawyers. However, the champion was always in suspicion not to fight with full dedication for financial reasons or for self-protection.

Michael Wert traces the origins of the Japanese art of fencing at the transition from the medieval to the early modern period with special focus of the meaning of the "Military Mirror of Kai" for the self-image of the samurai and the development of different fencing styles. In the article ""The Military Mirror of Kai": Swordsmanship and a Medieval Text in Early Modern Japan" (pp. 407-419) he shows that swordsmanship emerged as a new field of knowledge in early modern Japan in a time of relative peace while during the violent periods of Japanese history the sword was not the primary weapon of the samurai. The focus is on the "Military Mirror of Kai" a mix of fact and fiction and was widely read by samurai of the early modern period, becoming a foundational text for early modern warriors. The "Military Mirror" was the oldest widely available text in the early modern period that described famous swordsmen and their styles. The anecdotes about them are brief, but they influenced the many origin stories retold by many swordsmen who trace their history into the mythical medieval past.

The volume concludes with twenty reviews of current publications from different fields of Medieval Studies, which, however, are not related to the topic of the volume discussed (pp. 420-452).

In their introduction to the volume, the editors state that the articles approach the phenomenon "duellists" in an interdisciplinary dialogue (p. 247). This is probably due to an attempt to present the volume in a better light, as well as the declaration the issue would illuminate the topic from a protagonist-centred perspective (p. 243). Strictly speaking, only Wetzler and Jaser really write about duellists. Bauer and Wert write about fencing masters and Burkart and Gehrt about the function of written sources. At least the latter would be hard to do in a protagonist-centred perspective. However, "duellists" suits as a more general umbrella term, since the written sources are mainly about duels and since fencing masters teach mainly duelling. Also, the interdisciplinary dialogue could be questioned. Only Burkart uses insights of another article of the present volume in his contribution (p. 256, note 7), but obviously without knowing the article completely. Other texts differ from one another (for example the differing information about the manuscript Leeds, Royal Armouries, MS. I.33 in the introduction and the articles of Burkart, Bauer, Gehrt and Wetzler or the information about the office of Paulus Kal in the articles of

Burkart and Bauer). The present volume is therefore better described as a multi-disciplinary anthology.

But these issues do not diminish the good overall impression of the volume at all. It only is a pity that for some Italian and Latin quotations, no translation is given.

Actually, the Volume is not at all in need to be presented in a better light because the contributions contain enough scientific potential on their own. All articles are well-structured scientific papers that provide a proper introduction into their subject, follow a stringent methodology, and clearly present their source material. Beyond that they present precisely traceable results, in some cases (self-) consciously contradictory with previous research. Precisely because of the thematic diversity of the contributions the volume is highly interesting and I'm sure that it presents some new foundations and new ideas for future research into historical European and Asian martial arts.